Living Countertestimony

Living Countertestimony

Conversations with Walter Brueggemann

Walter Brueggemann
with
Carolyn J. Sharp

WESTMINSTER
JOHN KNOX PRESS
LOUISVILLE · KENTUCKY

First edition
Published by Westminster John Knox Press
Louisville, Kentucky

12 13 14 15 16 17 18 19 20 21—10 9 8 7 6 5 4 3 2 1

Book design by Sharon Adams
Cover design by Dilu Nicholas
Cover illustration courtesy of Columbia Theological Seminary

Library of Congress Cataloging-in-Publication Data

Brueggemann, Walter.
 Living countertestimony : conversations with Walter Brueggemann / Walter Brueggemann with Carolyn J. Sharp. -- 1st ed.
  p. cm.
 Includes bibliographical references.
 ISBN 978-0-664-23425-6 (alk. paper)
1. Brueggemann, Walter. 2. Theology. I. Sharp, Carolyn J. II. Title.
 BX4827.B66A5 2012
 230.092—dc23   2012010608

Most Westminster John Knox Press books are available at special quantity discounts when purchased in bulk by corporations, organizations, and special-interest groups. For more information, please e-mail SpecialSales@wjkbooks.com.

In acknowledgment
of the growing throng of contemporary
"aliens, orphans, and widows"
(Deut. 24:17–22)

The notion of "countertestimony" arises from the Bible itself and gives insistent voice to those who are marginalized from the economy and forcibly, often violently, displaced from their homelands. Indeed, the Old Testament is such a peculiar tradition because it insists on the legitimacy and centrality of this otherwise voiceless population. In our contemporary social context, the great systems of economic and political power (with military enforcement) continue to generate more and more such refugees. I cannot think of a more poignant acknowledgment for a volume on countertestimony than to call attention to our contemporary setting in which the war on the poor is waged "from above."

WB

Contents

Foreword

Most of us know little or nothing about the authors of the books we read. We have access to their published thoughts on particular issues, but seldom do we know the mind, soul, and spirit that move authors to write what they write. *Living Countertestimony* departs from convention by inviting readers to meet the author behind the words he has written. One need only scan the bibliography included here to recognize that Walter Brueggemann has been a dominant and generative voice in the Church and the academy for more than forty years. His published works, however, do not tell the whole story; they are but the public iteration of his deep and personal engagement with God, the world, and what he calls the host of "kingdom scribes" who treasure what is old and seek what is new.

As one of the friends invited to share a meal with Walter early on in this project, it seems to me in retrospect that the primary requisite for a place at the table was the capacity to laugh. Serious issues came up in the course of our conversations, but on this occasion they were derivative, not primary. Shared memories of the first time we met Walter; his dramatic flair in the classroom, including his bawdy description of God's message to Jeremiah; his dancing in front of the ark; and his way of staring an audience into silence by looking over the top of his reading glasses, which Walter concedes he used as a pedagogical tool, prompted laughter leavened with mutual experience. Spliced into the laughter about Walter's contagious charisma were anecdotal reminiscences on his grace and charity. Affirmations around the table focused on his eagerness to encourage others with handwritten letters applauding their completion of an essay or a book. Perhaps more inspiring for Walter's colleagues at Columbia

Theological Seminary was his habit of coming early to the office in order to hammer out on a manual typewriter the prayers that launched each day's lecture into the stratosphere of divine realities yet unimagined.

Genuine dialogue requires that both parties to the conversation be willing to make themselves vulnerable to the other. In this case, we readers listen in on the conversation prompted by the questions posed by Carolyn Sharp and Walter's responses. Sharp's questions are specific and directive. They probe Brueggemann's publications with questions that ask "Why?" Why did you take this particular position? Questions that fail to elicit answers become monologue, which Brueggemann resists; for as these "conversations" make clear, he is restlessly engaged with the dialogic imperative to hear, imagine, speak, and embody the truths that Scripture discloses, both with God and against God.

In response to Sharp's questions, Brueggemann candidly acknowledges his abiding fear of failure. He is "haunted" by texts like Jeremiah, Ezekiel, and Job that press him to go where he has not gone; he is terrified of failing as a biblical scholar; he is endlessly unsure of the importance of what he writes; and he admits that his preoccupation with the Church has been criticized by his contemporaries in the guild as second-rate exegesis that lacks the gravitas of serious scholarship. As a "Church scholar," Brueggemann concedes, with palpable disappointment, the guild has marginalized him. "You pay a price . . . for deciding to be a Church scholar, and that means that instead of doing technical work, you run toward preaching, which in the academy is considered second-rate stuff." Equally revealing is Brueggemann's discernment of how his work has been reviewed by his peers: "I think the real heavyweights in the field suspect that I don't do very good critical work. And I suspect that too . . . and that's okay with me." Terrified of failing, Walter looks back on his career and affirms that he has learned how to "rest in God's grace."

In view of Brueggemann's self-assessment, readers should not be surprised that he appropriates exile as the defining metaphor of his life. He reflects on his pietistic grounding in Niebuhr; the injustices experienced by his father, a pastor in the Evangelical Synod, the antecedent of the United Church of Christ; and his own struggle for identity and voice within ecclesial families. Confronted with the twin pathologies of "denial and despair," Brueggemann lives and writes as one whose words the status quo has marginalized. His compulsion is to envision a breakthrough, a way beyond current debates, which engages God by taking God seriously. As Brueggemann puts it, "the dominant trajectory we are on . . . is

X Orthodoxy vs Modern *context*

a trajectory of death. It is to us that an alternative has been entrusted, and we can't sit around counting *dageshes*."

Chapter 5 is strategically located at the center of these conversations. This entry eschews conversation. Walter preaches a sermon titled "Where Is the Scribe?" to the National Theological Conference at Trinity Wall Street Church (Episcopal) in New York. In a succinct but comprehensive survey of the nineteenth-century battle between the "orthodox" and the "rationalists," Brueggemann discerns that we have argued ourselves into a cul-de-sac. The old battles are no longer worth fighting. As he puts it, "The failure of nation-states, the emptiness of scientism, and the exploitative injustices of the market (all seductions faced by the Church) create an environment in which the old quarrel no longer compels." The enigmas of our contemporary world necessarily require us to move beyond the old question—"What happened when?"—to a new quest. Those who would be "kingdom scribes," Brueggemann says, must focus on a new and more demanding question: "What is being imagined [in Scripture] out beyond the givens of historical 'facticity'?" His answer serves as a summons: "scribes trained for the kingdom have two responsibilities: to treasure what is old and to offer what is new. A failed scribe may linger over what is old but offer nothing new. But kingdom scribes, scholars who serve the secret of God, work at the artistic pivot point of old and new, of tradition and interpretation, of crucifixion and resurrection." Modesty likely prevents Walter from equating himself and his work with the "kingdom scribe," but we, his readers, abide no such cautions. "Where is the scribe" who embodies the mission to which we each are summoned? We recognize him in the faithful work of Walter Brueggemann.

The title of this book—*Living Countertestimony*—is instructive. The noun, "countertestimony," is apt as a summative nominative for Brueggemann's work. The adjective "living" is a potent reminder that Walter Brueggemann's work, and ours, is not done.

SAMUEL E. BALENTINE

Challenge of today's Theologian/exegete.

Chapter 1

"Arguing with the Text"

A Dinner Conversation with Walter Brueggemann and Colleagues
Boston, November 22, 2008

This dinner conversation brings together some of Brueggemann's former colleagues at Eden Theological Seminary and Columbia Theological Seminary, two of Brueggemann's former students, and others who have worked closely with Brueggemann. The high-spirited and sometimes irreverent contributions from these colleagues range over many topics of interest to theological educators. Here are teaching anecdotes from Brueggemann's seminary classroom, reflections on ways in which Brueggemann's example has inspired and daunted other scholars, an analysis of Brueggemann's significant influence on contemporary Christian homiletics, and candid acknowledgments of the benefits and occasional annoyances experienced by those witnessing Brueggemann's celebrity at close quarters. Here, too, are unexpected revelations concerning Brueggemann's thoughtfulness as a mentor and the moments of vulnerability that have shaped his professional development as a prolific scholar and sought-after speaker in churches.

CJS

Attending were:

The Rev. Dr. Samuel E. Balentine, Professor of Old Testament, Union Presbyterian Seminary

Dr. Timothy K. Beal, Professor of Religion at Case Western Reserve University

The Rev. Dr. Walter Brueggemann, William Marcellus McPheeters Professor of Old Testament Emeritus, Columbia Theological Seminary

†Stephanie Egnotovich, Executive Editor, Westminster John Knox Press

The Rev. Dr. Anna Carter Florence, Associate Professor of Preaching and Worship, Columbia Theological Seminary

Dr. David Greenhaw, President, Eden Theological Seminary

†Dr. Jim Griesmer (Kathleen O'Connor's husband, a computer scientist)

Dr. Tod A. Linafelt, Associate Professor of Biblical Studies, Georgetown University

Dr. Kathleen M. O'Connor, Professor of Old Testament, Columbia Theological Seminary

The Rev. Dr. Carolyn J. Sharp, Associate Professor of Hebrew Scriptures, Yale Divinity School

The Rev. Dr. Christine Roy Yoder, Associate Professor of Old Testament Language, Literature, and Exegesis, Columbia Theological Seminary

CAROLYN SHARP: This will be more interesting the more we can get at what's at stake in Walter's work and the impact he's had on the guild and the arguments that have ensued in the guild around some of the claims that he has made. We'll want to think about how his work is useful for the Church, what we've seen that the Church has not noticed but could really benefit from, and so forth. Let's introduce ourselves by saying who we are and how we know Walter.

KATHLEEN O'CONNOR: I hold Walter's chair at Columbia Seminary. I am the William Marcellus McPheeters chair—they gave it to me because I could pronounce it! I am so happy to have it, because Walter has written so many books and articles that have influenced the field and inspired my work and hopes. My first recollection of having a personal conversation with Walter was after he published his review of the three Jeremiah commentaries: Robert Carroll's, Bill Holladay's, and William McKane's commentaries.[1] And what he said in the commentary [review] is—I think it was the last line—"The Church deserves more than this."[2] That was such a breath of fresh air for me! I felt so constrained by the way the conversation was going, that what we had to be concerned about was the little, little details of texts that had historical significance but seemed to have no theological meaning. And that's my first recollection of talking with you. I remember where we were; I don't remember what city it was, but it was an SBL meeting and we were up on the top floor somewhere, and I sat next to you and told you how much I liked it. And you said, "Yeah, but there are a lot of people after me!" [laughter]

TOD LINAFELT: I'm Tod Linafelt. I was a student of Walter's at Columbia Seminary from 1989 to 1991. I did a master's degree there. And I was also hired to clean his house— remember that?—and I adopted his dog, which they were going to throw out into the cold, cruel world. The family dog! But I showed up. So I'm a student who wanted to do a PhD and went on to Emory and now teach at Georgetown University in Hebrew Bible. I showed up at Columbia Seminary not really having much interest in the Bible at all. Didn't know who Walter Brueggemann was, but just happened, by luck, to end up—just because of the schedule probably—in his Pentateuch class. All of a sudden the Bible was interesting, and he quite literally took me aside one time, I remember, and said, "You know, you can do this for a living." [laughter]

O'CONNOR [merrily]: Not much of a living!

LINAFELT: Never in my life had I thought I would be a college professor or a scholar. But he said, "You can do this for a living." I said, "Well, how do you do that?" "You gotta go to graduate school!" and "you gotta learn to write, you gotta learn to read well." So, quite literally, he changed my life. He not only made the Bible interesting, he was a real mentor with regard to helping me along the career path. But his house was very dirty, though, when I first arrived. After I worked on it, it was a little bit less dirty.

TIM BEAL: I'm Tim Beal, and I came to seminary the same year Tod did, and we've been confused ever since. I had heard about Walter from my wife, Clover. She wasn't my wife at the time, but at Seattle Pacific University where we had been, Walter was legendary. He was on the faculty at Eden Theological Seminary. Rob Wall and Gene Lemcio and Frank Spina talked about him all the time as the next generation after Brevard Childs, and said that everybody "needed to go to Eden." As soon as Walter moved to Columbia, everybody "needed to go to Columbia." So that's why Clover and I went to Columbia Theological Seminary. So we'd heard about him, we'd heard stories about him in the classroom. Should I quote the most well-known one? Can I use profanity? because that's what I remember. . . . I think it was Jeremiah, that what Jeremiah was saying was—and I can't say it with the passion that Walter does, because I've learned, after fifteen years of teaching, that I don't have that charisma. But the point of Jeremiah was that [in a Brueggemann voice, with accentuated r's] "Yahweh is not your [expletive deleted], Yahweh is your lover!" [much laughter] I've quoted that so many times!

DAVID GREENHAW: He never said that!

LINAFELT: I've been in class when he's said that!

BEAL: All he said in our class was, " 'Can you f* a missile?' That's what Jeremiah is saying." Which, I don't know. But anyway, that was all before we went to Columbia Seminary. And I'd heard about him dancing in front of the ark in some dramatic way—clothed or unclothed, I wasn't sure. But what I remember more than anything else was that when I took the Pentateuch class with Tod, the first thing we were going to read was Gerhard von Rad's "The Form Critical Problem of the Hexateuch"[3] and that I'd better be ready to summarize that argument in full. I've never read an article more carefully than I read that article! I spent maybe twenty hours reading that article and taking ten pages of notes in preparation, just in case I had the opportunity to summarize that argument. And I can't even remember whether that opportunity arose or not.

BRUEGGEMANN: But it was well worth the effort!

BEAL: It was well worth it. I still use Deuteronomy 26:5–9 in my intro classes all the time, and so from there, well, we'll talk later.

LINAFELT: No class has ever been as exciting as that one on "The Form Critical Problem of the Hexateuch"!

CHRISTINE ROY YODER: I'm Christine Roy Yoder, and I taught for many years—seven years? eight years?—with Walter at Columbia Seminary with Kathleen. My first memory of being aware of Walter's work was when I was a doctoral student at Princeton, where I was taking an Old Testament theology seminar with Pat Miller, and Walter was working on his Testimony/Countertestimony[4] with his preliminary articles—you were probing that work—and that became part of our syllabus that semester. And I remember after having gone through Gabler and all the way up, how animated the seminar was around your notion of testimony and countertestimony, and how the whole feeling of the seminar shifted in light of the possibilities that opened up for thinking about Old Testament theology. And then, of course, to have the fortunate opportunity to interview at Columbia and come be with two stunning colleagues [pointing to Kathleen and Walter]. . . . One of the things I want to be sure to highlight in the conversation tonight is that I've learned so much from your writing. I've also learned an equal amount from you about collegiality and institutional-mindedness, and about fidelity, and about good citizenship. And so I want to underscore, as a colleague of yours, that you've shaped me in ways far beyond your writing and work. There are stories to tell! Our offices were right above the classrooms in which Walter would teach, and the sounds from the classrooms below should have been recorded!

O'CONNOR: Not only that! You could tell the story about students coming, and—our three offices were right together—they'd really want to talk to Walter, and our doors would be open, and they'd say, "Is he there?"

YODER: Like we were his secretaries. . . .

O'CONNOR: And we'd say, "You could knock on his door and find out!"

YODER: I was often assumed to be your secretary. [Brueggemann laughs] The other piece was, I was teaching and preaching at a church in Denver, and I was introduced—this is a true story—the pastor introduced me to the congregation as "she whose office is across the hall from Walter Brueggemann." And I was perfectly happy with that. I was perfectly delighted to be associated with you.

GREENHAW: I'm David Greenhaw. I'm professor of preaching and worship and president at Eden Theological Seminary. And I was a student—in those days (you know how people change their names?), he was "Walt Brueggemann," and it's been hard for me to make the shift to "Walter," because everyone called him "Walt," but these changes happen—I was his student in the 1970s. In fact, what I remember most . . . is that there was an election in the fall of 1976 when I started seminary, and we students were all talking about it. Walter was walking across the campus, and we stopped him and we said, "What do you think about this election?" And he was incredibly restrained. He didn't say, "Vote for Jimmy Carter," and I'd grown up in a Republican family, and I was really debating what to do. He was incredibly restrained. Today, it would be hard to be restrained this fall, to tell the truth. But I want to say this one thing—I want to tell this one best story, and some of you have heard this before. I've had several lives at Eden Seminary. I came back later and served as director of admissions and student services, or something like that. I lived in a house two doors up from where Walter lived, and at the time, his two sons were about fifteen and seventeen, and mine were three and five. Do you know this story? I'm cutting the lawn, and he's cutting his lawn. He stops his mower and walks two lawns over to me, and he says, "David, you have two sons up there, both willing to cut the lawn but not able. I have two sons who are able, but not willing." He said, "There's a period of about ten days when they're both willing and able. Take my advice: cut the lawn every day during that period!" [laughter] I've actually thought about that theologically: about the incredible odd combination of will and capacity, and how rarely they actually come together.

SAMUEL BALENTINE: I'm Sam Balentine. I teach at Union Theological Seminary in Richmond, and unless I'm mistaken here, I'm the only one at the table who's never been a student of Walter's or a colleague. I've never taught alongside him or had the privilege of sitting in his class. I must say, I've heard some of these stories through the grapevine, but it's much better when I hear them firsthand! I think we met for the first time at Oxford when I was a student. But the first clear memory that I have, just after you reviewed my first book,[5] was when I was delivering my first paper at SBL. Since I'd been in England, I didn't do like a lot of students in this country and read papers before I was done. So I think it was the first paper I read at SBL. A relatively small room, but it was overfull. Mine was the second or third paper. By the time I got up, the crowd had spilled down the middle aisle, and at the front of the middle aisle was Walter with his pen in hand. The whole time I was speaking, he was writing furiously, and I was watching out of the corner of my eye. I thought, "Well, this could be good, or this could be bad." I finished the paper and left immediately, and we had no conversation. That night was the presidential address, which I never go to—[to Brueggemann] not even to the one you gave, I must say. But this time I went, after having been at dinner with a longtime friend of mine and probably—no, certainly—after having had at least one drink more than I should have had. I showed up at the presidential address, and Walter was sitting a couple of seats in front of me. I don't remember the address or who was giving it, and I'm not sure I stayed awake for it. Afterwards, Walter turned around and said, "I enjoyed that paper today. Would you write a book for me on the subject?" [to Brueggemann] Do you remember that? That's where that came from.[6] I walked out with my friend and said, "Tell me what he just said!" [laughter] But there's one other thing I have to say. I had read his stuff and had already begun to plow some of the same fields that Walter had plowed before me. Every time I thought I had a good or maybe new idea, I discovered Walter had been there before me.

O'CONNOR: Yes, yes, yes!

LINAFELT: Worse than that, he's published on it already!

BALENTINE: We had letter correspondence back in those days. This goes back to the late '70s, early '80s. After about ten years of teaching, and we'd had some conversation but not a lot, I lost my job and was without a job for nearly two years. And I was bold enough to ask Walter to help me as I applied for anything from community college on up. Which he did, without question. But what I didn't know was that he was seeking opportunities for me without my asking—that he was writing letters and making phone calls on my behalf that I never knew about. [to Brueggemann] I'm not sure I would have ever gotten a job if you hadn't been on my side. Really, it really does matter.

STEPHANIE EGNOTOVICH: I was never a student of Walter's, but he taught me nonetheless. When I first met him, I was at Fortress Press and I was a brand-new editorial assistant. And his editor was John Hollar. And their mutual loyalty and love for each other were absolutely mind-boggling. Walter just gave John book after book after book! I watched that and I thought, this is the model of what an editor-author relationship should be. That was one of the outstanding lessons I learned about publishing. I've tried to apply it to the work that I've done over the past twenty-five years. [to Brueggemann] Thank you.

BRUEGGEMANN: John was everybody's editor.

EGNOTOVICH: Yes, he was.

GREENHAW: He died while he was editing something I was working on.

EGNOTOVICH: He died while coming home from the Frankfurt Book Fair.

ANNA CARTER FLORENCE: I'm Anna Carter Florence, and I first met Walter as a pastor, or came upon Walter as a pastor. It was 1990. I had only been in the ministry for two years; I was already burned out; I was twenty-eight years old; I thought I was going to quit. And my husband and I (he was a pastor too) went to the peacemaking conference in Washington, DC. It was sort of a last-ditch hurrah. We met up with a bunch of seminary friends. None of us had kids yet, at that point, so we all sort of knew this was a pivotal moment. Walter was the lecturer, and Allan Boesak was the preacher. There were a thousand people there, and Walter was giving lectures that were to become *Finally Comes the Poet*.[7] And sitting there in this room of over a thousand people, I thought: this is what I have been yearning for! This is what I believe about preaching! And no one had said it to me before in a way that I felt could sustain my ministry.

Book to buy

I came back from that conference (which was also the week that Nelson Mandela came to the States and did the ticker-tape parade down Wall Street; so with Nelson Mandela, Allan Boesak, and Walter Brueggemann, it was quite a week). I came back and of course I was preaching that Sunday, because it was summer and the senior pastor was away. The text was Exodus 2. It is the only sermon in my life that I have written in two hours. That was a sermon that later won a prize and opened all these doors—and became, as a friend of mine said, the sermon that's going to follow me through life. And [to Brueggemann] that was you! That was you. It's never happened since that I sat down and wrote a sermon like that. So my first experience was sitting out there as someone who was starving.

In 1997 when I came to interview, I was coming to do my lecture—Christine and I were coming at the same time—and they said, "Oh, you know, all the faculty are going to come hear this lecture for your interview," and I was like [mimics an anxious response]. So the door of Campbell Hall bangs open, and down the way strides this persona. He marches toward me—I was out in the hall throwing up—and he said, "Hello, I'm Walter Brueggemann. I'm in the Old Testament department." And I said, "I know who you are!" [laughter] I gave the lecture and got the job, and the first thing I received in the mail from anyone from Columbia was a book from Walter that was signed, "In anticipation." Which I held like this [miming reverential care], as if it were a relic! A month later, I'm thinking about my dissertation, which is on testimony, and I haven't started at Columbia yet, but Chuck Campbell, my closest colleague, and I are in constant conversation. Chuck writes me this letter: "P.S. Walter Brueggemann has just written an enormous book on testimony. You might want to check it out." [laughter] So that became the linchpin for me. And as I've gone out with pastors now, as I'm on the other end of things—and I spend a lot of time with pastors—routinely, *routinely*, when I offer them the language of testimony-countertestimony, and the way of the Church's *Muttersprache* [mother tongue], it's like the scales fall from their eyes and the burdens fall from their backs. They come up to me with tears in their eyes and say, "I think I can make it now for a couple more weeks." Everywhere I go, I say that the most important thing written for preaching in the last thirty years is *Theology of the Old Testament*. So that's just the first part—I have a lot of other stories. I started on one end, and now I find myself on the other end, but [to Brueggemann] I find that the person who still feeds us is you. And the only reason they buy my book is because he wrote something on the back![8]

BRUEGGEMANN: Well, I just want to say this is wonderful and more than a little embarrassing, but the agreement with Stephanie and Carolyn is that you must be honest and not just flattering. The only thing I said to Carolyn is, do not invite James Barr and do not invite Bruce Waltke![9]

GREENHAW: I had an office next door to Barr for three years.

BRUEGGEMANN: Well, there you go!

SHARP: I'm Carolyn Sharp. I teach at Yale Divinity School. I've never studied with Walter. I have read a lot of his work and look forward to poring over every page of his work over the next eighteen months or so in service of this project. I guess I just want to say a word about how this started for me, how this whole project of *Living Countertestimony: Conversations with Walter Brueggemann* got started.

It started in an over-compensatory moment in my pretenure career at Yale, when I decided to take on Walter in an article. Which I then proceeded to do.[10] It is, I have to say in retrospect, the one piece in my oeuvre that I would pull back, if I could. [Brueggemann laughs] I am living with the consequences of a very sharp tone in that article. It was me at the time responding to pressures in my environment and so forth—I'm not excusing it, but—me wrestling with historical criticism on the one side, trained in historical criticism at Yale and yet deeply interested in literary and theological questions. And I was really drawn to what Walter was writing. I was—if we want candor here—envious of your eloquence, and trying also to please my "masters" in the historical-critical paradigm. For whatever reasons, I took the gloves off in a way that, honestly, I'm ashamed of now. But *c'est la vie*—it is what it is. Well, he can dish back, too, right? [laughter] But here's the thing that helped me to come to the place of wanting to do this project. I know—without going into details—that Walter had an opportunity later to take me down if he wanted to, and he chose not to do that. He showed incredible generosity of spirit, which taught me as a Christian and as a scholar how to move out of the over-compensatory place that I was in, in my context.

YODER: Wow!

SHARP: So that caused me to want to come up to Walter at an SBL meeting two years ago (or maybe just last year; I honestly can't remember). I think it was San Diego, and I saw him standing at a bank of elevators. At first, I literally ducked back around the corner—[to Brueggemann] I don't know if you saw that part—because I was feeling convicted of my own earlier aggression in that article. But then I said to myself, "Be a grown-up and thank the man for his generosity." So I came over to you and haltingly tried to say that I was grateful for what you did and that I was indebted to you. I didn't get too into it because I didn't know how much you wanted to hear. But then we had coffee. You graciously invited me to have coffee later, and we talked for an hour, at a table in the book exhibit. And you started reminiscing about von Rad and some things that you had seen earlier in your career. And I thought that (a) I wanted to know more about what formed you as a scholar and as a Christian and so forth, and (b) that a lot of other people would like to hear those stories too.

O'CONNOR: Yes, yes, yes!

SHARP: So the genesis of this project was actually in that conversation, and it developed from there. So I'm really delighted that you're interested in doing this, and delighted to see each one of you here as well.

O'CONNOR: That's lovely. It's lovely about you, and it's lovely about Walter.

SHARP: It's very lovely about Walter, is what I would say!

O'CONNOR: Very lovely about Walter.

JIM GRIESMER: This is Jim Griesmer. I'm Kathleen O'Connor's husband. I certainly would share, I think, our gratitude to Walter, because he was instrumental in Kathleen's coming to Columbia Theological Seminary and just so grateful to him for Kathleen's sake as well as for my sake. Among the things that I enjoyed about being with Walter, he's my favorite movie reviewer! If there's a movie Walter hasn't seen, I'm not aware of it. But he'll tell you if it's a dog. More seriously, I'd like to thank Walter for the books of prayer that he has given to us. His most recent one, *Prayers for a Privileged People*,[11] was really an inspiring book for me to use daily and think about. Of course, in this day and age, at this moment in time, I'm not sure how privileged I am any more. [laughter] But we do have a new president, so. . . . I've certainly enjoyed the fifteen years that we've had Walter with us and the times that I've been able to spend with him.

O'CONNOR: The thing about Walter that you may not know is the way he writes letters to his colleagues. (You know that, probably, David.) You would say something in public, and no one else would even notice that you said it, and he would write you a letter about it. Handwritten. You couldn't always read it, but you knew it was well-intentioned and beautifully put, even though you couldn't quite tell what it said.

GREENHAW: What about cartoons?

O'CONNOR: Oh, cartoons!

GREENHAW: When our children were born, he clipped a cartoon out of the paper that was appropriate and sent a note to them, written to the children.

O'CONNOR: We haven't mentioned the golf cart. This is in Samuel, and it occurs as the ark of Yahweh is being returned from the Philistines. The ark seems to come all by itself. And Walter is the best impersonator of a golf cart, as he stands in front of the class and he drives the ark of Yahweh!

YODER: One of the things that Kathleen and I love is—we team-teach the Intro to Old Testament course, and we would ask Walter to come in and give a couple of lectures during the course of that time. And that was one we consistently asked him to give. Both of us just loved it, every year! It's almost as though Walter embodies the text in front of the students. And his energy level! [to Brueggemann] You are in full perspiration when you finish. The focus that he gives to the students! He says things that we've said a thousand times, but because he says it, they are hooked by it and transformed by it. He's able to say it in ways that are far more eloquent than I think we wrestle with, the two of us. But the embodiment of this cart has become just a delight. We wait to watch Walter do the cart.

BRUEGGEMANN: You know, I never thought about it, but James Muilenburg embodied the text. I think it must come from James Muilenburg.

BALENTINE: Did you see it?

BRUEGGEMANN: I saw it occasionally. I didn't see it a lot.

BEAL: Frederick Buechner wrote a tribute to James Muilenburg. I can't remember where it's published, but it ended up in a book somewhere, and he described James Muilenburg and the way he taught. When I read that, I shared it with Tod and Clover and other people, because it sounded so much like Walter as a teacher. That mantle was passed. You really demonstrated that very embodied kind of teaching that, I gather, James Muilenburg must have practiced.

GREENHAW: There's a connection. Muilenburg was a very influential figure and wrote almost nothing. Walter is a very influential figure, and he's written quite a bit—have you noticed? [laughter]

BEAL: At one point Walter was ill, so Tod and I were asked to teach some of your classes at Columbia. We were PhD students at the time.

YODER: Oh my God!

BEAL: I had all my notes from when I took Samuel with you, and I thought, I'll come in and do what he did.

O'CONNOR: "I'll do the golf cart!"

BEAL: Yeah. "I'll dance before the ark!" I remember going in thinking I couldn't possibly do better than what Walter had done in his class. I went in there to do that, and I presented it, and the students started asking questions, and suddenly none of it made any sense! [laughter] It was a real moment of self-revelation for me: I could not be Walter. There was something about the charisma, the presence of that interpretation, the embodiment of that interpretation, that I did not have. So it was on the one hand an appreciation of who you are as a teacher, but on the other hand, a realization that I've got to come up with this for myself.

BRUEGGEMANN: Tim told me when he taught at Eckert [College] that for the undergraduates, you had to do everything but tap dance.

BALENTINE: I was going to ask you a couple of questions, since I wasn't ever your student. Do you write your lectures out?

BRUEGGEMANN: Not any more. I did for the first ten years.

BALENTINE: So when you began teaching, you were pretty well crafting a lecture line by line.

BRUEGGEMANN: Yes. And it was all historical criticism.

BALENTINE: When you were doing the ark stuff with Muilenburg in your background, did you craft in your mind, before you went into class, the embodiment? Did you think before you went in the class that you were going to act this out?

BRUEGGEMANN: No.

O'CONNOR: It was spontaneous.

BALENTINE: That happened on the spot. And did you realize that you were echoing Muilenburg?

BRUEGGEMANN: No, I didn't. I realized that much later.

O'CONNOR: I bet Muilenburg was boring by comparison. I bet! I didn't know Muilenburg.

BALENTINE: I think that's the way good teachers work. They model things in ways that plant seeds that come to fruition in ways that we—in this case, you—don't realize until you step into it and blossom out.

GREENHAW: If the night gets away from us and I don't get to say this, it will be bad. I've been thinking about this a lot, because Eden Seminary in the evangelical heritage is huge in Walter, and it's hard to figure out who this person is without that heritage. And as president of an institution that's the carrier—inasmuch as there is such a thing—for that heritage, I've thought about this. At the core of this German evangelical heritage is something called the "irenic spirit." The word "irenic" means "peaceful," mostly, and those of you who know Walter know that he is not peaceful, really, in this sense. He's actually very polemical.

O'CONNOR AND YODER: Yes!

GREENHAW: And I'm trying to figure out: is he a true child of this heritage or not? And in some ways I want to say he's not. He's aberrant for this heritage. The real carrier for this heritage was his colleague Eugene Wehrli, who was irenic all the way through. Walter has a much more polemical character. And I've thought about the postmodern question that you asked. I believe this heritage, and I'm an adopted child of it, so, I'm an outsider trying to learn to speak a foreign language. I grew up as a Congregationalist in the U.C.C., which is god-awful. If you are in Boston it's all right, but when you are in St. Louis it's the devil! Walter's kind of chemistry, as I've figured this out about you, and I may be wrong about this, is that in the irenic spirit, what you do is you have a sense that the subject of your devotion is God. And God exceeds your capacity to grasp. Therefore God is more than you can understand, and whatever you do is partial and incomplete. Therefore you have a sense of openness to the Other, because the Other represents a way to understand this subject that you're so devoted to that's important. And so you're peaceful to the Other; you embrace the Other—there's more to get, there; you need this complement. On the other hand, there are things at stake here, because God's important. And the thing at stake here because God's important is the side of the evangelical heritage that Walt in many ways has embodied over against the academy in which he was trained, that failed to take the subject with the seriousness with which it needed to be taken. When I think about who you are and what you've done, I think that's where you've been. You've fought against a group that you valued but that denigrated the serious core. And yet you also were irenic and wanted to hold them together. So that's my reflection on that heritage and where you are.

SHARP: Walter, I'd like you to address the tensive relationship that you have with historical criticism. Because it matters to what you do, and yet you have pushed back so strongly against it.

BRUEGGEMANN: Yes.

SHARP: The relationship that you have with historical criticism is, I think, a really complicated one.

BRUEGGEMANN: Yes, it is.

SHARP: It's not a simple thing to understand how you are indebted to it, how you are impatient with its limitations, or with the artificial limitations that some of its practitioners have put on it. So I wonder if others of you have comments on that: on how Walter has positioned himself with and over against historical criticism.

BRUEGGEMANN: I am a part of that generation . . . droves of people went into biblical studies because of the biblical theology movement. We are all retiring now; Terry Fretheim is one of the last ones left. The shock for me when I went to graduate school was that they weren't going to let me do biblical theology. They made me do all this other stuff, which was endlessly frustrating for me.

SHARP: What about Childs in that regard?

BRUEGGEMANN: Along with Gottwald, Childs is the most important influence on my adult life in Old Testament, after my teachers, von Rad and Muilenburg. I figured out that what Childs was trying to do was to turn the Old Testament into *Calvin's Institutes*. And that's a killer. As Paul Riemann has shown in his recent article on Calvin and the Psalms,[12] there is just too much in the text that will not fit Calvin's scheme. The problem is not Calvinism. The same is true of every package of Church reductionism about the biblical text.

BEAL: Oh, man.

Brueggemann: I decided that his reactive way was to resist all the new movements. And I decided I didn't want to be a part of that. So I learned so much from him, but I didn't want to do what he did.

Florence: Can I say something about that from the standpoint of pastors? Here's what I see when I go out as a homiletician and talk to pastors around the country who have reached the limits of quoting other biblical theologians in terms of their preaching lives. What they love about Walter is that Walter does not ask them to quote him, but gives them the freedom to be interpreters who are part of a larger conversation. And not only interpreters, but provisional—to use a word that Kathleen used today and that Walter uses quite a bit. You know, that your sermon does not have to be the last word said about Christian faith. This is a new thought! What Walter has offered pastors is a way to say, it is enough to engage a text. It is enough to model a way of engaging and reading texts that is part of a larger movement of interpretation within the Church. And not only that: if all you do is quote other people, you don't enable anyone to be literate. Biblical literacy becomes something that is centered only in the academy, and the rest of us just quote it. But if you engage this way of knowing and entering texts, then you become an interpreter engaged in the lively, dangerous work of the community interpreting texts. And that is a life-saving thing to pastors who have reached the limits of their own relationship with the text. I think it's like a marriage: your work allows pastors to fall in love with the text again, and then fight with it, and not just quote other people about it, carpool around, you know? So that's one thing that I've noticed as pastors engage your work: you aren't asking them to archive you. And that saves lives, in congregations.

Linafelt: I have two things to say about that. (That's what Walter would always do, but it was usually three or four "things to say about that." And when he says it, he has no idea what they're going to be; but he then generates four things.) I have two things to say in response to that. One is that I haven't preached a sermon in eighteen years and hope never to again. But one of the things I remember in relation to what Anna Florence said is that by focusing on the text and not quoting experts—by not saying, "You've got to believe this because the best biblical theologians are saying this"—you can introduce all sorts of radical ideas. And if people don't like it, you can say, "You don't have to argue with me or with Brevard Childs, you've got to argue with the text!" That doesn't mean they're going to believe you. That doesn't mean, "Oh, now I'm going to read the text your way." But the argument becomes, how do we interpret it. So it's not, then, "We're the experts telling you, and you'd better believe this," but rather, "we are all around this text, interpreting, and here's what I think it says, and let me tell you why I think it says that, and you show me why you think maybe it doesn't say that." So, "don't argue with me; argue with the text"—or, "let's argue together," or "let's engage the text together." The second thing (Tim and I have talked about this recently) is that the single greatest practical influence from Walter's classes that both of us took is that he constantly made us pay close attention. He was so exegetically oriented, so oriented toward close reading. I've made a career of that. I've learned to read closely—he made us read closely. Every time he said something, it was, "show me where you're getting that," or, "come up to the board and show us: map that out." He constantly made us do rhetorical maps, he constantly made us interpret the text. And that's where I learned to do that. I've built a career because he made us pay close exegetical attention.

BEAL: And we still don't exactly know what "map the rhetoric" means! [laughter]

GREENHAW: Amen! Preach it!

SHARP: What do you all do in your scholarship and your teaching that Walter didn't do? Where do you push back or go your own way? I need to ask a question that's sort of the "edgy" kind of question now. And I should ask it of myself as well as the rest of you. So: history matters to me because it's the witness of real people trying to speak out of their pain and their joy and trying to testify to a God who is real in real lives. You've seen that I worry a little bit about Walter's focus on rhetoric apart from—not entirely apart from history, but saying that there is not enough that we can know about history. I don't disagree, but I worry. So that's one place where I worry. I try to think about history in ways that are rhetorically sophisticated but taking somehow—maybe naively—taking historical witness seriously too. [to Brueggemann] That's one place where I have unresolved feelings around your legacy.

YODER: I would second that. I was educated in a time when historical criticism was still dominant but newer methods were emerging, particularly feminist criticism, which had been going on for a long period of time but was finally being taught. When I was a doctoral student at Princeton, it had worked its way into the PhD curriculum alongside rhetorical and literary methods, but I was still heavily tied to the historical framework. And I do think that's been a place where I like the language of "worry." [to

Brueggemann] I appreciate the move and I think it's an important move, but I constantly found myself placing more value on the historical context than I heard you doing, and appreciating the difference, and being challenged by the rhetorical move in light of the sociohistorical. So I would echo some of Carolyn's caution.

O'CONNOR: Well, I think actually Walter has always been historically connected. The social criticism that you do is historical. And historical criticism—I don't even really know what it means anymore, and as a method—I think it's dead, D-E-A-D, dead, dead, dead!

SHARP: No, what do you really think?

O'CONNOR: Ultra-dead! And that we need to put things into historical context, but it's not learning what happened then that matters about this literature. And I think you help us do that. I think that you are historical, and I think that you push students and readers into the historical context that produces the literature. But it isn't what it says only as historical construction of the texts that matters, it's how the text makes meaning then and makes meaning now. And that's all that matters! Because I think historical criticism leaves it as dead literature.

GREENHAW: That puts me in mind of Walter Wink. I remember learning this from Walter Brueggemann, who is not always in sync with Walter Wink. The opening line of that book is, "Historical criticism is bankrupt."[13] It is not without assets, but it doesn't have the capacity that needs to be delivered. There's still information there, but I have to say frankly that I don't find it all that interesting! It's old stuff. But no one has paid any attention to it, so it's exciting. But if you talk about what the Church needs, the Church doesn't need to be introduced to historical criticism. The Church needs the energizing capacity to see these texts as transformational! And I'm worried that we're so excited about this "new thing" that Jesus didn't write these texts. I mean, this was known a hundred years ago. More—eight hundred years ago!

FLORENCE: Walter, this is something I maybe have not said to you, and others maybe have not said to you: you're a performer of texts, in some ways. And here's why I know this: When the students come into class, they imitate you. They imitate how pissed you are! They imitate how angry you are—for the moment as Jeremiah, for the moment as David, for the moment as whomever—about X, Y, or Z in the historical period. I think what they take from that is the importance of going back and embodying, performing the text. And of course they try to perform you, and we have to take them back to performing the text. Because they can't do it like you do! They can't spit like you do, and all the rest. They can't roar like you do. But the point is, you have shown them how powerful it is to be really angry, really riled, or really passionate, or whatever it is. You've shown them in relation to the text what that looks like, and what that could have looked like for David or some other person. So they want to try to do that now. Then what we have to do, because we're homileticians—we're their preaching teachers—is to say, "Don't do him, do the text. What he's doing is the text, right? You got that? This is the script, so do the script! That's what he's doing." I don't know if anybody has ever told you what an actor you are, in the pristine and beautiful sense of what acting ought to have been—what the Greeks meant, what Chekhov meant. So it's not a dead text, not dead biblical historical whatever.

Brueggemann: On the history question, I think I am in the transitional generation, because I know the history—I once knew it year by year—and I assume it, but then when I teach, the next generation doesn't get it. So I trade on stuff that I don't teach, and I think that's a hazard.

O'Connor: Yes!

Yoder: I think that's true in your *Intro to the Old Testament*, for example. We've used it for several years and we so value the theological richness that it offers—the one you coauthored particularly, but also your more recent one. And I agree with Kathleen. I think your work assumes it. But I like the way you just said it, that the students we're teaching don't know the history. So some of what we would potentially do is fill in some of that, in light of the theological wisdom you brought to it. I think that's a helpful distinction.

Greenhaw: Every year you did teach it, because I took an exam on it, and I had to know it. You were teaching the very historical stuff, earlier.

Linafelt: Walter's written quite a bit and talked quite a bit about Ricoeur's idea of "second naïveté." That's another way of putting what y'all said, which is that you can't have a second naïveté if you haven't gone through the criticism first, the historical. There's a sense in which historical criticism has a place, of course. It's dangerous to say we're just going to do the textual, we're just going to do theology; then you fall into a first naïveté. That's different from having gone through and making students come through the critical workout before saying, "All right, now we know all that. Let's go back and do what you thought we were going to do, but you won't do it the same way." I think that gives it more of an edge. And it's not an abandonment of historical criticism.

BRUEGGEMANN: Right.

LINAFELT: Like Kathleen, I think it's very much a part of your work. Although historical critics may not see it that way.

BEAL: Coming to Walter Brueggemann's work as a student, I hadn't read much of it. I think I had tried to read *The Prophetic Imagination* before coming to seminary, and maybe was kind of compelled by it. But what really impressed both Tod and me was what you did in the classroom, which was different from what you do in your writing and even in your lecture-based classrooms, which was the kind of text-based work that Walter does, which he calls rhetorical criticism. I'm not sure exactly how closely related it is to what James Muilenburg called rhetorical criticism. I remember the first exegesis paper we were assigned to do, and we asked him, "What does that mean? What are we supposed to do?" And you said, "Well, just map the rhetoric." And we didn't know what that meant, and you said, "Read James Muilenburg's presidential address, 'Beyond Form Criticism,'" which we did and it helped a little bit. And I remember you said, "Look at the particles," but really what you modeled in the classroom, the way you'd draw a provocative idea, an image, that quote you have from Wayne Meeks in the handout you gave us about images that are counterintuitive . . . those kinds of images and ideas that you drew out. . . . You'd map this rhetoric out on the board from this text, and you'd see something emerge out of the details of this text. It's a different experience—that kind of revelation in the classroom, out of those details of the text—that you can't do in print. And that's where we started, and then we were reading the text and it was a completely different experience. A countertestimony.

SHARP: In the classroom and in the faculty ranks, did Walter's celebrity ever cause problems?

O'CONNOR: Walter's celebrity creates internal problems for anyone who is his colleague, because everything he does is stellar. But Walter spent so much energy encouraging his colleagues that if you said anything, if you published a paragraph, Walter spent huge energy telling you how wonderful it was. So I think that Walter's presence among us was the most encouraging. In the school where I taught before I came to Columbia Seminary, one of the principal things I taught was Walter's words. And when I came to Columbia Seminary, I realized I couldn't really teach Walter's words anymore, because he was in the room next door to me teaching his own words. So I had to have my own. Walter, that really was part of your ministry among us: to encourage our words and to tell us we could find them, and that when we find them, they're good. That is such a gift!

GREENHAW: On the celebrity issue, for Stephanie's sake, I'll say something honest here. Carolyn had this question in her prompt notes asking about a book of Walter's that you wouldn't use. *David's Truth* is the book I wouldn't use. I was living next door to Walter at that time——and when I read that book, I read it through the eyes of what was going on in his life. And he has a phrase in there about Saul "losing authority." If I'm getting this right, it's something like, "when you're not in charge any more, it's hard." And Walter had left the deanship in that period. I think I'm right that it was a painful and hard period, and you were struggling with the president of the seminary mightily, and you left to go to Columbia Seminary. I think that book was very autobiographical.

BRUEGGEMANN: All of them are.

GREENHAW: Of course! That's right. But it was the period I was living in the most. So it was interesting in that way.

SHARP: Can you say more about that struggle?

GREENHAW: Well, I think this is a fair thing to say, those of you who know Walter, and [to Brueggemann] you're sitting right here, and I can say this about you: I don't remember a room you didn't walk into and fill up. You fill up the room! And when a new president came, a sweet man but not strong, there was a lot of tension and conflict. It was a hard period, I think, and the David book, for me, reflects that. I've read it three times, and I keep saying, "Oooh . . . let's go to *The Prophetic Imagination* instead."

BALENTINE: Walter, what do you mean when you say that everything you've written is autobiographical?

BRUEGGEMANN: Well, I am always amazed at colleagues who have research programs——.

FLORENCE: What is that?!

BRUEGGEMANN: ——because I don't have a "research program," I just do what seems to be next. So much of my writing has grown out of my church lecturing, and when you do church lecturing, you get to talk about anything you want to. You know, I think I would lecture about what was on my mind, and what was on my mind was on my heart. So that's what I mean. It grew out of what was going on with me. I think lots of it was that way, probably a lot more of it than I was aware of.

O'CONNOR: I think there is very little scholarship that is not our own, out of our own autobiographies. The best scholarship is when you know about that. It's when you don't know about that, but it's still there, that it cripples your capacity to see the work well with your original eye. That's a postmodern idea.

BRUEGGEMANN: The analogue to Saul that I had in my mind was Richard Nixon, from whom the spirit departed! He couldn't govern any more. So now I have to do David and Richard Nixon and me.

FLORENCE: Should we say something about the faculty meetings at Columbia? When Christine and I first started in the fall of 1998, at the end of every faculty meeting they would announce who had written what, and they would all clap. This was a big deal. You know, once a year or so, somebody gets something out, and we're all, like, "Yay!" And it got tiring that almost every month Walter would have published something. The person who announced this would make a big effort to lift up those of us who were clawing our way—

YODER: —with each article—

FLORENCE: And we'd go, "Yay! Yay!" and then she'd say, "and Walter wrote another book," and we'd all go [affecting a bored, listless tone] "yay." This was every month, practically. And then I was reading Annie Dillard's *The Writing Life*, in which she says that there are maybe only thirty people on the planet who write one usable page a day. And I thought, [sarcastically] "Well, fabulous . . . one of them is down the hall from me." Thirty people on the planet, and this is where I land. [to Brueggemann] Fabulous—thanks a lot! [laughter] But it did make me feel better that this is, like, planetary and not the norm.

BRUEGGEMANN: Well, Old Testament at Columbia is disproportionate. Three of us at Columbia have gotten the Luce fellowship. Nobody gets it outside of Yale or Harvard—except Columbia!

O'CONNOR: If you asked Walter to write a recommendation for you, you'd end up getting it!

BRUEGGEMANN: All of these people in Old Testament have gone well beyond me in terms of the theories to which they appeal. And at my age, I'm kind of locked into my theoretical base, and I'm not going to go beyond that. And it's perfectly clear to me that this happens with all of these people.

YODER: The point about celebrity and the observations about what it is to serve on the faculty with you: I said something similar to this at your retirement dinner, and it's hard to say it, but [becomes teary]. . . . Those couple of years, I learned that you would come in early, as is your custom, and get to work, but at a certain moment you would move to a manual typewriter to type up prayers that you would use at the beginning of class. You knew the texts of the day. Many of these have since made it into prayer collections, which is wonderful. I was across the hall, and I learned very soon as I was trying to work on my dissertation in the early morning hours, to leave my door open so I could hear you make that move to your manual typewriter. And the sound of your typing with a prayerful presence was a spiritual discipline. I was grateful for it. And it was not just the click-click-click of the typewriter, it was that you were so thoughtful about, "How is it that I take the text that the students are picking up this day and translate that language and the point of the text into a prayerful word for this community at this moment in this world?" And that discipline has crafted my own thoughts about prayer and about how to model for students the incorporation of biblical language into prayerful, thoughtful communal engagement.

GREENHAW: How many of you pray before teaching? [Florence, O'Connor, Sharp, and Yoder raise their hands.]

O'CONNOR: If you don't pray, our students will tell you. If you skip it, they tell you. [to Linafelt] You mean you don't at the Catholic university called Georgetown?

BRUEGGEMANN: Mary[14] used to say that if they listened carefully to the prayer, they wouldn't have to hear the lecture!

BEAL: Clover and I went to Seattle Pacific University, and one thing that struck us about those prayers was that it was kind of the I-Thou thing. There was never an address. You just went straight into second-person, and that was it. You never left that I-Thou, second-person language, which I thought was very profound.[15]

BRUEGGEMANN: In the late '60s I went through my Harvey Cox period.[16] I went for a long time without naming the Name. [to Balentine] Do you pray before class?

BALENTINE: I find it unsettling.

YODER: Why?

BALENTINE: Well, because in my tradition, prayer too often serves as a way to camouflage what is important. So I go with the rabbis on this and insist that study is prayer.

YODER: Yes . . .

BALENTINE: So I don't pray. I call attention to myself by not praying, and insist that the study is the prayer. Everything we do from the moment we begin is prayer.

O'CONNOR: Amen.

GREENHAW: Tenure would have been at risk if I had prayed where I was, when I was across the hall from James Barr. And therefore praying, nonetheless, was a reconstitution of the class. So I understand what you're saying. There is a kind of political edge to prayer that is significant.

SHARP: What makes Walter different from someone else—for example, Jack Neusner—who publishes a whole lot and who may not be known to be so original in every single work? There's this risk with being so prolific: Is every idea original? Is every contribution new? Now, I'm not making any analogy between the two of you; I think your work is very different from his. But there's that question of prolific writing—I don't know if anyone has ever used the word "obsessive" about your writing. . . .

BRUEGGEMANN: I have!

SHARP: And then the flip side of that coin: what are some the things that you all wish Walter would write about that he hasn't written about? What do you wish he would address? I have some things I'd like to learn more about.

GREENHAW: I saw that in your prompt questions, and I said to myself, "Good God, I won't answer that, because I haven't read everything he's written!"

O'CONNOR: I would like Walter to write even more autobiographically—even more than in *Pathway of Interpretation*.[17] I'd love to hear more deep, deep self-reflection.

BRUEGGEMANN: We're doing that here!

O'CONNOR: We're doing it now, and the next book is emerging from this conversation. I would love to hear that, just because I'd love to hear it but also as a model for people who pray and live in the muck of their lives, which is what you've written about. And you didn't go back to the question about Walter's particular essays and issues, and the lament questions that are so central to the work you've done, and the power in the Church that you have had. I've addressed this in my own work, and I'd love to hear you write about it.

GREENHAW: The most important essay that I know was an old Interpretation essay called "The Formfulness of Grief."[18] I think that's the turning point for me. It was such a powerful thing! I have to say one last thing. The fifty-year graduates were gathered at the seminary in the spring, and Walter was among his classmates. And I always ask these graduates whether they were preachers' kids, or this sort of thing, and somebody said this one thing that was incredible: "My father was a socialist." I asked them how many of them were, and nearly three-fourths of them were socialists. The meaning of this is really important, and I'd like to know more about that. This is significant. And I don't know what it means, exactly—I need to think more about it and read more about it.

BRUEGGEMANN: Well, it was somewhere between Franklin Roosevelt and Reinhold Niebuhr. In the old Evangelical Synod, my father was a pastor, and Niebuhr wrote a weekly one-page column in what was called *The Messenger*. In the Evangelical Synod, all the pastors went to Eden Seminary, and they all read *The Messenger*. They all read Reinhold Niebuhr, and they all preached Reinhold Niebuhr!

[Brueggemann orders vanilla ice cream for dessert]

FLORENCE: No way! I never would have thought you to be a vanilla-ice-cream kind of man!

BRUEGGEMANN: You heard about the guy with a bad head cold who went into a store and said, "I'd like some banilla ice cream, please"? And the clerk asked sympathetically, "Adenoids?" And the man said, "No, just banilla." [laughter]

O'Connor: Typical Walter. Faculty meetings would be transformed by jokes.

Brueggemann: So what happened is that the pastors of my dad's generation were all into the Social Gospel, largely because of Reinhold Niebuhr. And if you're going to be into the Social Gospel, that's going to tilt you toward socialism.

Sharp: So what else is missing in Walter's work?

Florence: I've got a thought. I'm the mother of two sons who were quite taken with you—had dinner with you on several occasions and even last spring said to me, "Could Walter come to one of our lacrosse games?" to which Walter said, "No thanks, don't want to do any more of that!" I would really like to hear you, as someone who has dedicated many books to your grandchildren, write to those children, to this upcoming generation that fancies itself emerging or whatever it is. I mean, I know the body of work is available to them and all the rest, but I would like to hear you say something to those grandchildren of yours and to the children of mine.

Brueggemann: I just gave a lecture recently on—I'd be curious to know whether you all know this verse—in Exodus 10:2 there's a place where Yahweh says to Moses, "I have conducted these plagues in order that you may tell your grandchildren that I defeated Pharaoh." So I got to lecture on what happens to the grandchildren if the grandparents do not tell them about the Exodus. The lecture is called "Antidote to Amnesia."[19]

Florence: Well, I would love to see you actually say that to them, because our children need the privilege of exposure to something bigger. So when you're ready, just let us know.

Sharp: Stephanie, why do Walter's books sell so well?

Egnotovich: It's just smooth marketing at Westminster John Knox! [laughter] I've had conversations with colleagues, not just at WJK but at other houses as well, about Walter and his books. People in publishing talk about Walter's books, and why on earth they sell. He connects with people in a way that not very many authors do. That's the essence of it, I think. So people wait for what he's going to say next. And I don't know how to get other scholars to do that. I think he's unique.

Florence: He really understands them.

EGNOTOVICH: Yes, I think that's it.

FLORENCE: [to Brueggemann] They know you understand them—the pastors. You should see the pastors waiting at the Festival of Homiletics. There are two or three thousand of them, and when it's time for Walter, they're just like this [dramatizes waiting in open-mouthed anticipation]. Really! Walter comes and there's this hush, because what he always says at some point in the lecture is, "What you do is the hardest thing that anyone does," and it helps get them through.

EGNOTOVICH: And he does not hide behind language. He uses language to bridge gaps and to leap over obstacles. There's an immediacy to what he says and the way he says it that makes his books extraordinarily relevant.

LINAFELT: I have two things to say about that. [laughter] And maybe more. Maybe why his books are so popular is that you get his personality in the books, which is very unusual. We are mostly trained to write in the so-called objective voice. And most of us don't have that much personality anyway! So, you know, you hear his voice and there's a real presence there. It's not the same as picking up any other book on the prophets or any other book on the psalms. So there's that sense of voice, I think, that appeals to people. I think content-wise, there's the fact that—maybe this is starting to be less the case than it used to be, but—he says things that other people won't say, especially in the pastoral context, about God. He's recently been called a blasphemer and a heretic in print, by a credentialed biblical scholar.

O'CONNOR: Who said that?

LINAFELT: I think Waltke.[20] You do take a chance if you say the sort of things that Walter will say about God having this ambivalent inner life and God's tensions—all this non-Calvinistic theological stuff. You take a chance with the doctrine police. But clearly the pastors and the people in the pew respond to it. They may not always agree, but they want people to say these kinds of things, so they can think about them and argue about them. Most people won't say that, and certainly wouldn't have said it twenty years ago. You couldn't take those theological risks.

FLORENCE: Like that "God is good all the time"! It's very permission-giving.

LINAFELT: Right. The common assumption is that the problem is always with us, the problem is always with humanity. Walter is able to say, "Maybe there are problems on both sides. And in fact, the Bible gives you ample witness to this. So if you want to argue, argue with the text, not with me!"

GREENHAW: Grabbing God by the collar! Can you see it?

YODER: Those are really good observations. Another thing I would add is how you're a bridge-builder between disciplines. The fact that you read voraciously in many other disciplines and integrate their vocabulary or frameworks of meaning in your work allows for this broader audience that many of us who speak largely in "guild-speak" tend to lack. The fact that you are so deliberate about the broader conversations, without regard for disciplinary boundaries, makes you hugely attractive to a wider audience.

LINAFELT: I have one thing to say about that.

BEAL: Only one?

LINAFELT: Only one. At Columbia Seminary when I first went to do the Master's degree and started studying with Walter, he inspired you to want to learn more and to read more, because he did seem to have read everything and brought it into the classroom. So this was a period for me when I first started doing a lot of reading. I'd go to the library and every single book I checked out—no matter what the topic was—had one signature on it, and it was Walter Brueggemann. On occasion there would be two, but mostly it would be a book that no one else cared about. But no matter what it was, Walter Brueggemann had checked it out and read it. He read everything.

BRUEGGEMANN: I had a big argument with the library when they started removing those [card catalog] cards and putting the information into the computer, because I think the history of the book and who read it matters.

O'CONNOR: I've noticed that. I haven't really done this, but I've watched you inspire yourself by reading. And then you write, and then you teach.

BRUEGGEMANN: That's right.

O'CONNOR: Your reading feeds you, and it's inspiring to me that you do that.

LINAFELT: As a student, you would see him wrestling with whatever he was reading. He'd say, "So I just read these poems by Czesław Miłosz," or, "I just read this biography of Freud," or, "I just read . . ." It might be something outside of the field completely. And that energizes you to want to learn, to bring things to bear.

BEAL: But this could be a moment of shame for some students, too. I remember that in the hallway, students would have books they wanted to sell for the next class. I remember a list of theology books for sale, and Walter had written in his distinctive handwriting, "These are worth keeping!" [much laughter] They were selling their souls.

SHARP: [to Brueggemann] Is there anything that scares you?

BRUEGGEMANN: My great struggle is to not be afraid of the Harvard/ Yale reviewers. I had a memorable conversation with Doug Hall, and he instructed me, "If you're going to be a theologian of the Church, you just have to pay that price and go on." Now, he didn't have to pay it, because he was a systematic theologian! It's what they expected him to do. Nonetheless, it was a very important conversation for me, because he kind of called me on it.

O'CONNOR: What brought the topic up?

BRUEGGEMANN: Oh, I think I was grieving about some review I got.

LINAFELT: Maybe it was Carolyn's article. . . .

BRUEGGEMANN: No, it was before that! [laughs]

O'CONNOR: I've heard you talk for many years about your role as translator, translating guild scholarship for use in the Church.

BRUEGGEMANN: That's right. What those people do is very important. It's a good thing that those sorts of scholars do what they do, as I depend on them for what I do. And I could not do what they do. It's a good thing that there are varieties of gifts. It has taken me a while to recognize and embrace my gifts, to focus on that work and leave the rest to others who can do it better than I can.

O'CONNOR: Walter, you are not a translator. You are the inventor and the creator. You may translate some stuff, but in the process, you're the inventor and the creator.

BRUEGGEMANN: But I depend on the deep critical work.

O'CONNOR: Mostly you don't agree with it, though.

BRUEGGEMANN: All art is derivative.

O'CONNOR: All art is derivative! Of course, of course.

LINAFELT: In the Psalms class, we got a lot of Gunkel, a lot of Westermann, a lot of Mowinckel, in ways that we would never have gotten by *reading* them. We were really getting them. You were translating, but it was even better than if we had read them, because we were getting something else with them. It's hard to make Mowinckel interesting for seminary students. [Brueggemann laughs]

GREENHAW: I remember going to an AAR/SBL meeting in St. Louis while I was a seminary student, and Ebla had just come out.[21] A large group of Italian scholars presented on their discovery, in heavy accents. I am sure it was interesting to someone, and Walter thought that this was good for us to go to. But they went on and on and on about the value of these texts, and it was sooo damned boring!

BRUEGGEMANN: As it turned out, it was terribly overstated.

GREENHAW: Way overstated!

SHARP: I have a question for you, Walter. What do the people at this table not know about you, that you are a little anxious about sharing but nevertheless, in the spirit of the good will and congeniality of this gathering, you will share? What do we not know about you?

BRUEGGEMANN: I can think of two things, because I'm instructed by Tod to think of "two things." One is how deeply propelled I am by the abuse my father got from churches. That propels me on the justice question.

SHARP: Say more about that.

BRUEGGEMANN: Well, he was poorly paid and treated badly, so that by the time I left high school, we lived in the only house in town that didn't have a furnace. And so on.

    The other thing that I keep hidden—though you all may have discerned it—is what an incredibly poor linguist I am. It is the professional curse of my life that I never learned German well. I should have learned it at home.

SHARP: [joking] There's still time, Walter.

BRUEGGEMANN: No, it's too late—it's much too late! When I went to graduate school, all of the important books were in German. My first seminar with Muilenburg—it was Jeremiah. On the first day, he said to me, "You'll report next week on Baumgartner's monograph on Jeremiah's use of the Psalms," which at that time was not translated.[22] That was near the end of the world. Then I flunked my German exam. I took eleven weeks of French at the University of Cincinnati, when I was doing my last summer of field education, and I passed my French! I had studied German for four years and flunked it. So the language stuff is terrible. When I took Ugaritic, I took Ugaritic from Isaac Mendelsohn at Columbia University, across the street from Union. So the class met, about eight of us, around a table in his office. And I'm never late for anything, but I was twenty minutes late to class because I couldn't find it. So the only chair left was to his left. And he believed in inductive teaching. He thought if you knew Hebrew, you could just read Ugaritic. So all the teaching he intended to do was twenty minutes. I sat down, and he said, "Well, we'll just start reading. Here!" [laughs ruefully] I never did catch on to that. A lot of that stuff, I didn't catch on to. Which is probably one of the big pressures in my turning away from history to rhetoric, to give me something to do.

O'CONNOR: It was providential!

BRUEGGEMANN: [laughing] Yeah, right!

SHARP: Well, I just want to add a footnote: that frees me up a little bit. The wall that I hit was with Akkadian, and boy, was it a hard wall! Akkadian is fascinating, but damn, it's hard! I remember at one point in the fall during my first semester of Akkadian, our daughter was six months old—I had just had a baby and started the doctoral program. I did not have eight hours a day to devote to Akkadian, aside from my other three classes. I couldn't do it. I remember walking down Wall Street in New Haven with tears streaming down my face as I was going to class, because I knew how hard it was going to be and I knew that I had not mastered it. It was very difficult. So I appreciate your sharing that story.

O'CONNOR: But how much does Akkadian have to do with your actual work now?

SHARP: Zero. Thank you!

LINAFELT: I know the Akkadian logograms for "beer" and "god." I figure that's all I need to know.

BALENTINE: [to Brueggemann] On the language issue: one of the things that I've watched and wondered about in your writing, especially given your intense interest in lament literature and exilic literature and poetry, is your distance from Job—which we've talked about, you and I, a little bit. So I'd like to hear you talk about that. You have explained it to me as a language issue.

BRUEGGEMANN: Yup. I don't know enough Hebrew to read Job.

BALENTINE: I'm not sure I'm buying it. I'm not sure you've convinced me yet. And you take a rather conventional view on Job, for someone who knows so much about lament and who feels it so keenly.

BRUEGGEMANN: Yes. I never have felt up to Job. Maybe a lot of it is linguistic, but even beyond the linguistic, I couldn't manage Job. I just find it forbidding and overwhelming, and I don't even know how to walk up to it. That's the reason. I accept Westermann's analysis that Job's speeches are collections of lament complaints, or something like that, but I don't think I know enough to do that. That's why I want to always stay close by your side![23]

FLORENCE: What's the difference between knowing enough to do it and feeling enough to explore it?

BRUEGGEMANN: Well, I don't feel enough . . . or I could feel it without knowing it.

GREENHAW: From my history with you, I think it has a lot to do with a fight against Wisdom literature. Is there something to that?

BRUEGGEMANN: Well, in my early work I wrote that book *In Man We Trust*, which was my foray into Wisdom literature. Phyllis Trible tried to stop that title. I was not yet sensitive to the gender issues with that language. She intervened at John Knox Press about the title. But the editor, who was Dick Ray at that time, was a very conservative guy, and he just went through with it. I didn't know enough. I can get the wisdom traditions from the outside, but I can't go deeply into them. I don't know why. I'm quite aware that I can't, but I don't know why. Christine and Sam have covered the corpus, so. . . . It's kind of a puzzle to me. I think, David, if you take wisdom as the revelation-and-reason thing, then I come down all on the side of revelation, and I'm not sure I understand that. I'm clear about it, but I don't know why.

GREENHAW: Can you talk about Doug Meeks at all, in relationship to your later writing?

BRUEGGEMANN: Doug Meeks, who you may know is a theologian at Vanderbilt, taught the gospel and the economy. He and I team-taught for twenty years. Most of the theology I know, I learned from him. He was a student of Moltmann and therefore of Barth. I think that was an important influence in another direction for me.

GREENHAW: Weren't wisdom tradition and natural theology associated with Schleiermacher?

BRUEGGEMANN: That's right. And when I got to Columbia Seminary, Shirley Guthrie's Barthian influence was so strong you could hardly do anything else. But, Sam, you must have had some hunches behind the way you said that.

BALENTINE: Well, I remember writing a piece for you in a Festschrift. It was on Job; it was a reading of Job.[24] I was immersed in Job, and I'm pretty sure the trigger or catalyst for whatever insight I had came from having talked with you. We had been in conversation for a very long time, and we had been friends for a very long time. And you never said a word about the article, except for a perfunctory thank-you.

BRUEGGEMANN: Yes, until much later.

BALENTINE: Until much later, when things were very different in your life. Somehow the conversation came up again, when we were at dinner one night. And I said, "Well, now, Walter, I already said this to you, and for you, once before." "Oh, when was that?"

BRUEGGEMANN: I had missed it completely.

BALENTINE: It was in the article, and you read it and appreciated it in the usual way. And you wrote me back after that dinner conversation and said, "I've reread what you said. I wasn't in a place to understand what you were saying when I read it before."

BRUEGGEMANN: The text was Job 40, I think, where God says to Job that He created the crocodile: "I have created this ferocious creature like you"—like you! I think, Sam, that I got to rereading that after eight years of psychotherapy . . . something like that. Then I got it.

SHARP: Want to say anything about what you learned that you couldn't see before?

BRUEGGEMANN: What I learned is that my Pietistic tradition, which I learned from my father, taught me essentially self-effacement. Sam's article was confirmation of my psychotherapy—that you don't have to be that way. That's how that comes together for me. So I had so much to unlearn before I could read it.

SHARP: Was it liberating for you, the second time you read it?

BRUEGGEMANN: Oh, yes. Sam's article was an extraordinary act of friendship—it showed me something that I had initially missed.

BALENTINE: That's an important contribution to our conversation, that you see it as an act of friendship. And your understanding of what friendship means. What loyalty means. Right?

BRUEGGEMANN: That's right.

BEAL: We were sidebarring about that before it came up. I had written a piece on Job, and yet ironically, this is something that you have not written about. I feel the same about Job. I'm no more linguistically qualified to do so—less so!—than you are. I haven't written anything on Job where, every sentence, I haven't thought about you and thought about your influence. We went from Columbia Seminary, Tod and I, to working with Carol Newsom on Job at Emory.[25] But everything we brought into that Job seminar, and into student teaching in the seminary on Job, was all coming out of our time with you and out of your influence. So it's kind of ironic that you feel like you don't have a voice vis-à-vis Job, and yet here's Sam talking about this, and we had this experience.

BALENTINE: I wonder whether it isn't the language, really. Somebody earlier said something about the piece you did earlier on the formfulness of grief. (This is just anecdotal, from my experience.) You cannot write an article with that title, let alone write what you wrote in that article, unless you know something about—and have yourself been formed by—grief.

FLORENCE: That's right.

BALENTINE: It's not a language issue! It's way beyond that. And so, I think—this is just by way of self-reflection but also to contribute to the general conversation—my sense is that your interest in rhetoric, which I share, with a kind of aloofness to the history, which I share, is formed by a real existential passion. And one can't go where your passions haven't taken you yet. That's both a blessing of what you've given us—and I guess in our different ways what we practice—and it's a limitation of what we do.

FLORENCE: There's something interesting in what you say about that. [to Brueggemann] I remember one of my early conversations with you, in my early years, just in this sort of fraught sense of my late 30s: how am I going to write about *x*, how am I going to write about *y*, when I haven't experienced it? This is the homiletical dilemma. And you said, "I think the issue is access." Access! To me that's been huge. Because access is different from experience. It has a sense of proximity and taking-on and saying yes to it.

GREENHAW: And pastoral responsibility. Because pastors have access to pain that exceeds their own pain. And to be able to have access to that pain is incredible. And the responsibility to form that pain into language on behalf of the whole Church is very, very important. [to Brueggemann] I think growing up as a PK [preacher's kid] is the key to your life; I've heard you say that, and I think that's really important. Because your father got abused by these people—not treated well. But he served them by going to the places of pain in their lives in incredible ways. And that is fuel for your capacity in great ways.

BRUEGGEMANN: I was in a Lilly seminar twenty-five years ago that went on for three years. To start the seminar, what they agreed to do was for everybody to get to know each other, to adopt a metaphor that would disclose our life. My metaphor was exile. I can trace all that exilic business, and I think that's behind everything I do.

LINAFELT: On the issue of your inability to write, to some extent, on the study of Job: I think a lot of what you do is to take texts that seem very settled—where everyone thinks they know and things are comforting, or that we think are settled—and show how they're not. You show how these texts are actually deeply unsettling. They're much more agonistic than folks realize. They're much more challenging. But with Job, it's all there. You don't need to take Job and do that to it. I think that connects with what you were saying about people's lives. We've talked a lot about, you know, walking out of the church and everybody says, "It's fine, pastor. It's fine," and of course, it's not fine. Part of what you do is to stir that up, in a painful but necessary way. You do that with biblical texts. But Job—it's all stirred up already. So you don't need to come and tell us about how Job gives you an ulcer if you live with it, because that's obvious to us. But we didn't know about the Psalms necessarily; we didn't know that about the book of Samuel or these other books.

YODER: Beyond Job, are there texts that haunt you? That you've wrestled with and engaged on multiple occasions and that still haunt you?

BRUEGGEMANN: Oh, I think Jeremiah. I wish that I could get my head around Ezekiel. I just can't. So I'm haunted by my inability to relate to that text, but I am haunted by Jeremiah. I think I learned that from Muilenburg. You know, Muilenburg had a whole commentary written on Jeremiah that he provided to us but never published, because he thought it wasn't good enough. He thought it wasn't good enough, where he was really doing rhetoric in Jeremiah and some Psalms.

BALENTINE: Your friend, Terry Fretheim, told me once when he was writing a commentary on Jeremiah, after having had immersed himself in it for a very long time (Kathleen's listening!) that he found himself going to bed at night weeping, because he had been so deeply immersed in the text. And then he would wake up in the morning weeping because he knew what was waiting for him when he went back to it.[26] Do you connect with that?

BRUEGGEMANN: Yes, although I wouldn't have been able to be that articulate about it. But it seems to me that Jeremiah just goes to the bottom of everything.

BALENTINE: Is that what you mean when you say it haunts you?

BRUEGGEMANN: Yes.

O'CONNOR: Part of what we all do—and we need to do it with so much more consciousness!—is that connection between our pain and our joy that informs the passions of what we see in a text. That's why you speak to so many people. Because whether you know it or not, that pain and grief and loss and abandonment in you come through the text to the people's hearts. That's why I want you to write an autobiography. I want you to write about your life through the text. Because there's still something there, some life! I think that's what we should all write about—that which hurts us the most and speaks to us the most. This whole pretension that we could make that out-there, "objective" reading of the text is so false.

GREENHAW: But do we have to be so naked to do that?

O'CONNOR: Yes! And if we do that, we'll touch the world. If we stay back here, we don't affect anybody. And I don't know how he [Brueggemann] does it, but he does it.

GREENHAW: How do you not?

FLORENCE: You don't need to say anything about yourself for us to know everything about you. When you show us you as an interpreter, you show us you! When pastors ask me about your life—"Where is Walter now? What is he doing now?"—none of the details of the joys or sorrows of your life are surprises. They hear it in your work, in the way you come at the text and the depth with which you do it.

BRUEGGEMANN: As you were saying, David, that really is the mystery of being a pastor. Just imagine what any community would be like if you took the pastors out of it! I'm not talking about "the Church," but even so. . . . As Kathleen knows, I was in Rome in early October at the Basilica of St. Paul, which is manned by Benedictines. And all of these confessional booths had Benedictines in them for the pilgrims. You know, Protestants dismiss all that, but it struck me that there's a place to put all this stuff. And Protestants do it differently, but we do it too: we put it with the pastor. It gets turned into bread, somehow. And Kathleen, you're right about all that. It's a question for all of us in the biblical guild: how much of that can you do and maintain your credibility in the guild?

O'CONNOR: Who cares?

BRUEGGEMANN: Well, I care.

LINAFELT: Everybody cares.

O'CONNOR: But you don't need it.

FLORENCE: Here's what I hear pastors say: "He's a friend of mine. I e-mail him on occasion. Tell him I said hello." I think they are ready to hear whatever you want to share.

O'CONNOR: I think you've already done it.

GREENHAW: I was a dean with a professor who was really into literary stuff and ignored the historical stuff; it was like foam on the surface. There's a history here—heed the history, and then you can do the literary stuff. This is what I admire most, the tension between the attention to historical criticism and the refusal to let it all stay there. That's so valuable! The tension is right, but if we resolve the tension without the historical stuff, it's meaningless. You have to do both.

BRUEGGEMANN: The way I see myself positioned, you have to do two refusals. You have to refuse historical criticism, but you also have to refuse canonical criticism.

O'CONNOR: Yes!

BEAL: Tying that to what Kathleen was pushing you about, I think there's also a tension between self-revelation and self-effacement or self-concealment. And complete fulfillment of desire for revelation is always profoundly unfulfilling.

O'CONNOR: It's not so much self-revelation as it is self-consciousness. It's not about you, but it's about what you're aware of.

BEAL: Readers feel that self-consciousness without that complete self-revelation.

O'CONNOR: Oh, they do. They do.

BEAL: There's a tension there—I don't know.

FLORENCE: That's what the beauty of a sermon is, in terms of the connection it provides between the interpreter and the text and the listener: what is not said. The sense of redemption that you feel to all these things is beyond words.

BALENTINE: An observation is triggered by a small memory that lingers, and yet, explodes.[27] [laughter] Early on in my tenure at SBL meetings, about thirty years ago, watching you come into a room that was overfull, spilling out the doors, take the lectern as the first, second, or third in a panel, stand there while there was a lot of rustling around, glasses down [imitates Brueggemann glaring over the top of his glasses at a crowd; much laughter] . . . you all probably saw this every day . . . until he had stared the audience into silence. And then there was this "No, no"—the defiance that you're talking about. It was clearly, "This is who I am, this is what I've come to say." There was clearly a defiant note in it, which as a child of the '60s I didn't need to be persuaded about—I was a kindred spirit. But there's also a "Yes." It's not only a "No," there's also a "Yes" that stares us into silence. Which I learned from you. I do this, or try. I don't come to the lectern and start speaking; I come to the lectern and I stop. Whether what I've got to say is worth listening to or not: "Listen!" I got this from you. And it's not just about saying "No," which you're better at than anybody I know. It's about saying "Yes: this is the alternative." But I got it from this. [slides glasses down and glares across the top of them]

BRUEGGEMANN: When I first started wearing these, a woman said to me, "You know, you can get the whole lens." I said, "These are not for seeing. These are a pedagogical device." [laughter]

GREENHAW: You talked about Gottwald, and Gottwald is important. I remember the transformation of the SBL. Gottwald had published *The Tribes of Yahweh*.[28] And they put it in a little, bitty room, a tiny room in a hotel in New York. They misjudged how important it was. And you responded. It was you and Gottwald in the corner of a hotel room, and they came in the room and down the hall forever, and it was clear that this was what was happening at the SBL. It shifted the SBL! I believe that's what made you able to be the president [of the SBL] in that way.[29] It was a major change in your appreciation of what Gottwald was doing. But more than the sociological stuff, it was really the meaning for the Church that was so critical. And you took Gottwald and helped Gottwald speak to the Church in a very powerful way. That was New York, in the '80s.

BRUEGGEMANN: I remember the room!

SHARP: It's time to close. Our thanks to all of you for participating, and to Stephanie and Westminster John Knox for their generosity in making this conversation possible. I want to thank Walter for his candor and all that he has shared. It can't be easy to be on the spot, to be asked and probed about all of your commitments.

BRUEGGEMANN: And thanks to Carolyn, not only for this but for taking on this whole initiative.

LINAFELT: Maybe this will make up for that article.

SHARP: Oh, I'll be working on that for some years yet, I think.

BRUEGGEMANN: What was the phrase? She accused me of "ebullient romanticism." When I wrote a letter of reference to support her tenure, I said, "Even though she accuses me of ebullient romanticism, I still think she's terrific!"

BEAL: I just want to say, is there anyone here whose professional life has not been greatly enhanced by Walter's personal and professional commitments? [general murmurs of assent]

O'CONNOR: I sometimes fear that I'm just an impostor and that I'm here only because Walter supported me, and that if Walter had not supported me and encouraged me and brought me to Columbia Seminary, I'd be working for Wal-Mart.

BRUEGGEMANN: I have to tell you about when we interviewed Kathleen. She had come to the seminary to interview, but Doug Oldenburg was determined to have a Presbyterian.[30] And we interviewed Kathleen, and we didn't even take a vote. We just understood. The hell with "Presbyterian" or "not Presbyterian" —we wanted Kathleen! [laughter]

Notes

1. See the review essay by Walter Brueggemann, "Jeremiah: Intense Criticism/Thin Interpretation," *Interpretation* 42 (1988): 268–80.
2. Brueggemann's last few lines in the *Interpretation* 42 review are, "In another context, it would be sufficient to say these are splendid, competent studies. Our locus in this journal, however, requires that these commentaries be reviewed not only in the environs of the scholarly community but in the presence of the church and synagogue, and with a yearning, frightened eye on our world which is collapsing. In the very long run, one wonders if a verdict will be given about us, that we let the text have its powerful say in ways that mediated faithful human options in our time; or if we will be judged to have kept the text at such distance that the larger questions from these texts were not permitted and the daring hints of resolution were not made available."
3. Gerhard von Rad, "The Form Critical Problem of the Hexateuch," in *The Problem of the Hexateuch and Other Essays*, trans. E. W. Trueman Dicken (Edinburgh: Oliver & Boyd, 1966), 1–78.
4. Walter Brueggemann, *Theology of the Old Testament: Testimony, Dispute, Advocacy* (Minneapolis: Fortress, 1997).
5. Samuel E. Balentine, *Hidden God: The Hiding of the Face of God in the Old Testament* (Oxford: Oxford University Press, 1983). Brueggemann's review: *Catholic Biblical Quarterly* 47 (1985): 310–11.
6. Samuel E. Balentine, *Prayer in the Hebrew Bible: The Drama of Divine-Human Dialogue* (Minneapolis: Fortress, 1993).
7. Walter Brueggemann, *Finally Comes the Poet: Daring Speech for Proclamation* (Minneapolis: Fortress, 1989).
8. Anna Carter Florence, *Preaching as Testimony* (Louisville, KY: Westminster John Knox, 2007). Brueggemann's endorsement on the back cover reads, "This is a delicate, artistic blockbuster of a book that is sure to alter our thinking, our talk, and our practice of preaching. Anna Carter Florence begins with compelling 'case studies' of preachers—all uncredentialed women!—who have stepped outside the box and given voice to the new truth that has arisen from their bodily venture in faith. From there Florence probes the way in which such bodily truth—textually grounded—dares to insist upon articulation, even when such articulation defies 'the System,' runs risks, and shakes the settled world. Florence brings subtle theological thought to her argument, but by the end of the book her words soar and sing with concrete speech and with practical theology of a most practical kind. The utterance that Florence sounds and invites cannot be left unsaid. Preachers will find in this book a guide, a companion, and a goad to fresh truth-telling. This book is indeed a blockbuster that will, if we attend to it, bust all our blocks!"
9. James Barr offers an extended critique of Brueggemann's work in *The Concept of Biblical Theology: An Old Testament Perspective* (Minneapolis: Fortress, 1999), 541–62. Bruce K. Waltke sharply criticizes Brueggemann's *Theology of the Old Testament* in

his (with Charles Yu) *An Old Testament Theology: An Exegetical, Canonical, and The-matic Approach* (Grand Rapids: Zondervan, 2006), 69–72.

10. Carolyn J. Sharp, "The Trope of 'Exile' and the Displacement of Old Testament Theology," *Perspectives in Religious Studies* 31 (2004): 153–69.

11. Walter Brueggemann, *Prayers for a Privileged People* (Nashville: Abingdon, 2008).

12. Paul A. Riemann, "Dissonant Pieties: John Calvin and the Prayer Psalms of the Psal-ter," in *Inspired Speech: Prophecy in the Ancient Near East: Essays in Honor of Herbert B. Huffmon*, ed. John Kaltner and Louis Stulman (London and New York: T. & T. Clark, 2004), 354–400.

13. Walter Wink, *The Bible in Human Transformation: Toward a New Paradigm for Biblical Study* (Philadelphia: Fortress, 1973), 1.

14. Brueggemann's ex-wife.

15. "I-Thou" refers to the intimate relationality of God and the believer as expressed in Martin Buber's classic work of Jewish philosophical theology, *I and Thou*, originally published as *Ich und Du* (Leipzig: Insel-Verlag, 1923). The English translation most influential in North America in the twentieth century was that prepared by Walter Kaufmann (New York: Scribner, 1970).

16. For example, see Harvey Cox, *The Secular City: Secularization and Urbanization in Theological Perspective* (New York: Macmillan, 1966).

17. Walter Brueggemann, *A Pathway of Interpretation: The Old Testament for Pastors and Students* (Eugene: Cascade Books, 2008).

18. Walter Brueggemann, "The Formfulness of Grief," *Interpretation* 31 (1977): 263–75. Reprinted in *The Psalms and the Life of Faith*, ed. Patrick D. Miller (Minneapolis: Fortress, 1995), 84–97.

19. Brueggemann gave this lecture at Lipscomb University (Nashville) on October 15, 2008, at a conference on the book of Exodus.

20. Waltke, *An Old Testament Theology*, 70, quotes Brueggemann on the dialogical, pro-visional, and open-ended nature of biblical rhetoric and responds, "Is it too harsh to recall that the Serpent also asked, 'Did God really say?'" On p. 71, Waltke evaluates Brueggemann's theological position regarding the capriciousness of divine sover-eignty as blasphemous; on p. 72 Waltke writes, "Brueggemann draws his heretical theology from his flawed exegesis. . . ." Brueggemann responded to Waltke on a review panel discussing Waltke's *Old Testament Theology* on November 24, 2008, at the SBL annual meeting in Boston.

21. In 1975, archaeologists working at Ebla in Syria discovered many thousands of ancient clay tablets dating to the late third millennium BCE. The tablets, inscribed with Sumerian writing and a hitherto unknown Semitic language that came to be called Eblaite, included economic texts and other documents.

22. Walter Baumgartner, *Die Klagedichte des Jeremia* (Giessen: A. Töpelmann, 1917). Brueggemann assesses the significance of Baumgartner's work in pp. 162–67 of his *The Theology of the Book of Jeremiah* (Cambridge: Cambridge University Press, 2007), citing the English translation, *Jeremiah's Poems of Lament*, trans. David E. Orton (Sheffield: Almond, 1988).

23. Balentine has written a commentary on Job, published by Smyth & Helwys in 2006.

24. Samuel E. Balentine, "'What Are Human Beings, That You Are Mindful of Them?' Divine Disclosure from the Whirlwind: 'Look at Behemoth,'" in *God in the Fray: A*

Tribute to Walter Brueggemann, ed. Tod Linafelt and Timothy K. Beal (Minneapolis: Fortress, 1998), 259–78.

25. Carol A. Newsom subsequently wrote *The Book of Job: A Contest of Moral Imaginations* (Oxford: Oxford University Press, 2003).
26. See Terence E. Fretheim, *Jeremiah*, Smyth & Helwys Bible Commentary (Macon: Smyth & Helwys, 2002).
27. The allusion is to Brueggemann's *Texts That Linger, Words That Explode: Listening to Prophetic Voices*, ed. Patrick D. Miller (Minneapolis: Fortress, 2000).
28. Norman K. Gottwald, *The Tribes of Yahweh: A Sociology of the Religion of Liberated Israel, 1250–1050 B.C.* (Maryknoll: Orbis, 1979).
29. Brueggemann served as president of the Society of Biblical Literature in 1990.
30. Douglas W. Oldenburg was president of Columbia Theological Seminary from 1987 to 2000.

Chapter 2

"Redescribing the World"

Boston, November 24, 2008

The following conversation sheds light on the roots of Brueggemann's sustained engagement as a biblical theologian not only in and for the academy but also in the public square. Brueggemann reflects on formative family relationships and the ways in which his passion for economic equity and commitment to political justice were nurtured at Elmhurst College decades ago. Brueggemann allows us to glimpse the surprising beginnings of development of his powerful scholarly voice: as a shy, young man lacking confidence in intellectual ability, he was too daunted to major in philosophy or literature and, by his own admission, was "terrified" throughout his three years at Union Theological Seminary. As the conversation unfolds, we see that academic leadership in his first position at Eden Theological Seminary helped Brueggemann to find his footing in the guild. The conversation then moves to explore a highly visible public interaction with biblical scholar Bruce Waltke at the annual meeting of the Society of Biblical Literature in 2008. It closes with reflections offered by Brueggemann on prayer and worship.

CJS

CAROLYN SHARP: It's such a pleasure to think about the impact of your work, to think about the influences on your thought and stories from your development as a scholar. I'm sensing that there are lots of great stories that I don't know, and I can tell from your colleagues that there's a lot that people want to share. Let me start with college as your first formative academic experience. You were at Elmhurst and you took a B.A. in sociology. Why were you interested in sociology?

WALTER BRUEGGEMANN: Well, my brother was a year ahead of me, and he majored in sociology. I followed him all the way through college and seminary. I knew I wanted to be in the humanities or social sciences—that was the limit—and I was too intimidated at the time to do philosophy or literature. So I ended up in sociology by default. At Elmhurst, it was really a one-man department. There were a couple of adjuncts, but. . . . I took about 25 percent of my college work from him.

SHARP: Who was that faculty member?

BRUEGGEMANN: His name was Theophil Mueller, and he was a really contrarian figure. This was in the 1950s, and he still drove a Model A. He was very authoritarian, in which the pedagogical thing was to memorize what he said and give it back to him. But it was just incredibly shaping because in addition to knowing sociological theory, he really had the passion of a Christian prophet for justice. And that got bootlegged in with it. So it was a defining thing for shaping me about social justice, public theology, and all those points.

SHARP: Was he interested in the sociology of the poor and marginalized in the community, or power structures? Say more about the "prophet" part of it.

BRUEGGEMANN: Well, I took all the courses: the sociology of crime, sociology of family, rural sociology, urban sociology, sociology of race. I was in his class the day that the Brown-versus-Topeka school opinion was rendered.[1] He danced in class, because he had been locally working on race questions. You know, the way that they worked on it in the '50s. It wasn't radical or anything, but he had a passion about it. So he was interested in the "haves" and "have-nots" and all those kinds of questions. I don't know that he was terribly activist. When I went to Elmhurst College, the sociology majors were largely pretheological students, so he knew he was shaping future pastors. And in retrospect, I think the influence of Reinhold Niebuhr on him was great. The Niebuhrs went to Elmhurst, and at that time they were kind of in the woodwork of the place. I went to college out of a small rural high school; there were twenty-seven kids in my high school.

SHARP: Where was that?

BRUEGGEMANN: It was in rural Missouri. I knew nothing, and I was so intimidated about everything and everyone. Which I think was the reason I sort of followed my brother. He had a little more courage than I did. So I decided, "I'll just do what he does."

SHARP: What's the age difference between the two of you?

BRUEGGEMANN: He's a year older. And in the last year of seminary, he took an intern year, so we did our senior year together and were ordained together.

SHARP: And he's ordained now? In which denomination?

BRUEGGEMANN: He's retired. But he was in the U.C.C. Actually, we were ordained a few years before the U.C.C. was formed. It was an antecedent: the Evangelical and Reformed Church.

SHARP: Have you stayed in conversation with your brother?

BRUEGGEMANN: We had always stayed in conversation, but we grew apart until I was divorced three years ago. He has rallied to me, and I talk to him almost every day. He's been terrific about my transitions and all that.

SHARP: It's great to have a loved one step in during a time of crisis, a time of change. Do you want to say anything about what the "growing apart" was about? Do you have any insight into that?

BRUEGGEMANN: I think we just both got busy. There wasn't any hostility to it particularly, but I think when I went an academic route—we never talked about this, but my hunch is that he probably was a bit put off by that, because he's not an academic type. He's a very practical guy. And I think it was just the complexity of having families and stuff like that. Probably we were both kind of neglectful more than anything else, just didn't put the energy into it.

SHARP: You speak so eloquently to the church. Is it possible that in part you're speaking to your brother?

BRUEGGEMANN: What I would think more is that I am echoing my father, who was not a well-educated man, but he had all the right passions. I think that in an odd way, my vocation is an echo of his. He was a fierce guy for justice in rather stumbling ways, because his generation didn't know how to do a lot of things that we've since learned about all that. I think that connection is much closer than with my brother.

SHARP: You lost your father at a premature age. How old were you?

BRUEGGEMANN: I would have been in my late thirties. We never had any abrasion, but I wasn't as close to him as now I wish I had been. But I've become aware of how much I'm like him. People tell me my gestures are the same as his, and all that kind of stuff.

SHARP: I want to ask another question about Elmhurst. Was there a class you hated, a professor with whom you had conflict, anything you really didn't like about that experience?

BRUEGGEMANN: Well, the two low points were in my first semester. I had to take Biology 101, and I almost flunked it. I have no capacity for anything scientific. [laughs] Partly it was the problem of learning how to study and being a disoriented college freshman and all that. The other course—I'm no good linguist, and I took introductory German, and that was a hassle for me. But as soon as I had gotten past those required things and could do what I wanted, it was better. I suppose it was the end of my sophomore year in college before I computed the fact that I could really do this. I hadn't gotten on top of it until then.

SHARP: If it's any consolation, I'm happy to hear that you had trouble with biology, because I got a C in "Chemistry for Poets"—that was the title of the course, "Chemistry for Poets"—and I barely pulled off the C.

BRUEGGEMANN: [laughing] Even "for poets"?

SHARP: Yes. It was terribly boring to me, and I skipped ten classes in a row. Got scolded by the professor and everything. So thank you for sharing your trouble with biology! Tell me about the extracurricular side of your life in college. Did you join the debate club, or sing, or play sports?

BRUEGGEMANN: I belonged to two clubs, which in retrospect didn't amount to anything. We had a pretheological society that brought in speakers to talk about ministry, and then I belonged to the sociology club, the high point of which was when we brought in Norman Thomas. He was a socialist who ran for president about seven times, and a great old warrior by the time we had him in. I'm no athlete, so I was the manager for the cross-country team, I was referee for junior varsity basketball, and in the season, I spent every late afternoon at the track, setting hurdles and timing sprints and doing all those things that didn't require any competence! [laughs] I suspect that in our college, I was the number one informal cheerleader for basketball and football teams, all of which were dreadful. We hardly ever won a game.

SHARP: They needed a cheerleader, then!

BRUEGGEMANN: That's right! So for about two years, junior and senior years, in the local U.C.C. church, as a student I led the liturgy every Sunday. And on Saturday night I always had lost my voice . . .

SHARP: . . . from the cheering!

BRUEGGEMANN: Yes, right. So it was always a bit of a crisis.

SHARP: So let me ask you this, then: on Saturday night, would you have been in the library or on a date?

BRUEGGEMANN: I never dated. I was shy and embarrassed, not knowing how you do that. I would have probably been in the library if it were open, but it wasn't. So I just hung around the dorm and didn't do much.

SHARP: So you must not have met your wife in college, then. [Mary Miller Brueggemann, his first wife]

BRUEGGEMANN: Not until graduate school. So not through seminary did I date. Either I didn't have time because I was studying, or I compensated for not doing it by studying!

SHARP: An experience that's familiar to many, I suspect, in the scholarly arena.

BRUEGGEMANN: That's probably right!

SHARP: I want to hear about the B.D. at Eden, about with whom you studied Bible and how your hermeneutical sensibilities started to be formed.

BRUEGGEMANN: Well, the B.D. was just the M.Div. back in those days, and it was a fairly set program. You didn't have a lot of options, and seminary was really a good time for me. I was really on top of it; I could do things. I got my only B in a preaching course!

SHARP: No, you didn't!

BRUEGGEMANN: I did.

SHARP: Was there a comment on a paper that you remember?

BRUEGGEMANN: Oh, I remember it very well. We had to do a series of sermon outlines—in those days, you did the outline business—and I did the characteristic thing that seminarians do when you don't know how to read a text: you make an outline of ideas. And my teacher said, "That's not what we are looking for here. We're looking for you to handle the text." I didn't know how to do that.

I had two Old Testament teachers, neither of whom hardly ever published anything. One of them was in his last years. He had been my father's seminary teacher, and he was a storyteller. He is the only person I know who studied under both Albright and Gunkel. He just told Bible stories. When I got to graduate school, I took my lecture notes along, and what I discovered was that in telling stories, what he was doing was giving us Gunkel's complete taxonomy of forms. You know, legends and myths and so on. But he never told us he was doing any of that. So he got me interested in it.

Then I had a younger teacher at the time, who introduced me to von Rad. Von Rad in the '50s was just coming on the scene. There wasn't much in English yet. That was really the impetus. I was the bookstore manager of our little bookstore—it didn't amount to much. When the faculty would order special books for themselves, I would often keep the book and read it before I told them it was in! Because I didn't know how to find a book to read—I didn't know anything like that. One of those books was Davie Napier's little book, *From Faith to Faith*.[2] It really was the first English replication of von Rad. That's what it was, although I didn't know it at the time. And he had a chapter in there on Genesis 1–11 that von Rad did, and one on the succession narrative. So I like to say—and I've told Napier—that that's really the book that got me into Old Testament study.

SHARP: What fascinated you the most about that? What drew you in?

BRUEGGEMANN: I think it was von Rad's artistic sense and his patterning and his ability to see how these texts interrelated to each other. It was an inchoate sense about rhetoric that I wouldn't have named at the time.

SHARP: He waxes poetic about the Yahwist, doesn't he?

BRUEGGEMANN: Oh, yeah. It's just incredible. I was in Heidelberg for a year when von Rad was old but still active. They told me that there in the university, when he preached at the university church, all the graduate students came to hear him just for his rhetoric. They weren't interested so much in what he said as in the power of the rhetoric.

SHARP: What year were you in Heidelberg?

BRUEGGEMANN: 1970–71. Von Rad died the next year. The other thing about going to graduate school—this is what my family says—is that Eden Seminary had a very rigorous field-education program. The first year, everybody spent the year at the inner-city settlement house. My assignment was to run a weekly club for seven-year-old inner-city girls. And my family said that's why I decided to go to graduate school. [laughs] Because I wasn't too good at that!

SHARP: What about the spiritual formation side of seminary life? Did you go to chapel a lot?

BRUEGGEMANN: Oh, yes, I was a good institutional citizen. I did everything that was expected.

SHARP: Did you balk at any of it?

BRUEGGEMANN: No, no, I never have really balked at any of it. Probably I should have, but I didn't.

SHARP: And this was all in what became the U.C.C. mode.

BRUEGGEMANN: Yes, this was the other side of the house, the Evangelical and Reformed side. But in those days, we didn't talk about spiritual formation. You were being formed, but it was never talked about that way. In that kind of seminary, there never was a split between the academic side and the other side. You and your teachers were all deeply involved in the church. When I think back on it, none of it happened on a very high level. The academics weren't on a very high level. But the phrase that was often used for the third-generation immigrant community was "the German church on the American frontier," and you didn't have to be too erudite to be a pastor in those churches. You just had to love people.

SHARP: Still a good thing to do! Tell me about Union. I'd like to hear about James Muilenburg and others with whom you studied.

BRUEGGEMANN: The younger of the two Old Testament teachers, the one who introduced me to von Rad . . . I had never heard of graduate school. I didn't know anything about anything like that. So that teacher shepherded me into it. The only place I applied was Union because it was not so competitive in those days. I had never heard of Muilenburg. So I went to Union and was terrified. I spent all three years being terrified.

SHARP: Terrified of what?

BRUEGGEMANN: Failing. I think that the impetus of my academic life is to keep trying to prove that I can do it.

SHARP: Wow. I think you've proved that to many people, quite decisively! But not to yourself, perhaps.

BRUEGGEMANN: I think those deficits continue to be there. So: Muilenburg was an incredible force. Everybody in the seminary turned out to hear his Introduction lectures. Other faculty members, too. Everybody went to the "performance."

SHARP: He was dramatic?

BRUEGGEMANN: He acted out everything! There's a story they tell. I wasn't there, but he was lecturing about Mount Sinai, and he held up his two hands as the two tablets of the commandments. He lectured for the longest time holding up his two hands as the two tablets. A secretary came in and said, "Dr. Muilenburg, there's a phone call you have to take," and he said to a student, "Will you hold these?" [laughs]

His graduate seminars were hit-and-miss. And they were anxiety-producing, because you could never quite figure out what we were doing or what he expected.

SHARP: Was it all about process at the spur of the moment?

BRUEGGEMANN: Well, it seemed like it to me! I think I had three seminars with him, and I sat in on some lectures. The first one was Jeremiah, and the first day he said to me—he didn't know me, he just said, "You come in next week with a report on Baumgartner's monograph on Jeremiah," which at that time wasn't translated.[3] I nearly had a stroke.

SHARP: Did you have someone help you? How did you do it?

BRUEGGEMANN: Oh, I just guessed a lot! I had George Landes, probably his first year, for archaeology and ancient Near Eastern texts, or something like that. And the third member of that faculty was Sam Terrien. Terrien was a brilliant lecturer, but it seemed to me his seminars mostly didn't go anywhere. I was probably not a good member of seminars—I wanted somebody to lay it out for me!

SHARP: I find that hard to believe, because you are such an independent and original thinker in your own work.

BRUEGGEMANN: Well, I wasn't then! It took me a long time to get there. I had Ugaritic and Akkadian with Isaac Mendelsohn, and I had "Text and Canon" with Harry Orlinsky. Those were side issues. So there's basically Muilenburg and Terrien.

SHARP: What courses at Union did you take in theology? Tell me more about the broader education you got there.

BRUEGGEMANN: Oh, I didn't take anything outside of Old Testament. What you had to do (I've never heard of any other program doing it this way) was, you had to take six entrance exams to the doctoral program: Old Testament, New Testament, church history, history of doctrine, philosophy of religion, and I don't know what the sixth was. So it was assumed that you had that stuff under your belt. One of the great regrets I have about my time there is that I was so intent on getting it right and getting it done that I completed it in three years, and I never went to any other lectures. That was pretty dumb, given who was there. But I was very single-minded about all that.

SHARP: Whom do you regret having missed while you were there?

BRUEGGEMANN: Niebuhr, particularly. But John Knox[4] was there in New Testament, Wilhelm Pauck in Luther studies, Cyril Richardson in patristics—I should have exposed myself to those people. But if you do that, then you don't get out very quickly.

SHARP: Did you have any female teachers?

BRUEGGEMANN: None. In the seminary there were a couple of women in Christian education, but otherwise there were no women teachers.

SHARP: And Phyllis Trible taught there later.

BRUEGGEMANN: Phyllis Trible and I were contemporaries. She was there before me and after me, and she really was like Muilenburg's daughter, they were so close.

SHARP: What was it like, being a peer of hers?

BRUEGGEMANN: It was pretty intimidating. She knew what was going on!

SHARP: Was it a competitive ethos there or supportive?

BRUEGGEMANN: It wasn't competitive. I'd say it was mildly supportive, because we knew we were in it together.

SHARP: What about your Ph.D. in education? You took the Th.D. in 1961 and the Ph.D. in 1974. What happened in between?

BRUEGGEMANN: When I got my doctorate, I immediately went to Eden Seminary and started teaching. The early '70s were in such incredible upheaval, and I started thinking—I was completely wrong about this, but I started thinking that seminaries were going to close at a rapid rate and there wouldn't be any jobs. So the reason I went to that doctoral program was, I thought I'd better create some options for myself. St. Louis U. was there, so that's why I did that. The whole thing was sort of foolish, but I learned a lot. The terrible thing is that I had to take three courses in statistics, and I nearly died!

SHARP: This was concurrent with work at Eden?

BRUEGGEMANN: Yes. Not only was I teaching a full load, I was the academic dean. But they had all these courses at St. Louis you could set up for late afternoon, because they were wanting school teachers to take those courses. So it worked.

SHARP: Sounds like a feverish life.

BRUEGGEMANN: It was a feverish life indeed. But in those days I was high-energy and could do a lot.

SHARP: Some might say you still are, with your publication rate! How long were you academic dean?

BRUEGGEMANN: Fourteen years. The only reason I did that was we didn't have an academic dean. Richard Niebuhr had been the dean for four years back in the '30s, but you didn't need a dean, because everything just went along in a rut. And it turned out, at the time, that we had presidential leadership that was greatly beloved but that needed help with an increasingly complex seminary program. So the faculty created this post. And I did it that long because in that faculty, there really wasn't anyone else to step into it at the time.

SHARP: Now who was the president at the time that you were academic dean?

BRUEGGEMANN: It was Bob Fauth, who was a wonderful pastor from Chicago. He came to be president, and he was a wonderfully gracious man. What happened is I had all this responsibility to make it work, but I really didn't have any authority, because he wouldn't give me any authority. So it was a hard place in which to live. We didn't have any conflict. He was so nice that you couldn't have conflict with him And we remained great friends—I spoke at his funeral. But it was so hard, because in the early '70s, the seminary was filled with draft dodgers who weren't really interested in education.

SHARP: So what did you see as your goals: curricular goals, hiring goals, changing how admissions worked? What were you involved in?

BRUEGGEMANN: We did a lot on curriculum. In those days, we thought we needed to break up the old disciplinary patterns and get it connected to other cultural and institutional elements and the like, in the city and so on. All of which took enormous energy. And probably didn't have much impact. [laughs ruefully]

SHARP: Ah, educational reform. Was there resistance among the faculty to what you wanted to do?

BRUEGGEMANN: Yes, there was. We were a small faculty, and for the most part, faculty were on board about all that. But my institutional ambitions were not very realistic in terms of the resources of the school and the human energy that it took. In retrospect, it probably wasn't a very good use of my energy. But you do it.

SHARP: When I think of faculty meetings I've been a part of, I think of two extremes. See if either of these sounds like faculty meetings you saw at Eden. One is where decisions are all made in a back room, and then you come into the faculty meeting, and the people in power just tell you what they've decided, and you're done. Which can be very disempowering for everyone in the room. Another kind is where true conversation goes on, and maybe even yelling and conflict, but it is a real dialogue. Is either of those models what happened when you were there?

BRUEGGEMANN: There wasn't much back-room stuff. And there wasn't much quarreling. Funny thing about it, there were about fourteen of us, and Elmer Arndt was the teacher of the history of doctrine and the strong man on the faculty and the secretary of the faculty. And the faculty meetings largely consisted of one-on-one interaction with him. And when he thought we had talked long enough, he wrote down what we had decided! It wasn't terribly abrasive because people pretty much trusted him. He had always done his homework, and he was smart. So it was reasonably peaceable. The other thing is, in a simple institution like that, there weren't a lot of life-or-death decisions to be made.

SHARP: Not a whole lot of drama, then? No scandal or campus crisis?

BRUEGGEMANN: No. In a small faculty like that, everybody knows what everybody is doing. The vexation was that we had one faculty member who was fighting the authority of faith and was smitten with Jung. He always deliberately positioned himself as the odd man out. We tried to operate by consensus, and that means that one person who wants to be that way can create the need for lots of energy and so on. I felt the brunt of that as the dean, trying to make things go forward. Later on—I guess I was still dean—we had just one occurrence of a scandal where a faculty member got hooked up with a student. No, I think I wasn't dean any more then.

SHARP: Blessedly.

BRUEGGEMANN: Yeah, right.

SHARP: I want to switch gears and see if you are interested in filling in a couple of blanks.

[Brueggemann is given a short form to fill out. It is reproduced here with his answers:]

I hope that I will never lose my ability to ____ *hear and speak* ____ .

I wish I knew more about ____ *critical theory* ____ .

The biblical book that terrifies me the most is ____ *Ezekiel* ____ .

I write so much because, ____ *(a) it satisfies me* ____
____ *(b) my endless sense of deficit* .

I am thankful that ____ *I have good work, good health, & good folks* ____ .

I will be a better interpreter when ____ *I can work on a larger screen* ____ .

I am hardest on myself about ____ *getting it done—over pressure about work* .

My quirkiest scholarly habit is ____ *excessive note-taking* ____ .

BRUEGGEMANN: I say to my students, "Someday you'll give thanks that you had one teacher with no idiosyncrasies!" [laughs] It'll have to be someone other than me, probably. [Musing aloud on his "excessive note-taking" answer:] When I retired, I threw away two big file cabinets filled with 3-by-5 cards. This was precomputer times. I kept notes on everything and never looked at them.

SHARP: Taking the notes is what gets it in your brain, right?

BRUEGGEMANN: That's right. [Mulling his " larger-screen" answer] By that I mean, have a larger sense of what's out there in terms of pop culture and intellectual culture. I tend to be very . . . [imitates a laser focus]. And because I stay focused, I get a lot done, but then the connections aren't always as good as they need to be.

SHARP: That's interesting, because I think many would see your work as already quite broad and interdisciplinary, in terms of homiletics and theology and so forth.

BRUEGGEMANN: The other thing I wish I knew more about is science. I have no prospect of completing that.

SHARP: "Critical theory": what would you like to know more about?

BRUEGGEMANN: I would like to understand more about Horkheimer and Adorno. What I would particularly like to know more about is the Jewish component of what they were up to. I've read a lot of that, but I always feel like I don't get it. And I've been influenced by Ricoeur—I don't think he should be slotted into "critical theory," but . . . Ricoeur has influenced me greatly, but I never quite feel that I understand what he's talking about. I just wish I understood that whole European conversation better—Levinas, and all that. I have a student now—I mean, he was my student; now he's studying with Carol Newsom—and he is urging me into Lacan. Well, I try to read that stuff, and I cannot understand anything. I just don't have any philosophical depth.

SHARP: You need psychoanalytic theory for that too, right?

BRUEGGEMANN: That's right.

SHARP: Hardest on yourself about getting it done?

BRUEGGEMANN: Yeah, I just can't let go of stuff until it's all done.

SHARP: Do you obsess about a project until it's completed and accepted by a publisher?

BRUEGGEMANN: Yeah. Well, even e-mail—I don't like to let e-mail sit. I think it ought to be answered promptly. So when I get a little writing assignment, I work quickly, and I've been penalized. Two editors had invited me to contribute articles to books they were going to do. So I get those articles finished, and six months later I get them back and hear,

"Sorry, we couldn't get a publisher." So I should have waited. I'm sure no one else had written an essay yet!

SHARP: I'm sure that given your academic credentials, you could place anything you've written! In the time we have left, I want to think with you about the panel this morning with Bruce Waltke.[5] Then I want to think about teaching and faith issues, to get some groundwork laid in these areas so we can revisit it and go deeper in future conversations. So first, the panel today. This was interesting to me, and I heard a number of people say that they thought you acquitted yourself very well in that encounter. Waltke said in his critique of your *Theology of the Old Testament*, "You can't build a theology on adjectives and nouns and verbs. You have to use the whole text." Has he misunderstood what you're doing?

BRUEGGEMANN: Oh, I think so. What I concluded in general is that he did not have any sense of the theoretical base from which I try to do my work. And there's no use in trying to engage him about that. I mean, if he doesn't pay attention to how my argument works, then I can see why he would say that. I probably have said to you that my statement that God lives nowhere but in the text is the most problematic statement in the book. But it would be hopeless to try to explain to him what I meant by that. I should have written that sentence better. I regard as a tautology the [evangelical] claim that God lives in the Bible. If you want to talk about who this God is, you have to talk about God in terms of the Old Testament's representations of God. Or you get something else.

SHARP: If we're talking about textual interpretation, then we are talking about the rhetoric of the text. If you're talking about your experience of God in prayer, then that's different. Or your sense of God in worship: that's not the text. That's a different experience.

BRUEGGEMANN: Right. Even after the panel was over, I went up to shake his hand and we had another unpleasant exchange.

SHARP: What was that about?

BRUEGGEMANN: I said something that I thought was gracious, because I just wanted to leave it there. But he responded with something, and I always take the bait. I don't remember details. He said, "Well, we just disagree." And I said, "No, we really don't disagree at all, but you have no patience to listen to how I'm saying it." I thought it was unfortunate because when the guy's got his magnum opus[6] and he's an old man, there's no use in being contentious, but I also thought I couldn't just let it go. It was interesting that a prominent evangelical scholar said to me, both before the panel discussion and afterward, "You have to say something about this," and then afterward he said, "What you said was what many of us who are in his circle also want to say."

SHARP: Yes. There is more hermeneutical diversity in evangelical circles than Waltke seems to want to concede.

BRUEGGEMANN: A younger evangelical scholar said to me, "Bruce [Waltke] is always very sure. His opinion may be different five years from now, and then he'll be very sure again."

SHARP: One aspect of what Waltke said interested me a lot. He's talking about training evangelical pastors for the church, and says that your work undermines what he's trying to do with his students. Do you think evangelicals are right to fear your work?

BRUEGGEMANN: No! Absolutely not. I have many evangelicals who respond positively to my work, and I engage with them. I thought the clue was, he said, "I want to protect the faith." And what I want to say is, "It doesn't need protecting! It just needs elucidating in imaginative ways." If being evangelical is reduced to a fixed package of truths, well, that's not what evangelical faith is about. I know a lot of evangelicals for whom that's not what it's about. When I was at Regent for three days, I did not know that was his school. So I was with some younger faculty, and I was talking about this panel upcoming at the SBL, and then I found out that he was their colleague! They were saying, "Yeah, well, that's just Bruce! That's how he does it." I don't think the younger ones have any trouble with my work, and they're zealous evangelicals.

SHARP: I would think that the imaginative aspects of what you do—the way of thinking about "redescribing the world" in a way that's open to God's truth—I would think that would be quite congenial to at least certain streams of evangelicalism.

BRUEGGEMANN: Oh, I think so too.

SHARP: And the way in which you run at status-quo constructions of the world and power—that should also be appealing. An exhortation to be "in the world but not of it"—that's what I hear in your words, which, again, should be congenial to evangelicals.

BRUEGGEMANN: In October, I was at a clergy conference with two hundred Church of Christ clergy. Not United Church of Christ, but Church of Christ. We had a marvelous time, and they're very conservative.

SHARP: Was it in the South?

BRUEGGEMANN: It was in Nashville.

SHARP: Wow—they're still inviting you?

BRUEGGEMANN: They are!

SHARP: Let me just ask a couple more questions—not about the text, now, but about your experience of God outside the text. When do you pray? What kind of praying do you do?

BRUEGGEMANN: I do a lot of my praying by writing prayers. And I pray at night. My prayers of late have seemed to be prayers of thanksgiving, because I am in the best place of my life I've ever been in. But I'm not a very disciplined pray-er. I guess eventually I would take refuge in the notion that—as [Michael] Fishbane has said—study is prayer. I think that's what I do.

SHARP: You pray through your work.

BRUEGGEMANN: I think so. Not in any mystical sense, but I do have the impression that I am—not all the time, but very often in my work—I am engaging in praise and obedience, which I think are the two facets of the Christian life. Because of my upbringing, the obedience side of it has been more pronounced. I've had to learn the praise side from Anglicans.

SHARP: Tell me briefly how often and where you worship, and then, what part of the worship service means the most to you.

BRUEGGEMANN: When I was in seminary I went to chapel a lot. I can hardly bear it anymore with all the dreadful student sermons! I now go on Sunday morning, basically, and I go to St. Timothy's Episcopal Church, which is in the neighborhood where I now live in Cincinnati. I used to worship in the Episcopal cathedral in Atlanta for about five years. It's very affluent, very upper-class, very wonderful. But this parish in the suburbs has the most wonderful music program—it's just wonderful.

SHARP: What kind of music do they have?

BRUEGGEMANN: Oh, they do Duruflé and lots of other things. The organist himself has just this incredible solo voice, and they do so much music.

I don't know how they can get it all ready every Sunday. It's not a big choir, but he pays a few people from Xavier University to come sing, and it's always fresh. We have more congregational responses that are fresh than I've ever experienced before. Oh, probably the singing means the most to me.

SHARP: Do you sing yourself?

BRUEGGEMANN: I do. I have no voice, but I sing!

SHARP: Do you sing tenor, baritone, bass . . . or wouldn't you say?

BRUEGGEMANN: I wouldn't say! But I love to sing. And the prayers are important to me, though I don't really like Episcopalian bidding prayers. It always feels to me like we are talking about praying rather than praying!

SHARP: Do you have a favorite hymn?

BRUEGGEMANN: My favorite hymn is "Love Divine, All Loves Excelling," because I think it's just an incredible narration of the whole story of the gospel. That's my favorite. So when I led chapel, every time, I chose that hymn!

SHARP: When I got married, I got to choose hymns, and I chose five. I didn't care that people might have wanted the service to be shorter, because you know what? I was getting married!

BRUEGGEMANN: And what were they?

SHARP: I know that the tune "Hyfrydol" was there—I think it was indeed "Love Divine, All Loves Excelling." Another one I choose whenever I can is, "Deck Thyself, My Soul, with Gladness," which is a gorgeous Eucharistic hymn. My husband loves "Holy God, We Praise Thy Name"—he's Roman Catholic, and it's from his childhood, so we chose that one. I can't remember the others.

BRUEGGEMANN: He's Roman Catholic? My son married a Roman Catholic, but they attended the Swarthmore Presbyterian Church—a wonderful congregation of thinking people.

SHARP: Presbyterians have a learned denomination. They ordain to teaching, don't they?[7]

BRUEGGEMANN: That's right. Related to your preface yesterday about the current division in the Episcopal Church: next March, I'm doing an address to the House of Bishops, and they've got a guy, a sociologist, who's written a book called *The Big Sort*. And it's about people changing red and blue jobs, and red and blue churches, and red and blue communities, and the bishops are concerned about that happening in our society and in our Church. So when the guy called me, I said [ironically], "Well, I'm sure I'm an expert on that too!"

Notes

1. *Brown v. Board of Education of Topeka, Kansas*, 347 U.S. 483, the 1954 United States Supreme Court ruling that segregation of black and white students in public schools violated the Fourteenth Amendment and was therefore unconstitutional.
2. B. Davie Napier, *From Faith to Faith: Essays on Old Testament Literature* (New York: Harper, 1955).
3. Walter Baumgartner, *Die Klagedichte des Jeremia* (Giessen: A. Töpelmann, 1917).
4. Dr. Knox was the Baldwin Professor of Sacred Literature at Union Theological Seminary from 1943 to 1966.
5. The panel was held on November 22, 2008, at the annual meeting of the Society of Biblical Literature; panelists responded to Waltke's book, *An Old Testament Theology: An Exegetical, Canonical, and Thematic Approach*. Brueggemann was one of the respondents.
6. The magnum opus to which Brueggemann refers is Waltke's (with Charles Yu) *An Old Testament Theology: An Exegetical, Canonical, and Thematic Approach* (Grand Rapids: Zondervan, 2006).
7. Presbyterians traditionally consider ordained ministers to be "teaching elders"; see http://gamc.pcusa.org/ministries/ministers/ordination/.

Chapter 3

"Disrupting the Cynicism of Despair"

New Orleans, November 21, 2009

This interview explores key concepts in Brueggemann's influential early scholarly work on the Israelite prophetic imagination. Reflecting on the twin evils of denial and despair, Brueggemann shares his understanding of the task of the preacher, namely, to resist the ways in which social and religious structures of empire continually tempt believers to abandon their baptismal identity. Brueggemann discusses the importance of practicing a posture of gratitude and muses on the human yearning for fidelity. The conversation moves to the dominance of historical criticism within the guild of biblical studies and the challenges involved in appropriating difficult biblical texts in the life of the Church. Brueggemann engages Bruce Waltke's critique of his *Theology of the Old Testament*, specifically addressing Waltke's charge that Brueggemann's critique of the God presented in the Hebrew Scriptures is blasphemous. The discussion closes with Brueggemann's reflections on exegesis and factionalism in the scholarly guild and his words of advice for new biblical scholars.

CJS

CAROLYN SHARP: I thought that today we might think about some of the points and themes and hermeneutical moves that you make in some of your best-known work. We can think together about ways in which you challenge the Church, ways in which you challenge the academy, and also ways in which you might respond to challenges yourself—if I dare!

WALTER BRUEGGEMANN: Indeed!

SHARP: I'd like to start with *The Prophetic Imagination*, which is a book that has had phenomenal impact. It's in a second edition now and is very well known; pastors and seminary professors reach for it all the time. In that book, you argue that the prophetic—what the prophet is about—is disrupting the cynicism and low expectations that seem to characterize human life in community. You talk about new gifts, the prophetic articulation that redefines how people experience life and makes way for new gifts to be given. And you said short of that, short of this prophetic witness to newness or acceptance of newness, life for us becomes a "dissatisfied coping," a "grudging trust," a kind of managing that dares never ask too much. So people become dissatisfied and just "settle."

The question facing ministry is whether anything can be said, done, or acted in the face of this hopelessness. In place of cynicism and hopelessness, the prophets are calling us to a more vibrant kind of life, out of this hopelessness, and cutting through, as you say—these are your words— "cutting through the despair" and penetrating the dissatisfied coping that seems to have no end or resolution. This is interesting to me. You wrote that in 1978. I want to ask you first whether you think it is still true that our common life, either as a society or as a Church, is this sort of dissatisfaction and settling for what is, without daring to reach for real hope. Is that something that you still think?

BRUEGGEMANN: Yes, I do. In fact, sometimes when I look back at that book from 1978, I'm astonished that I had seen that much that way, because my mind hasn't changed. The way I frame that now is to say that the twin pathologies are denial and despair. You've probably seen that in some of my other essays.

SHARP: Yes.

BRUEGGEMANN: Denial is the numbed pretense that it's all right, and if you penetrate the denial, then you do fall into despair. I think now with these hopeless wars and with the collapse of the economy, I think that hopelessness and despair are primal marks of our society. I think that the rage from the right wing is not really about any particular issue. What it's about is that we now find ourselves in a world that we don't understand and that we don't like, and we don't know how to manage it. So I would maybe nuance it somewhat differently, but I think that's about right. I could imagine in the Old Testament in the sixth century [BCE] that there must have been that kind of despair. Jerusalem is defeated, and we're never going home, and there's no new impetus to be expected.

It's a great oddity to think that trusted speech can open things. I often think of Martin Luther King's "I Have a Dream" speech, in which that's exactly what he was doing. He was opening vistas for social possibilities that nobody thought were possible. It seems to me that in his capacity to do that, he was faithful to and echoing that sixth-century promissory speech.

SHARP: It is, in a way, scandalous to have the kind of hope that King suggested, or the kind of hope that we can see at the end of Amos, or the kind of hope that Isaiah offers. Because it really argues for the revolutionary power of God to transform things, and if denial is a hallmark of our age, I don't know that people are all that willing to be transformed!

BRUEGGEMANN: I think that's right. The tenured West tends to think, "It couldn't be any better than this, so why would we want to change anything?" I suppose that's why a good theology of hope always wells up among the disinherited who can't hope otherwise. When the Jesus Seminar voted that Jesus didn't say anything apocalyptic, we had an African American custodian at my seminary, and he read something about this. So I told him what was going on, and he said, "Boy, if they eliminate that apocalyptic stuff I'm out of business." He didn't have any trouble entertaining hopes that God was going to do something new that would change this. So I think a lot of our despair is situated sociopolitically in a context that makes serious theological claims impossible.

SHARP: And I think that fuels a lot economically. Not blaming, of course, our government alone—or at least, I would not blame us only—but generally global capitalism. There's a reason it thrives on the marketing of bodies and lives in the way that it does.

BRUEGGEMANN: That's exactly right.

SHARP: There are people who are vested in denial, and also people who just don't see a different way. There's the hapless ones and the ones who are vested in driving it.

BRUEGGEMANN: That's right. And there's collusion between those two forces.

SHARP: Speaking of collusion: how does the Church collude in maintaining denial? Does it? I'm thinking in particular about Karl Barth and his dissatisfaction with the liberal program that reduces Jesus to a nice teacher who had some good ideas, who wouldn't have said those apocalyptic claims or make those messianic claims for himself regarding the radical in-breaking of the kingdom of God—if that is the liberal program.

BRUEGGEMANN: Oh, I think that's exactly right, and I think that the mainline churches have so accommodated ourselves to that that we've lost our nerve about this. So you have to tone down everything in order to maintain the budget and the program. So I've been thinking a lot that what clergy need to do is to make a list of all the things they know they need to say and dare not say. I think that's what's so disabling for clergy, to live in that contradiction between what must be said and what cannot be said because it violates the norms and expectations of the Church.

SHARP: It's so tricky, because pastors want to be effective, and if you're run out on a rail you can't be effective for long. They also want to be pastoral, and there are questions about how far you can push a community or individuals and still be pastorally sensitive. And yet, how quickly does it become accommodation and yielding to the culture? I wonder whether you have been able to say some things that the average parish-based pastor cannot. Or do you find yourself holding back?

BRUEGGEMANN: One of the things I find about myself is that when I preach, I almost always preach to strangers, so I can write a hell of a sermon! My experience is that when I get up to preach that, and I look out there, even without knowing people, I feel like, "I can't say that!" I depart from my manuscript a lot. As an itinerant, what I try to do—although I don't always manage to do it—is to say things that the pastor dare not say, and hopefully to create a little bit more space about that. I do wonder whether people's awareness now of the depth of our crisis might create a kind of readiness for that. I just did six weeks of a Wednesday-evening kind of thing at my local church, which is a typical suburban church, St. Timothy's Episcopal in suburban Cincinnati—Anderson township. I did Daniel, on which I had never worked before. The way I set it up is that the empire was trying to talk Daniel out of his Jewish identity, and the empire today is trying to talk us out of our baptismal identity. What astonished me about that is that no one challenged my use of the word "empire." Now, they were Episcopalians, so maybe they were just being nice about it. But the drift of the conversation indicated to me that people sort of understood what I was talking about. I think that's a new sensibility among us. The dawning of the ideological hegemony of military capitalism, or whatever one calls it, is a bit more available and it does give pastors and preachers a bit more room to operate about that.

SHARP: Denial is really hard right now. It's still possible, but there are so many people who are hurting or losing their homes, their jobs. In moments of crisis, people can be more receptive to a new vision.

BRUEGGEMANN: That does push many people off, precisely, into despair, too.

SHARP: So hope is even more radical, because people don't have food, don't have money.

BRUEGGEMANN: That's right. When I talk about these hopes, one of the push-backs I get is, "Well, what does that have to do with the fact that my husband doesn't have a job?"

SHARP: What do you say to that?

BRUEGGEMANN: Well, I say that the local congregation needs to find a way to support the unemployed. It's a communal thing, and nobody has an individual crisis if we have any sense of church. And we have to take the first steps, even though we can't see the second step, about the ways in which we practice the economy ourselves. That's really hard, because we haven't had to think that way forever in the U.S. economy.

SHARP: It's also daring particularly for Episcopalians to hear that church is not—now, this is a stereotype—that church is not a social club that they can come to on Sunday. We are mutually accountable, one for another, in an existential way.

BRUEGGEMANN: That's right.

SHARP: That would be a little alarming to some Episcopalians.

BRUEGGEMANN: The senior priest at our parish, Roger Greene, really works very effectively about that on the local level. He is busy helping people connect the dots on that with each other. But in the face of long-established individualism, that's really hard.

SHARP: When you talk about the prophetic task disrupting the cynicism of despair, you suggest three different ways that a prophet can do this. The first thing you say is that the prophet offers symbols that are adequate to contradict hopelessness. Some kind of icon or way of meaning-making that is not just a Band-Aid, not just some flimsy, lovely little thing, but is actually adequate to address the hopelessness that people are feeling. And then the proclamation aspect of prophetic witness: bringing hopes and yearnings to public expression, which maybe we do less than we used to. And third, to speak concretely about real newness that comes to us—which sounds like testimony, to me. So I want to pursue each of those with you in terms of your own spiritual life. In terms of the prophetic contradiction of hopelessness, what kinds of symbols are meaningful in your life of faith?

BRUEGGEMANN: I'm interested that I used the word "adequate." One never knows whether they are adequate. I tend to gravitate toward specific texts. So the text that I focus on a lot is in Isaiah 65 about new heaven and new earth and new Jerusalem. But then the poem really unpacks that with great specificity about the economy and all of that.

SHARP: The blessings of life, right? Longevity, security. . . .

BRUEGGEMANN: Right. No more building and another inhabiting, no more planting and another eating, no more infant mortality. It's extraordinary. And then I suppose that while I'm aware of the patriarchal character of the phrase "kingdom of God," the way I cast that for myself is "regime change." If you ask what regime change is, the Old Testament prophets were good about that, but I think often about Jesus' parables. He gets very concrete: the kingdom of God is the way that a father and son relate differently. I continue to struggle with how to relate to my sons, so that's important to me. You can argue that the kingdom of God is like the Good Samaritan. That relates to health care policy: am I willing to pay for this guy's health care? And that lets me turn it back into critique of the present regime and how that has been organized. So I think we preachers are very lucky that we get to talk about this, and I find myself, through my preaching, talking myself into it!

I think it is the task of proclamation or interpretation for people to be able to leave the meeting with some buoyancy and entertain the thought that some things are possible that we did not know were possible. It seems to me that's what prophetic promises are always doing. And whether one talks about new covenant in Jeremiah, swords and plowshares, lions and lambs—those kind of particular poems I don't find very hard to translate into ethical mandates or ethical possibilities in my life, particularly about money and about time, which are the ways in which I organize my questions. I believe that the spheres in which evangelical obedience comes to me primarily are in how I manage my money and how I manage my time.

SHARP: Say more about money and time. Do you give to particular charities or volunteer? Or are you talking about the writing that you do with your time?

BRUEGGEMANN: First of all, about my time. Time is a big crisis for me, and I can think of better uses for my time, but the first question for me is to disengage from my aggressive use of time in my work. I can factor that out: I ought to have more time for the neighborhood and for volunteer projects, but the first thing is, I need to make time for myself to *be* rather than to *do*.

SHARP: Sounding a little like Type A, driven, working all the time.

BRUEGGEMANN: That's exactly it. And the money thing is about generosity and attention—security and all of that. So I'm not always so intentional about it. When I'm intentional, then I try to ask, "What if these promises were true? What would the new regime look like? What would my membership in the new regime look like?"

SHARP: Living as though it is true.

BRUEGGEMANN: That's right.

SHARP: I pause to note an ironic dimension of you talking about the fevered working pace that you have and wanting to pull back a little from that, as part of acknowledging this new regime. Because, the ironic part is, everything you produce has a way of proclaiming the kingdom of God and inviting people into Scripture and the truth of community. So, ironically enough, if you write less, then others will be waiting for that invitation!

BRUEGGEMANN: So maybe it's a noble addiction!

SHARP: Yes, and those of us who are workaholics will salute you. I am actually not at all the person to challenge workaholism, unfortunately.

BRUEGGEMANN: When I did this six weeks at my local church, I talked with the pastoral staff about a way that would be an alternative to military capitalism. And we wondered, "Yes, but do you have to say it just that way? Can't you say it in a different way: 'an alternative to the rat race,' or something like that?"

SHARP: Well, yes and no. The "rat race" is about individuals striving to get ahead and maybe not even seeing how they're slaves to financial competition and economic gain.

BRUEGGEMANN: Yes, but if they don't see it, it's because it's situated in that ideology.

SHARP: That's just it. And you are a very powerful voice in terms of challenging that whole structure, the larger social structure. It's not just that a few individuals need to get it through their heads that they should be more present to one another.

BRUEGGEMANN: That's right.

SHARP: It's the whole—if I may employ this over-used term, the whole military-industrial complex. You are big on challenging that, and it's not reducible to the "rat race." Even though people might not want to hear it, I think it's important that you are saying it.

BRUEGGEMANN: In the *New York Times*, one of their daily reviews last week was titled, "Gratitude." I thought it was rather good at explicating what the author was saying about gratitude, but then at the end was sort of dismissive of the whole argument, like, "What does gratitude get you? What can you do with that?" I think that gratitude is the only impetus for an alternative way of life.

SHARP: Gratitude to whom?

BRUEGGEMANN: Well, that's just it: you have to have a God, or a Giver, or something on the other end. And I don't know that the reviewer got that out of the book. But for the reviewer, it was sort of a novel category, and that shows something of where we are, sociologically if not theologically.

SHARP: I'm sure the old certitudes no longer hold and can no longer be taken for granted in our society—religious or other, really. And yet, maybe in the general population, the Enlightenment model is still sort of a tacit foundation.

BRUEGGEMANN: Yes.

SHARP: But as old certitudes are disrupted, where people are anxious or uncomfortable around religion, they don't know what to replace it with. So it's either personal empowerment, or I don't know what else, but it's a difficult place for people to be in.

BRUEGGEMANN: Which is why the articulation of the whole gospel narrative is so important, from creation on. I think even in church people get it only in bits and pieces. They don't see the whole narrative.

SHARP: Even in lectionary-based churches, that's true. You still don't hear the whole thing.

BRUEGGEMANN: That's right.

SHARP: I'd like to ask you about your unease with certitude, with monologue, with the sort of confidence that we see in what you've called texts of orientation in Scripture.

BRUEGGEMANN: It does come up in a lot of ways for me, doesn't it?

SHARP: It really does, and it's one of the things that makes your work so appealing to so many different kinds of people—even, ironically enough, to those people who are vested in the structures of power. They're never us, right? We're all reformers and on the cutting edge—somehow it's never us.

BRUEGGEMANN: Right!

SHARP: I could have chosen any of a number of your works to go into, but I chose *Interpretation and Obedience* from 1991 to think about this, to think with you about certainty and assurance and "establishment" ideology. Those things fail. They are not to be trusted, and in fact you say in a number of different ways that they "lock down" the imagination in unhelpful ways.

BRUEGGEMANN: Yes.

SHARP: You prefer the unsettled, the dialogical, the unanticipated or surprising. This is, now, my assessment of your temperament as a theologian, both in terms of interpretation—in how you read the text—and perhaps in community as well. And so you have a phrase about "holiness dwelling precisely in ambiguity." And then you extend that, in this particular passage, to thinking about community, about brothers and sisters who are troublesome to us or inconvenient to us. You say that they are not obstacles to be gotten around, that they are rather "the means and shape of life"—this is what life is, in all of its unpredictability and unsettledness, perhaps even discomfort. So, here comes a question that would be radical for Walter Brueggemann. Other people would find radical a question about ambiguity and unsettledness, but you love those things, so I want to ask you a question about certitude. Do you have any cause for certitude these days, perhaps something that you might not have "owned" earlier in your career?

BRUEGGEMANN: Well, I should say first that all this talk against certitude to some extent is a wish rather than a reality. I have to say that because people who know me well wouldn't credit me with over-amounts of this. I do think that the older I have gotten, the more I have been able to move away from essentialist understandings of reality. And a good bit of that is long years of psychotherapy. So the way I now formulate it is, one has to juxtapose certitude and fidelity, and I think certitude is essentially a cognitive category—one we use in theology and many other places. And so the churches prosper when they provide certitudes, but that's a misplaced yearning, because we do not in fact yearn for certitudes. What we yearn for is fidelity, which is a relational category, not a cognitive category. I think this is so clear from Jesus' statement, "I am the way, and the truth, and the life." The truth is not the Chalcedonian formula about Jesus, it is the faithful presence of Jesus. So I have come, slowly and not very far, to see that what really is important to me are people upon whom I can rely who image the God upon whom I can rely. I think we always want to engage in reductionism, producing a formula about relationships and then trusting the formula rather than relationships.

To say it all another way, I think that much popular classical theology has taught us that God is a fixed point—omnipotent and all that kind of business—which we try to move; whereas it seems to me that in the Old Testament, both parties are on the move all the time, finding out how to position themselves vis-à-vis each other. And that change of model for me has been very important in trying to understand myself as an agent underway rather than as a fixed identity. So I am always at the edge, now, of thinking that a fixed certitude is likely to be idolatrous. Now, I don't know that one can follow that through consistently, because finally one has to say something. Except that when we have to say something, we need to remember that what we say as our best certitudes can be grandly pretentious. Our temptation is to absolutize.

SHARP: Being at the mercy of relationship is not easy for many. It's easier to orient to a fixed orthodoxy, to say, "I assent to this or that claim." It's challenging for everyone because we are vulnerable.

BRUEGGEMANN: That's right. It's like having a teenager in the house: everything has to be renegotiated all the time! Now, you might want to come back with, "No, not everything is renegotiated," but it really is.

SHARP: Even if some of the answers might be the same over time—"no, you can't have a sports car when you're fourteen." The answer will stay the same, but the reasons the question was asked may change.

BRUEGGEMANN: And then you'll have to have the conversation again!

SHARP: One more follow-up on this particular point. You write also in *Interpretation and Obedience* that "those who live at the edge are characteristically abrasive, restless, and challenging" as they engage questions of certitude that they had thought were settled. "Abrasive, restless, and challenging": those are, I think, positive adjectives in your lexicon.

BRUEGGEMANN: They are positive except insofar that as a white tenured male, I don't experience them as positive. But yes, I think they are positive in terms of the health of the community.

SHARP: Right—salutary. You bring up your own status, and that's what I want to ask you about. In what ways are you part of the restless challenge that is pressed toward the center, toward the structures of power, and in what ways in particular—if you'd care to reflect on this—are you complicit in the complacency? Whether in your job or in another arena.

BRUEGGEMANN: I think I am complicit in many ways economically, politically, and sociologically. But I am also aware of belonging to the restless marginal, and I'm in the process of continuing to discover how that is so for me. It is so because I came out of a pietistic German community that was marginal as I was growing up, because of the war against Germany and my people. I think that I either had a not-very-good education, or I felt that I had a not-very-good education. And as you know in Old Testament studies, if you didn't go to Harvard or Yale, you're always playing catch-up.

SHARP: Or you feel you are.

BRUEGGEMANN: That's right. In the United Church of Christ, I come from the other "side" of the Church that isn't congregational. So in many ways, I think I feel that marginality that evokes a kind of strenuousness in me about, "This is not right," or, "This needs to be called into question." Now, having said that, I have enjoyed safe teaching positions and tenure and accommodating publishers and all those kinds of things, and I'm not unaware of that. So it's stuff that I have to continue to try to figure out.

SHARP: It's interesting because I see—I'll tell you what I see, and then you tell me whether you think it's right—I see your position within the academy as paradoxical. You are absolutely one of the best-known voices in biblical studies, certainly in biblical theology and in homiletics as well. You aren't a professional homiletician, and yet you are more famous than most of those who are professional homileticians. So you have this extraordinary visibility and stature. And yet you have an acute sense of marginality, of trying to get into a center that I don't think is actually there. Everybody thinks there's a center there. Even the people who did go to Harvard and Yale are playing catch-up too—they're just hiding it more than others. So there's a paradox there about your bona fide and very real power in the guild and your sense that that's not reliable.

BRUEGGEMANN: And it may just be that my "take" on the human predicament of anxiety is more to play catch-up. But I also know that you pay a price in the academy for deciding to be a Church scholar, and that means that instead of doing technical work, you run toward preaching, which in the academy is considered second-rate stuff.

SHARP: A "soft" discipline, to some, although of course they are incorrect.

BRUEGGEMANN: That's right, but there you go. On my lack of doing technical work: first of all, I find it profoundly boring, but I also am not very good at it. So I think what I do is probably a match for the gifts that I have, and I've sort of come to terms with that.

SHARP: I do agree with you that certain kinds of technical skills and knowledge are prized in the North American academy and the German academy too. Handily enough, the inadequacies of folks in those other areas—say, in pastoral application or proclamation—are not held against the practitioners of historical-critical method. But they seem to assume that everyone should have that foundational skill set, and then if you want to go preach in your spare time, go ahead. It's a really warped way, and an arrogant way, of limiting our understanding of the kinds of skills that are important, not only for the Church, but the life of the academy too—for reading these texts.

BRUEGGEMANN: And there have been, as you know, changes in the discipline of Old Testament studies, because when I started fifty years ago, there was nothing outside of historical criticism. That's just what you had to do. The moves and shifts about that are terrific and wonderful. Because if you think about your very important book about irony, such a book would not have been even thinkable if you were doing historical criticism.[1]

SHARP: And current interests in postcolonialism and "situated readings" these days—I hear, and you might still hear too, historical-critical colleagues being utterly dismissive of situated readings. So there's a ways to go, but there's a lot of energy around this in the guild, which is heartening.

BRUEGGEMANN: I learned that in an issue of the journal *Interpretation*, when they first did their feminist stuff. As I recall, the editor's preface kept talking about Phyllis Trible's article as being advocacy from a context, but continued to presume that nobody else's scholarship was either advocacy or from a context—it was just a given.

SHARP: So-called neutral, dispassionate, objective scholarship.

BRUEGGEMANN: That's right.

SHARP: There are those of us who have seen through that, but then there are those who haven't.

BRUEGGEMANN: And some never will!

SHARP: We've talked a little already about fidelity. I want to ask you about difficult biblical texts—texts that arguably use rhetorics of violence and that harm. Ethics of reading are important when we're reading any sacred texts. I wonder whether you would agree if I say that you have not challenged difficult Scripture texts very directly. You choose texts that are troubling and unsettling but in fruitful ways. Are there texts that are close to unusable in Scripture because of their violence, because of being "texts of terror," to use Phyllis Trible's phrase—because of their xenophobia, misogyny, war-mongering or jihadist mentality, and so on? Let me ask you about a concrete text, and then perhaps you could respond more generally to that whole line of questioning. So, the book of Joshua. Is Joshua readable today? What do you do with holy-war tradition?

BRUEGGEMANN: First of all, let me say, when you ask whether they are "usable," I think there are texts that are not usable in preaching and public liturgy, but that may be importantly usable in contexts of study and conversation. So you have to have a range of uses. But I tend to think about those kinds of texts out of my experience with my personal psychotherapy. My way of thinking textually about psychotherapy is that it is reincorporating into one's identity old texts that I thought I had gotten rid of by denying them. So I want to say that the book of Joshua is an old text in our community, and we can't pretend that it's not there, and we can't pretend that it didn't happen. We have to process it, but what one does with those texts inside of therapy is to embrace them and critique them and find out that they may not be true. Even though I remember that this is what my mother said to me, "blah blah blah," maybe I'll get free of it. I will not get free of it by pretending it is not there. I will get free of it by going through it. So—this is related to my argument that God is in recovery from violence—I've learned from Renita Weems and Carol Dempsey and a bunch of people that these texts are very dangerous to use because you may trigger the wrong reactions. But in safe pastoral venues, we have to revisit the propensity to violence that permeates our tradition and our history. And if you take these texts seriously, then God is implicated in all of that. We have to deal with that, and we have to press God to deal with that, and we have to move along to better ways. That's what I think. Now, that requires a certain kind of sophistication about texts and about self, and the problem is, in many church venues you don't have the opportunity to process all that. So it has to be done carefully and knowingly. But I am unpersuaded by the liberal evolutionary notion that we've now left those texts behind. I just don't think that works. And I don't think stuff like that can be explained away. It has to be dealt with and embraced and processed.

SHARP: Your point makes clear that it's not just that these are some texts that are a little disturbing, within a whole collection of texts. Rather, to use the family systems model, they represent a whole system of issues that we should be processing, whether we are doing so adequately or not. These texts are formational. They are root experiences that are going to be forming and deforming us whether we respond to them or not.

BRUEGGEMANN: That's right.

SHARP: The other risk, of course, is that when we ignore them, that has profound implications for the canon of Scripture as a whole, to be picking and choosing what we like and don't like.

BRUEGGEMANN: It does indeed.

SHARP: A problem with what one might call the "liberal agenda"—"oh, we just don't read that any more"—is, what about the revelatory power of the other texts? Where does that come from, if one is just going to pick and choose texts as if at a salad bar?

BRUEGGEMANN: Yes, and if you take the usual liberal position that the book of Joshua is just a mistake, it's a slippery slide. When you arrive at the claim that God is love, how are you not going to say that's a human projection?

SHARP: It astounds me that people don't see that risk! But it does go back to what you said earlier, that the opportunities in the Church—even the opportunities for forming pastors-in-training, even at the seminary level—are slim, few and far between, in terms of doing this really deep layer of work. One might have to . . . I don't know, write a lot of books over the course of a lifetime to try to get at that! That might be one way to address it.

BRUEGGEMANN: That's right!

SHARP: But you say, and I think you are absolutely right in this, that God is implicated when we look at these texts, and also when we look at what you call texts of countertestimony in Scripture, texts that push back on God. I want to bring up in this regard Bruce Waltke's critique of your work. Because he really doesn't like the idea that God is implicated in any of this. He is extremely uncomfortable with that.

BRUEGGEMANN: I know it! Have you seen his book?

SHARP: I have not read the whole thing—I have to be candid about that. But I have seen the part where he addresses your work. And so I thought I'd get a thought or two from you pertinent to this point. When he is reviewing what you say about Israel's countertestimony in Job's complaints, psalms of lament, and so on, he says, "This latter witness," that is, this countertestimony, "Brueggemann alleges, presents *I AM* as abusive, contradictory, and inconsistent, unreliable, and unstable."[2] Waltke continues to characterize your position by saying, "He blasphemously charges: 'In my judgment . . . Israel's text and Israel's lived experience kept facing the reality that Yahweh's self-regard keeps surfacing in demanding ways.'"[3] He thinks you're critiquing God in this, and—he makes this move a couple of different times in his review of your book—he says, "Is it too harsh to recall that the Serpent also denied that God is good . . . ?"

BRUEGGEMANN: Yes!

SHARP: ". . . and that Cain could not affirm that God was just?" So he sees your position as heresy, perhaps even as a position of Satan! If God is implicated, we can't rescue God, right? So what do we do with that, if God is implicated? Do we stay in a relational mode, praying and yelling?

BRUEGGEMANN: Yes, that's what I think. And truth-telling. In that SBL panel, Waltke said publicly that his vocation is to protect the Church from wrong interpretations.

SHARP: What do you think the Church needs to be protected from? Because I'd bet you and he have different views on what the Church needs to be protected from.

BRUEGGEMANN: Well, this will tell you where he goes—he has some pages in his book in which he draws the conclusion, from his ethical reflections, that according to the Bible, women should not have jobs outside the house. They should stay home and have families. So there you go.

SHARP: It's interesting, because that's not even in Scripture in so many words.

BRUEGGEMANN: That's right!

SHARP: If you wanted to say women shouldn't speak in Church, well, you could point to Scripture texts that say that.

BRUEGGEMANN: Right. What I think the Church should be protected from is idolatries. And I think we all have our idolatries, but Waltke's idolatries are so evident in his book: he imagines a nice little family and a nice little neighborhood, but God has not put us in that world any more.

SHARP: Even if God might have put you and me in that world, there are millions who are not there. When we think about countertestimony— railing at God or pushing back on God—I have an image of a statue that we've created of God that's going to crack when we push on it. And that needs to happen.

BRUEGGEMANN: That's right.

SHARP: Our golden calves. Even if we try as hard as we can not to create a "God" that's going to become an idol, I think it's almost inevitable that humans end up doing that, in our prayer, and so on.

BRUEGGEMANN: Oh, I think that's right. That's why the impetus of reformation is always at work. I want to say about the book of Joshua: somewhere, Elie Wiesel was asked whether he believed in God, and I don't know all that he said, but he said something to the effect, "Sometimes I believe against God."[4] It seems to me that is one way of taking these texts seriously: to engage enough with the God in the text to be against what God is up to. That's taking God seriously.

SHARP: Absolutely. And the fact that in Christian tradition, a dimension that Wiesel might not be able to draw on but that we can draw on has to do with the incarnation of God in the person of Jesus Christ, and what that means. Real life in all its messiness and contradictions and ambiguity—all those words: the unsettled, restless ambiguity of it—is honored by the presence of God living in it, rather than just looking down on it from on high. So we have to speak those truths, even if people get mad.

BRUEGGEMANN: That's right.

SHARP: Has anyone ever gotten mad at you? Have you ever had someone storm off because of something you said?

BRUEGGEMANN: Oh yes, a few times!

SHARP: What comes to mind, if I may ask?

BRUEGGEMANN: I was teaching in Atlanta, and I was talking about the military-industrial complex, and students were fine with it until I suggested that Coca-Cola was a part of that. A guy walked out of class. And I remember once, I was in the state of Washington in some church, and I said something imprudent about Ronald Reagan, and some people got up and walked out. So it happens. If you say something quite specific, so they understand what you're talking about, then . . . [laughs]

SHARP: I admire that you do get concrete. I'm seeing this in the addresses that I'm looking at.[5] You don't hesitate to get concrete.

BRUEGGEMANN: Well, if you are itinerant, it's fairly easy to do.

SHARP: You just get the hell out of there once you're done. Hop in your car quick!

BRUEGGEMANN: That's right! I don't think I've told you this, but my best shot at speaking the truth was when I was preaching at an affluent Presbyterian church here in New Orleans on Mother's Day. The assigned reading was from Acts 10, where Peter has that vision of the reptiles and so on, and God says they're clean. The way I set my sermon up was to say that Peter got these notions of clean and unclean from his mother—Mother's Day—who taught him Leviticus. My sermon was, it turned out that Peter's mother was wrong, and yours probably was too!

SHARP: Did you hear huffing in the congregation? I like it. As a mother, I would say that your point frees me up not to be the infallible source of all wisdom. The pedestal is a lonely place. And it's not a safe place, because you can fall off it. Which is the flip side of misogyny, of course—it's a long way down, if you fall off the pedestal.

You have critiqued the academy on the dominance of historical-critical methods, and I would say also that in a very gentle way—even a tacit way—you critique the Church for what it is not yet capable of doing, or the instances in which it shrinks back from what is necessary, what you call a "loss of nerve," although it's a very gentle, pastoral way in which you offer alternatives to the Church. Slightly less gentle with the academy, but that's fine—we can take it! So in these critiques, if I were to reflect on temperament assessment tools such as the Myers-Briggs Type Indicator, I hear the tones of a frustrated idealist. What would an ideal academy look like to you, a utopian SBL, or a utopian seminary? What would that actually look like?

BRUEGGEMANN: Given the immense pluralism of the guild now, ideally it would be an acknowledgment of its varieties of gifts and then a resolve to take each other's work with great seriousness. Because I don't want to get rid of historical criticism. I don't think, as Walter Wink does, that it's bankrupt.[6] But I learned from reading some Gramsci[7] about the organic intellectual, related to the revolution, that what we need are more organic scholars who are related to not just Church, but to the revolutionary, visionary aspects of the text, who rely on historical critics to do a lot of the homework that we have to have. And I certainly rely on people like that. So it would mean overcoming the ditch between the historians and the hermeneuticists, who never talk to each other. The SBL is a model of that: we have our little private meetings and we never have to interact with each other. I don't want to be romantic about the guild, but it would be like a family with many diverse siblings, all of whom take each other with great seriousness and who share a common inheritance for which they are all responsible. Something like that.

SHARP: I hear echoes of the Corinthian body—varieties of gifts—in the beginning of your remarks. There are three things I would like to pull out of what you said. One is the notion that may not be based on theology—because we're all from different traditions and different faiths—but somehow perhaps as intellectual seekers we are all of a body, with the eye and the hand and whatever, so there could be an organic connection to be honored better than we currently do. The two other things I hear are that you would like to see more interdisciplinary accountability to each other. . . .

BRUEGGEMANN: That's right.

SHARP: . . . I don't know if you'd say only in the theological disciplines or writ more broadly. And then the third thing is a generosity of spirit that is maybe not entirely lacking, but in certain times and venues definitely understated.

BRUEGGEMANN: Yes. I think many book reviews are actions of excommunication. And in the Church, I am continually astonished. I get around a good bit in churches, and I am simply astonished at the myopic denominationalism. In almost every denomination, they don't know that anyone else is out there, or what they're thinking, or anything like that! My own impression is that after you get by the shibboleths that we all have to reiterate, everybody's caught in the same problems and has the same possibilities. That's simply to say that ecumenism needs to be concrete and vigorous to break up our little camps of truths.

SHARP: That would be the ideal Church—not the fractured body of Christ that it is.

BRUEGGEMANN: Right. That doesn't have to mean uniformity.

SHARP: No—you don't like uniformity! It's boring.

BRUEGGEMANN: That's right!

SHARP: Your work has been striving toward making those possibilities visible. Some who might have been on the blunter end of comments from you might disagree.

BRUEGGEMANN: I tend to think that scholars need to be granted their premises. If they are operating from premises that are different from mine, that needs to be accepted as the starting point of the conversation. Whereas many scholars keep beating up on other scholars because they don't accept their premises. So generosity of spirit may not be easy for any of us, but it's really important.

SHARP: The academy seems to be built—maybe this is human nature, or culture, but—certainly the academy as it currently stands is built on "young Turks" unseating the fathers, and until we can name that dynamic and change it. . . .

BRUEGGEMANN: Right—what Harold Bloom calls the Oedipal urge. I was in a session once with a younger scholar, and he was lambasting older scholarship. Some older scholar very gently said in the session, "Someday you'll be the older scholar, so you need to pay attention to that."

SHARP: "First of all, we're sitting right here! Second of all, you'll be the old school that others think is totally inadequate soon enough."

BRUEGGEMANN: Exactly!

SHARP: I have five quick questions needing stream-of-consciousness answers from you, and then we'll close. What aspect of the work of a biblical scholar is most exciting to you?

BRUEGGEMANN: I love most the work with a particular text. After I do what critical work that is required, my delight is to "go inside the text" to see how it works. I am invariably surprised by what is there. From there the move to other texts signaled by that one opens new worlds almost every time.

SHARP: What disappoints you most about the current state of the guild of biblical scholarship?

BRUEGGEMANN: I think it is disconcerting that we are divided into "camps," depending on who our teachers have been and the scholarly tradition in which we live. Scholars who abhor religious authoritarianism are often quite prepared to practice similar authoritarianism about their work. This more or less divides into historical positivism on the one hand and hermeneutics on the other hand, but the number of "sects" is very large. I fail to understand why we cannot learn from those with whom we disagree. I am inclined to think that any credible scholar is serious about his or her work and deserves to be taken seriously on the terms of that work. That does not mean we cannot be critical, but the need to denounce or excommunicate seems to me a great misfortune among us.

SHARP: What advice would you give a young, idealistic doctoral student who wants to make a mark in the guild?

BRUEGGEMANN: Well, I am not sure anyone as old as I am has any useful advice to give, given the new ways of scholarship and the frantic pressure for tenure. I would say, do not publish too much too soon. Do not gel into hard judgments and commitments too soon. Do not make your dissertation your life work. Live with the issues for a long while, read in the history of the discipline so that we may know from whence come the questions in front of us. It is not so important to "make a mark" in the guild. It is important to do sound, reliable scholarship and find satisfaction in that. One may get "noticed" and openings may come, but I would not make that a principal passion. The work itself is what is important. There are few scholars who make a durable mark; when they do, it is partly a matter of being gifted and learned; it is also partly happenstance, so I would not use much energy on that. One other thing: keep the big picture in mind, and let work be related to other disciplines. We are in the midst of a large and deep revolution in the world, and we cannot afford, in my judgment, to have our scholarship excessively preoccupied with minute in-house questions.

SHARP: What do you wish you had realized before you embarked on your long and storied career?

BRUEGGEMANN: I doubt there is anything about my work that is "storied," but it is surely "long." I wish I had seen earlier that the first work is getting tools for the long haul. I missed important tools because I had no sense of the long haul. I wish I had understood more about the politics of journal publishing and the "family trees" of influence that pertain to that politics. I wish I had had clarity much sooner about the interface of guild and faith, and that I had not worried so long about Enlightenment positivism. I wish I understood sooner that almost all our scholarship is situated in old and deep narratives, most of which we keep hidden, even from ourselves. I wish I had been more alert to the ways in which "secret things" are not ours, but "revealed things" are our work [Deut. 29:29].

SHARP: Is there something you would like to say to the guild that you have never said publicly before?

BRUEGGEMANN: Well, the guild is diffuse and one cannot address it all, plus the "the guild" is not waiting for anything I might say, but. . . . I have no doubt that the particulars of criticism are important, and we need to keep at them. But the small matters of criticism, still largely framed in nineteenth-century categories, need to be kept in the purview of the large issues before us in the world and in our society. Biblical scholars, in my view, need to be players in the interdisciplinary work of contesting for a viable social world. To the extent that our work is preoccupied with critical matters, to that extent we have in many ways said that the big issues are to be left to others who can work from our criticism. I think this is a cop-out, and a down-playing of the deeply revolutionary, problematic text with which we work. This is not a plea for "relevance" or "contemporaneity" as much as it is a bid to recognize what it is that has been entrusted to us in this text. This entrustment requires a push beyond the expectations of graduate school over which we may linger too long. I have, of course, moved in those directions in my own work, but it has been not very intentional on my part. I wish that move were more intentional with other scholars who, for good reason, are preoccupied with promotion and tenure. We cannot just keep moving the deck chairs around.

SHARP: Thank you so much for your time and your energy for this project. I very much appreciate it.

BRUEGGEMANN: Well, what would one rather do than get to talk about one's own work! [laughs]

Notes

1. Carolyn J. Sharp, *Irony and Meaning in the Hebrew Bible* (Bloomington: Indiana University Press, 2009).
2. Bruce K. Waltke, with Charles Yu, *An Old Testament Theology: An Exegetical, Canonical, and Thematic Approach* (Grand Rapids: Zondervan, 2006), 71.
3. Ibid., quoting Brueggemann from *Theology of the Old Testament: Testimony, Dispute, Advocacy* (Minneapolis: Fortress, 1997), 303.
4. See Wiesel's comment, "The Jew, in my view, may rise against God, provided that he remains within God. One can be a very good Jew, observe all the *mitzvot*, study Talmud—and yet be against God." Quoted in Emil L. Fackenheim, Richard H. Popkin, George Steiner, and Elie Wiesel, "Jewish Values in the Post-Holocaust Future: A Symposium," *Judaism* 16 (Summer 1967): 266–99, at 299.
5. The reference is to a book of Brueggemann's collected addresses for churches, theological schools, preachers, and ecclesial judicatories: *Disruptive Grace: Reflections on God, Scripture, and the Church* (Minneapolis: Fortress, 2011).
6. See Walter Wink, *The Bible in Human Transformation: Toward a New Paradigm in Bible Study* (1975; repr., Minneapolis: Fortress Press, 2010). The famous first sentence of Wink's book is, "Historical biblical criticism is bankrupt."
7. Antonio Gramsci (1891–1937), Italian political theorist, linguist, and philosopher.

Chapter 4

"Practicing Gratitude"

Atlanta, November 20, 2010

In this conversation, Brueggemann engages questions having to do with the pastoral formation of those who read the Bible in the seminary classroom and in the church. According to Brueggemann, interpretation needs to generate new possibilities for understanding in new contexts; in this respect, he owns a "liberation hermeneutic" as being foundational to his exegesis. His career-long interest in opening up the imaginations of readers springs from two sources: his keen sense of the limitations and dark moments of life, and his sustained yearning for *shalom*. As this conversation unfolds, Brueggemann mulls the compartmentalization of the theological school curriculum, considers ways in which doctrinal commitments can unduly constrain interpretation of the Hebrew Scriptures, worries about the problem of the violence of God in biblical texts, and affirms his enduring hope that the guild of biblical studies might learn to foster an irenic approach to intellectual disagreements.

CJS

CAROLYN SHARP: Today I have a few questions related to the SBL and how you position yourself as teacher and interpreter here. The first one has to do with an SBL session in which I'll be participating tomorrow. It's sponsored by the Wabash Center and Westminster John Knox Press, and it's about helping students navigate faith challenges in the biblical studies classroom. It's supposed to be an interactive pedagogical conversation with small groups and so forth. My first question comes out of an e-mail interaction in preparation for that event. The premise of the event tomorrow is that it is valuable for us to help our students negotiate what comes up for them theologically and spiritually when they study the Bible critically. Now, different theological educators will do that in different ways—how one approaches those issues depends on one's context. If you teach in a public college or university, you'll have a certain set of constraints by which you have to abide. You won't wax confessional in the classroom in the way that you might in the seminary classroom. And I think that probably—painting this with a broad brush—different issues come up for students in a college setting than for those in a theological school.

WALTER BRUEGGEMANN: Sure.

SHARP: And it might be fair to say that students who encounter the Bible in college or university classrooms for the first time might be surprised or shocked at what's actually in the Bible, you know—many of them perhaps not having read it before. The violence, the misogyny that you can see in the text, the colonial or conquest worldview, rhetorics about obliterating the Other: obviously we do have texts in the Hebrew Scriptures that can be disturbing. Some of the issues for theological students might be the same as for those college students, but other issues would be different. Many theological students come with a deep confessional commitment to Scripture as the revealed Word of God. Some of them, in my experience, wrestle more with the disjuncture between narrative representations of the Exodus and the Conquest, on the one hand, and what they hear about biblical archaeology, on the other, since the evidence is not there for a massive, one-time exodus or a comprehensive conquest. They get worried sometimes, in my classroom, about multiple perspectives or approaches to interpreting Scripture, because they've had maybe just their pastor teaching them how to think about Scripture before coming to divinity school. And then ideological criticism of biblical texts: one of the things that you do so well is to look at voices on different kinds of power dynamics in the texts. I think that surprises people who have never engaged in critical inquiry into Scripture.

BRUEGGEMANN: Right.

SHARP: So people have various challenges when they come to study the Bible. My questions to you are these: When you think about your time at Eden and more recently at Columbia Theological Seminary, what kinds of crises or challenges did your students have in your classroom specifically? And how did you negotiate those or address them pedagogically?

BRUEGGEMANN: When I taught at Eden, which was a more liberal seminary, at that time what you had to do was to try to make the case that Scripture was important. When I went to Columbia, which twenty-five years ago was more conservative than it is now, there was no problem with the assumption that the Bible was important, but what you had to do with those students was to open it up critically, to see that you couldn't take it as a package. And I have found Ricoeur's scheme of the postcritical "second naïveté" to be helpful in both contexts. In a conservative context, you've got to move beyond the precritical to the critical, and in a progressive context, you've got to move beyond the critical to the postcritical. I think that my great insight is that while you're doing precritical → critical → postcritical about the Bible, you've got to do precritical → critical → postcritical pastorally about the self. So that a precritical self can tolerate a critical Bible, or a critical self can move to a postcritical Bible. That grid worked out with the precritical self is, "Everything's fine, and my parents loved me," and all that. The critical self is, "My mother really hated me." The postcritical self is, "My mother did the best she could, and she loved me in the way she knew how." And I think that when students have that sense of self-knowledge going on, they can tolerate that knowledge about Scripture. But if the self is simply unsettled and unruly, then those moves within Scripture can be very difficult.

SHARP: That's a really complex pastoral view into what's at stake for students when they're reading Scripture, as individuals. It probably translates, at least in some dimensions, into what's at stake for reading communities, as well—as regards their histories and how they understand themselves, both as individual parishes and as larger traditions.

BRUEGGEMANN: Yes. One of the unfortunate things about the compartmentalized curriculum is, reflection on that stuff is going on in C.P.E.[1] and those kinds of classes and learning experiences, but the different areas of the curriculum don't come together. So you can't easily communicate to students that these processes are parallel and related to each other.

SHARP: Interdisciplinarity, then, is important not just for the intellectual excitement of it but for the ways in which a set of questions from one discipline can interrogate the assumptions of another discipline. It may— this is so interesting, what you're saying—interdisciplinarity may actually be important for formation.

BRUEGGEMANN: For pastoral formation. That's right.

SHARP: I've never heard anyone say that before.

BRUEGGEMANN: And I think that a pastor, on any given day, deals with precritical, critical, and postcritical people. The pastor has to be extraordinarily agile about the pastor's own self in relationship to all that.

SHARP: To what degree is it important to host people in whatever stage they're in, in the classroom? Have you ever been tempted to say, "You know, it just didn't happen that way. Get over it!" or "This is the truth—just deal with it"? Because I have seen teachers in various disciplines who are very insistent about this or that point being the truth: "You can go deal with it with your therapist on your own time, but just deal with it." Of course you can hear in my tone how I feel about that position! I think it does harm.

BRUEGGEMANN: I can't do that. You have to be generous.

SHARP: Say you have in the same classroom a precritical student sitting in the front row, and a doctoral-bound student there too who is just in love with theory and doesn't see that anything is at stake in these issues theologically. How do you host them at the same time, in that learning environment?

BRUEGGEMANN: Well, I'm sure I don't do that very well. But what I try to say to students in those extremities is: what we're trying to do, given where each of us is, is to hear the gospel here. And we come at this in such different ways that we ought to recognize it's not very easy for any of us to hear the gospel in this text. Either because we're aware of how terrible the text is or because we've got it locked up in a doctrinal package. Neither way gives us access. I was at a lay conference not very long ago at which I was talking about the mutability of God and all that. This guy spoke up and said, "I think God does not change. That's what Plato said."

SHARP: Ah, so Plato's in the canon now.

BRUEGGEMANN: I came down on him rather hard and said, "Well, you can have a Plato seminar somewhere else, but that's not what this is!"

SHARP: A colleague of mine in theology draws on Plotinus to think about God, and she makes what I'd say is a secondary move to go back to Scripture and shore up this view that really is a Hellenistic concept of a timeless, eternally unchanging God. I have no problem with postulating that and naming one's sources—Plato, Plotinus, whatever. That's fine. But let's not then say that the Hebrew Scriptures are presenting that kind of God! Because that's so evidently not true.

BRUEGGEMANN: Indeed. When I'm in a Presbyterian church, I try to say as often as I can that the categories of the Westminster Catechism are simply not biblical![2]

SHARP: They're, uh, more recent.

BRUEGGEMANN: That's right! But we're all nurtured in that stuff, and we have so much to unlearn. Just as we have so much to unlearn about ourselves—about our essentialist sense of self.

SHARP: That makes me think, too, about your interchange with that disciple of Plato. What you were asking him to do was to be honest about where he's basing his claims and to name that, so that you could have the conversation. The conversation might be, "Well, actually Plato is next Tuesday somewhere else; we aren't doing Plato here today," but transparency is important. It can be valuable for our students to see what is at stake for us. If I get ticked off when someone says, "Oh, the Exodus didn't happen—get over it," or a scholar says brusquely that the resurrection didn't happen and students just need to deal with it, . . . well, what I want to ask is, what's at stake for us in the different ways that we read? Because we are the ways we are for a reason. Some of the causes are unfortunate and need to be remediated—there are villains out there, and parts of ourselves we don't like—but there are reasons why we read as we do, reasons why we pray as we do, and so on. So helping students learn to see what is at stake for them is a really important part of this.

BRUEGGEMANN: That's right.

SHARP: Would you reflect on what is at stake for you in the kinds of readings that you do?

BRUEGGEMANN: Let me say first of all, I probably never say to a student, "Get over it!" I do say sometimes—so that the whole class doesn't get dragged aside—"well, you and I will have to disagree about that for now." But for neither of us is that the final position, and we have to go on thinking about it.

SHARP: That's quite a bit more nuanced than to say, "Get over it!" That's a lovely thing to say, pedagogically.

BRUEGGEMANN: I think I'm very pragmatic about what's at stake. What's at stake is finding out that the tradition is generative of new historical-social possibilities. And I think that's why we arrived at a high view of the authority of Scripture. If we finally decide, in our own reading, that it is not generative of new possibility, then we are denying the intentionality of the canonical force.

SHARP: That's where Brevard Childs would agree with you.

BRUEGGEMANN: We agreed about so much, for all his objection to me.[3] I would want to go on to say to students, "Well, this isn't a perfect text, but name me any other generative text anywhere in the world, and you will discover that none of them are perfect either. So we got what we got."

SHARP: And the text is not God. Or shouldn't be.

BRUEGGEMANN: That's right.

SHARP: Thinking about challenges or crises that arise for students—and we're all students! we all continue to learn every day, from Scripture and from all the things we read—is there anything in Scripture that still challenges you, that has caused you to experience a bona fide "dark night of the soul"? You've been seasoned and eloquent for so many years on engaging Scripture, and on naming the unsettling and disturbing parts. Is there a voice or a text or a tradition in Scripture that still really gets up in amongst you and bothers you?

BRUEGGEMANN: I think all the violent stuff—you're going to work in Joshua, and I think that any Old Testament teacher has got to be haunted by that. You know, deep in the night, I think about the whole scandal of particularity: about the chosenness of Israel and the chosenness of Jesus and the chosenness of the Church. It's kind of chilling to think that that's how we've made our faith claim. I'm haunted by that stuff.

SHARP: Some of us can easily bracket or disclaim the expressions of particularity that are overtly xenophobic or that are overtly exclusivist—"this is the only way; the rest of you are going to hell." But nevertheless, deep down, even with all the "grace" words and the generosity and inclusivity that some of us on the left try to muster, it is chilling, isn't it?

BRUEGGEMANN: It is. And I think we're seeing the fruits of it in Israeli policy now about the chosen land and the chosen people. I think that transfers so readily to U.S. exceptionalism, which is the same idolatry.

The hardest challenge for pastors is to mount any critique of U.S. exceptionalism. People are incredibly vigilant about that not being critiqued, and I think it's rooted in these texts. We've taken that over in unthinking ways, and it's very, very big and deep for us.

SHARP: Pastors can get run out on a rail for that.

BRUEGGEMANN: That's right. My pastor simply said in a Fourth of July sermon that the United States sometimes is very arrogant, and a couple of people walked out.

SHARP: You'd think that would go without saying. No country is perfect! If they have Fourth of July hymns on a Sunday and you're in the pew, do you sing them?

BRUEGGEMANN: Well, I try to mumble. [laughs]

SHARP: One of my personal dislikes is anything patriotic in the church, which is the community of the people of God through time and across the globe—followers of Jesus Christ entirely apart from nationality. I have a problem with nationalism in worship.

BRUEGGEMANN: I once went with a group of students to Hungary on a seminary trip, and I preached during church, and I think it was the practice of that time that they sang the Hungarian national anthem—which is a kind of a prayer.[4] It's very theological. And then the organist thought, to be fair, we should sing the "The Star-Spangled Banner," which was really embarrassing! Ours, unlike theirs, is a war song!

SHARP: Being on site here at the SBL annual meeting brings up another kind of question. Either earlier in your career or later, when you were at Columbia, did you ever apply for any other job? Were you wooed by other schools?

BRUEGGEMANN: I never applied for another job. But I taught at each seminary for twenty-five years. I assumed that Eden Theological Seminary would be my life's location—that was my alma mater. I finally left Eden over a leadership controversy that I thought I shouldn't have to put up with. But I didn't apply. Columbia Seminary had contacted me a couple of years before that. I would not say that I ever was "wooed," but I was contacted by several faculties, and I was invited to join the Princeton faculty. But I decided I wasn't ready to do that.

SHARP: Why not?

BRUEGGEMANN: I didn't have the nerve for it. My conversations at Princeton were not very hospitable to the liberation hermeneutic that I pursue. In the interview process, I was interviewed by doctoral students, and they were concerned to find my weaknesses. I went home and thought, I'll never be able to think a new thought.

SHARP: That's remarkable, that doctoral students could make someone of your stature feel terrible!

BRUEGGEMANN: Yeah. Maybe that was my own lack of nerve, which is a recurring issue about that sort of thing. But I don't have any regrets about not going there. That's the appointment that Patrick Miller got, and he was much better for it than I would have been. So I've been very content with both of my appointments.

SHARP: So you don't have a "grass is always greener" kind of mentality?

BRUEGGEMANN: No, I really don't. I'm inclined to think that, not having had doctoral students, I had much more time and energy for my own work. Doctoral students take a lot of time and energy—I never had to do that! I've been very privileged to be where I've been, and I've been very well treated.

SHARP: Both are wonderful schools, absolutely. Your story does surprise me, because I'm guessing that you could have had your pick of positions, except for perhaps at schools that theologically disagree with you. I'm not saying that Gordon Conwell or Fuller would invite you to come, necessarily.

BRUEGGEMANN: Well, my own perception is that at the other extreme, I think the real heavyweights in the field suspect that I don't do very good critical work. And I suspect that too. It is what it is, and that's okay with me.

SHARP: That's interesting, because I've heard that in what you've said before, and we all have our baggage that we bring with us.

BRUEGGEMANN: Yes—that may be more my own issue.

SHARP: Thinking back to the precritical → critical → postcritical paradigm, it seems to me that you offer insightful critical interrogation of texts from a postcritical position. You've come through that journey. Now, I don't know how precritical you ever were, in your faith or in your intellectual views.

BRUEGGEMANN: Probably not much. The German evangelical tradition in which I was nurtured had settled its commitments to critical study already in the nineteenth century. And it was never hung up on the "substitutionary atonement" that now riles so many progressives. In retrospect, I think that my ecclesial tradition was well ahead of its time, but I did not know that earlier. It was a kind of innocent pietism that was able to work from a perspective of compassion and did not need to engage in such quarrels or reduce matters to scholastic categories, a reduction that vexes so many now.

SHARP: But I would say this: it may look to folks who don't understand what you're doing as if you're offering a simple reading of texts, but it's actually quite far from that. That would be their own lack of acumen in assessing what you're doing. That's what I'd attribute it to, if indeed you have encountered the opinion that you are not doing critically rigorous work.

BRUEGGEMANN: Well, I think the pastor who does postcritical work has to say it so that precritical folks in the congregation can think it's precritical. The object in teaching is not to scandalize people, but to empower them. There needs to be a bit of anxiety in learning what one does not know; but nothing is gained by shock and alienation.

SHARP: So there's something there to nurture their learning and their growth in faith. I do hear you about the university-based theological school, which is of course my own context. I have to tell you, the question I dislike the most, the question that makes me want to leave my job, is when a student comes up to me and asks, "What's that *dagesh* doing in that letter?" if there's a *dagesh* that's anomalous. I know the main reasons why *dageshim* are there, and I know some of the anomalous reasons why a *dagesh* might be there. But that question has become . . . not my bête noire exactly, but close. It's such a tiny thing. It's just a dot in a letter in a manuscript, but for me, it has come to represent all the ways in which I have never memorized Gesenius[5] and I don't have control of every idiosyncrasy of Hebrew philology. It's just not what I do! And on a good day, when I'm trusting that God has me where I'm supposed to be, I'm fine with it. But on a bad day, that question, "What's that *dagesh* doing there, Professor Sharp?" can be quite disruptive to my sense of self!

BRUEGGEMANN: And what's really going on there is, the student is trying to show you, "Professor Sharp, look, I can spot a *dagesh*!" Actually a student who does that comes off herself as a rather "simple *dagesh*"! [laughs]

SHARP: Indeed! That's helpful to me. And as in interpersonal conflict and so many other arenas, it's wiser to listen to what's being said beneath the words, and try to respond to that. But where we have our own reactive places or sensitive places, it's hard to respond wisely.

BRUEGGEMANN: That's right! What the student wants you to say is, "Oh, that's brilliant!"

SHARP: "Good job! You did it!" So it sounds like you don't have regrets about the choices you made professionally in terms of institutions.

BRUEGGEMANN: Not about that—that's right.

SHARP: Do I hear other regrets in the background of that statement?

BRUEGGEMANN: Well, one of the regrets I have is this: I was academic dean at Eden Seminary for fourteen years, and I regret how much energy I put into that. But it had to be done. I don't brood about it.

SHARP: There might have been another dozen books written . . . probably fifteen books, if you had not been academic dean! But service is important too. We do take that seriously, for sure. Here's my last administrative question. Let's think back on your time as president of the SBL in 1990— and you were vice president in training the year before, as is the custom. Do you have reflections on that time, either in terms of the leadership role that you were expected to play or in terms of the politics of the guild?

BRUEGGEMANN: I think they made a good decision when they separated the function of the president from the administrative chores of leadership. It's now largely honorific—you just do the address, and I think that's good. I was always playing catch-up on the administrative side, because I didn't know about that. Fortunately, I was in Atlanta, where the office of David Lull was, so I could get briefed before every time that I had to provide administrative leadership. The good thing is, the SBL has a sort of political life that doesn't depend on the leadership of the president. The other thing I think about is, I'm really delighted that I was nominated as president, but all you really need is two good friends on the nominating committee!

SHARP: Be that as it may, it really is an extraordinary honor. Not very many people have done it.

BRUEGGEMANN: Well, yes, it is an honor. When you review your own generation, you can identify people who have been skipped over that shouldn't have been skipped over, and so it goes. I was on the nominating committee, and we nominated Brevard [Childs], and he turned it down. He said, "I would have to criticize too many of my friends."

SHARP: Really? I would simply note that one does not have to say everything that's in one's mind.

BRUEGGEMANN: That's right!

SHARP: It's funny, thinking about vulnerability and whatever one wrestles with throughout one's life. When we consider the vulnerability that I've heard you express around certain kinds of historical-critical or philological engagement with Scriptures, you might think that being president of the SBL might have silenced that inner-critical voice.

BRUEGGEMANN: No. It's too strong!

SHARP: It does go to show that our inner critics are just too strong—even for the president of the guild! So that healing or integration clearly can't come from outside. It has to come from inside, from spiritual work or inner work.

BRUEGGEMANN: Yes, and I have reflected on that. It's kind of a mismatch.

SHARP: It's also wonderful, in a way, because it goes to your humility. I know on a bad day, one might experience it as vulnerability, but it also goes to humility, and that's a Christian virtue! Just wanted to note that.

BRUEGGEMANN: Right.

SHARP: I'd like to ask a couple of questions about *Journey to the Common Good*, your lectures at Regent College. You speak about anger. You open the lectures with an observation about impediments to the common good. You speak about the patriarchalism of Scripture, undue or particularist interests of race and sect and party and so forth, and you mention also layers of human and divine anger. Certainly anger can be harmful and distorting to human relationships, to sense of self and to communities. But I think also of the prophets in this regard, and of Jesus overturning the tables in the Temple. Anger can be an authentic gift and testimonial witness for advocacy. When integrity is threatened, anger can be an appropriate response that is not necessarily aggressive or shaming or harmful. So, would you reflect—whether in terms of politics or your own writing, what you've wanted to do—on whether there is anything that still makes you mad after all these years?

Whether it's a righteous indignation or the kind of anger that you'd prefer didn't arise?

BRUEGGEMANN: As a member of the Society [of Biblical Literature], I'm sort of a Rodney King: "Why can't we all get along?" "Mad" may be too strong a word, but I get very irritated that so many of our colleagues act like they have to defeat each other. Why can't we learn from the people with whom we disagree? I went to hear a paper a few years ago of Philip Davies's. There isn't anybody with whom I disagree more, and he and I have had some not-good exchanges. After the session was over, he expressed surprise that I would come to hear his paper! One of the problems now in the Society is that we are organized into little cliques, and we go only to papers of our friends who are on the same wavelength, and we never get these other exchanges. I think that it's much better if we can say, when we disagree, "More than one of us may be right about these things." So that's a preoccupation of mine. But I use less and less emotive energy on stuff like that now. I'm going to do my thing, and that's it.

SHARP: It would truly be a culture-changing thing in our guild if everyone who disagreed with someone else would first say how they had been instructed by that person, and then continue, "For me, what's still at stake is this, and I'm not satisfied that we've addressed it adequately."

BRUEGGEMANN: That's right. So many book reviews are written in a negative way. What the book reviewer often says is, "If I had written this book, this is the book I would have written. Alas, I didn't write it."

SHARP: To which one wants to respond, "Get over yourself—it's this person's project, not yours!"

BRUEGGEMANN: Exactly.

SHARP: Now I'd like to spin out for you an analogy that I have no doubt will embarrass you. It's about Moses and you. Fair warning, and you may completely discount it, if you like. I think about all the ways in which you use the Exodus story in your different writings, as this narrative or this cultural memory that awakens us to the captivity of the human spirit— that's your phrase, from *Journey to the Common Good*. "Captivity of the human spirit": there is the bona fide slavery of Israel in Egypt, and then there are analogues for communities of faith up to today, and for us as readers today, as well. You say that when our human spirit is held captive in today's world, that means we seem to be okay with, or at least don't actively resist, the temptation "to commit aggressive brutalizing war," "to tolerate acute poverty in an economy of affluence," and "to sustain policies of abuse of the environment."[6] When our spirit is held captive, at best we are perhaps a little uncomfortable about these things. We seem to permit these outrageous things to continue.

It's your use of the phrase "captivity of the human spirit" that finally helped me to see something I had not seen before. Your writing is always about using the text to open up alternatives. That is clear, and I've known that for a long time—alternative ways of seeing the text, alternative ways of envisioning community, new ways of understanding abundance, and so forth. But central to your witness in the Church and in the academy, I would say, is the way in which you speak boldly to "Pharaoh," whoever "Pharaoh" may be: the military-industrial complex or consumerist culture in North America, mentalities of anxiety and scarcity and paucity. When you talk about the academy, you name the hegemony of a narrow historical-critical approach. You also mention interpretive moves that don't account for the polyphony and rich dialogical nature of Scripture, although there, it's more that you show us how to do that—it's not so much that you whale on others who don't read as you'd like. Those kinds of things, I would say, represent "Pharaoh" to you. So you are engaged, then, in freeing the imaginations of your readers and calling on the carpet the "Pharaohs" of our day. So, go ahead and decline this analogy, if you want to, but it really did make me think of you as Moses—or, you know, "The LORD your God will raise up for you a prophet like me" (Deut. 18:15) as a Mosaic prophet.

If you were to stipulate the Moses analogy—just for a moment, let's agree that we can call you a Moses, even though I know that's probably embarrassing. I have some "Moses" questions for you. The first has to do with the manna in the wilderness of your own wanderings, when you have those times of personal despair or confusion, or you feel lost, in the guild or as you move through life. What is the "manna" that you keep coming back to, that gets you through?

BRUEGGEMANN: Well, I think it's the text. I find the text and the study of the text endlessly generative of myself. And I don't understand it, but I am sustained by pastors who live in much more difficult places than I do, and they tell me, from time to time, about the transformativeness of God, and they discern this in the midst of their ministry, which is again always a very particular thing. It typically takes a long time to get there, but I think now that in the concrete, specific detailed practice of gratitude in my life—and I have so much for which to be grateful—most of the time the recital of gratitudes will overcome the darknesses. And I am sustained in that by the liturgy and by the Eucharist. At this place in my life, I am really able to be sustained by the gospel narrative. I don't mean that I live completely there—I've got lots of other stuff going on in my life. But this turns out to be more adequate, and it's a recurring wake-up call to me. Obviously, at my age, I think a lot about frailty and mortality. I'm really agnostic about all that.

SHARP: Say more.

BRUEGGEMANN: I have no deep conviction about the end. God will be God. And that's really postcritical! But that's kind of where I put my buckets down. I also have to say, I've lived a very fortunate life. Other than the deep scar of my divorce, I have never had anything bad happen to me. I don't think I'm innocent about all that—I'm aware of more complexity than that. But I would say that the world in front of the text (Ricoeur's language) is sustaining for me, and I get that mediated to me by lots of folks.

SHARP: Here's another Moses analogy. Moses struck the rock and God provided water for the people, and they drank. But Moses is prevented from entering the Promised Land for some reason having to do with striking the rock—people have argued for centuries and centuries about what he did wrong. If you were to take on the mantle, even ironically, of Moses for a minute: is there something you suspect you've gotten wrong, that you just don't know how to figure out?

BRUEGGEMANN: Oh, I suppose lots of things. I think I am easily critiqued for being too credulous about the Bible, not severe enough about its patriarchy and sexism or whatever. I easily give Scripture the benefit of the doubt. That's who I am, so I suspect that ain't gonna change. But where I am socially located, the extent to which I do that isn't radical enough. I think in my *Old Testament Theology*, I don't know what I got wrong or said wrong, but it was maybe the cavalier dismissal of historical questions. I probably should have struggled more with that.

I don't think I want to take back anything about the main trajectory of my work, but I could have thought more or listened to more people or other people, or given better nuance to a lot of things. I suspect I am so much a child of the Church that I didn't push beyond that. I do think that the people that are extraordinarily skeptical and angry with the tradition are also children of the Church. They're just wounded children of the Church, and I have not been wounded much by the Church. So I understand myself fairly well in context, and that's how it comes out. There are a lot of specific points that I didn't get right, but I am continually pressed out by new conversation partners, so I'm aware that most of the stuff I'm now thinking wasn't anywhere on my horizon a decade ago. And I love that.

SHARP: That provides a nice segue to my next question. Let's talk about the Promised Land. This is my last "Moses" question for you. You've seen so much in terms of the growth of the guild, and especially in terms of methodological plurality in a group that, from what I understand, was originally fifty or a hundred North American males with one kind of language.

BRUEGGEMANN: That's right: Protestant.

SHARP: And they were meeting in a couple of hotel rooms. Today, the guild has many thousands of members and hosts a huge diversity of methods, reading strategies, and cultural interests. You are yourself—I think it's quite visible in your work—responsive to thinkers from Ricoeur to Levinas and responsive to these changes in the guild. On my analogy, this current generation that includes all of us, except "Joshua" and "Caleb"— I don't know who they might be—all of us here today will not get into the Promised Land of biblical interpretation. There is a "Canaan" that lies before us, that looks different—that is some kind of utopia. If you're standing on top of Mount Pisgah, looking over to that Promised Land: do you have any sense of the contours of that landscape?

BRUEGGEMANN: Of scholarship?

SHARP: Of biblical scholarship, or you might want to go for biblical theology. Whatever you've been journeying toward, these past forty years.

BRUEGGEMANN: I think that there are varieties of gifts. Thank God there are varieties of gifts in scholarship, because the historians and the archaeologists and the philologists—all those kinds of folks, and the things they do that I don't even understand—their work is acutely important. People like me depend on that work. I don't think we adequately appreciate the gifts that we subterraneanly give each other. So I don't want to imagine that we can get along without that. But I also think that our scholarship has to move much more toward what Gramsci, the Italian sociologist, called "organic scholarship." By which he meant scholars who are involved in the revolution, serving the reconstruction of social institutions, social structures, and social powers. Mostly, we can see that the old myth of objectivity is gone. So we are, willy-nilly, advocates.

I believe that the deep intentionality of Scripture is a world of *shalom*, however one details that. Our scholarship, as a body, needs to deliver more on that. I think we need to be more up-front in funding the church and synagogue, and in funding public discourse. The reason I think that's so urgent is that the dominant trajectory we are on, in our society, is a trajectory of death. It is to us that an alternative has been entrusted, and we can't sit around counting *dageshes*. I mean, *dageshes* need to be counted, but we need to go ahead and get that done! That may be a little bit romantic, because as soon as you talk about becoming an organic intellectual, we're not agreed on where to go with that. You remember my acrimonious exchange last year with Bruce Waltke, who is a very distinguished conservative scholar. We're not going to go in the same direction. So there it is. But I guess the matter of being public intellectuals is really important to our vocation as scholars.

SHARP: So that's an integrative approach to the intellectual discourse and the practices of helping to dismantle what exists or helping to create a new way forward—which might imply interdisciplinarity, talking across the divisions or "areas" of the theological curriculum, so that there's intentionality and risk taking in trying to talk across those boundaries, and not just in talking but in trying to embody an organic approach.

BRUEGGEMANN: That's right. And I think a lot of younger scholars are much better able to practice that with agility than most of us who were so compartmentalized earlier on.

SHARP: Maybe. I'd want to dissent from your phrase "most of us," because that kind of work is exactly what you yourself have been doing.

BRUEGGEMANN: Yes, I suppose, in the ways that I've known how.

Notes

1. Clinical Pastoral Education, a formal internship, usually in a hospital setting, is expected of seminarians in most theological schools.
2. In preceding remarks, Brueggemann is clear that he objects to calling "biblical" those ideas that we have gleaned from elsewhere, whether from Hellenistic philosophy or from the development of later Christian doctrine.
3. Childs was unsympathetic to interpretive efforts that discerned theological meaning only as that related to the original historical contexts within which biblical texts were composed and edited. He critiqued the earlier work of Brueggemann on that score:

see, for example, Childs's *Introduction to the Old Testament as Scripture* (1979; repr., Minneapolis: Fortress, 2011), 74–75. In *The Struggle to Understand Isaiah as Christian Scripture* (Grand Rapids: Eerdmans, 2004), Childs affirms that Brueggemann's "brilliant homiletical interpretations" are "often fresh, probing, and skillfully applied" (292). But Childs objects to what he sees as the relativistic postmodern slant of Brueggemann's readings more generally (293). Further, he deplores Brueggemann's focus on rhetoric as opposed to *Heilsgeschichte* ("salvation history," as construed by generations of Christian interpreters). Childs characterizes Brueggemann's eschewal of messianic and other traditional Christian readings as "a serious break with the entire Christian exegetical tradition" (294–95).
4. The text of the Hungarian national anthem, *Magyar Himnusz*, is reminiscent of one of the historical psalms in the Bible (compare Pss. 78, 105, 106, 136). Hungarian text by Ferenc Kölcsey (1823); English translation by László Korössy, www.korossy.org/magyar/himnusz.html.
5. The reference is to a classic grammar of biblical Hebrew written by German scholar Wilhelm Gesenius (1746-1842) that still enjoys wide use in North America and Europe: *Gesenius' Hebrew Grammar* (26th German ed., 1898; English ed. edited and enlarged by E. Kautzsch; 2nd English ed. by A. E. Cowley [Oxford: Clarendon Press, 1910]).
6. Walter Brueggemann, *Journey to the Common Good* (Louisville, KY: Westminster John Knox Press, 2010), 31.

Chapter 5

"Where Is the Scribe?"

Trinity Institute's 41st National Theological Conference,
New York City
January 19, 2011[1]

The "scribe" in my assigned topic, "Where Is the Scribe?" is the critical scholar of Scripture. The question posed concerns what the Church may learn and utilize from critical scholarship as it remains faithful to its engagement with the gospel as given in Scripture. The relationship between church practice and critical study is clearly vexed and problematic and has been so for a very long time.

WB

I

It is important to see that the rise of modern critical scholarship, as a university project in Germany and England, arose in the modern period of the Enlightenment, in the wake of the Reformation. Two matters may strike us as crucial about this beginning point of modern criticism. First, it was in the wake of the Reformation and was, for a very long time, a Protestant project. Indeed, Roman Catholics did not participate in historical-critical work until after 1943, and Jews took up the work of criticism variously in the modern period with Benedict Spinoza commonly cited as a beginning point. As you know, the Reformation sought to champion the free, unfettered Bible as the word of God, free of church domination in the service of clergy power. By the seventeenth century, however, both Lutheran and Calvinist traditions had been largely reduced to a scholasticism in which the freedom of the gospel had been reduced to absolutist theological formulations. The slogans of the Reformation were now used to work against the claims of the Reformation, the reduction of the biblical gospel to an absolutist package of doctrinal truth.

101

Second, in the seventeenth and eighteenth centuries, the option of Enlightenment rationality was utilized by liberal academics who found the alternative of "orthodoxy" unconvincing and unbearable. In the Old Testament, that initial question led to a challenge of the Mosaic authorship of the Pentateuch, and in the New Testament David Straus began to rethink the testimony about the life of Jesus. In both cases, the critique honed in on the central narrative of faith and began to challenge the absolute claims of the primal narrative. It is impossible to understand the critical enterprise except as a response to such absolutizing claims made by the Church; critical scholars, now empowered by autonomous reason that was impatient with the unquestioned claims of "the tradition," began to think and study outside the box of Church authority.

In the Old Testament, the project reached its culmination in the late nineteenth century with the definitive work of Julius Wellhausen, who summarized over a century of scholarship with the famous "Documentary Hypothesis" about JEDP.[2] That hypothesis was a combination of two very different claims. On the one hand, it was judged possible and necessary to identify different documents (sources, layers) in the Pentateuch that came from different periods and reflected different historical circumstances. Second, the documents were said to be credibly arranged in an interpretive sequence that moved from primitive to sophisticated, from polytheistic to monotheistic, from magical to ethical. That is, scholarship imposed an evolutionary schema on the text that continues to be commonly popular even now in the Church as one way of explaining away what is embarrassing in the text. The effects of the two-pronged argument were the conclusions that (a) no document could claim absolute authority; (b) every document or source reflects a human perception in a moment of history; and (c) the sequence is inherently supersessionist, so that each new document superseded the last, and one did not need to linger over what is primitive, polytheistic, and magical. This approach permitted scholars to take only what was "best," judged by European Enlightenment rationality, so that they could articulate from it a scheme or narrative that was considerably at variance with the attestation of the text itself.

The operational work of criticism was defined, in the early days, by the milieu of the "historical": thus, "historical criticism." That accent on the historical is given primacy by Hegel in his dynamism of change, came to expression in Darwin's judgment that all species have a history, and is taken up by Freud in his mantra that personal history reiterates cosmic history. Eventually the accent resulted in the conclusion that even God has a history (a history of human perception), so that everything, including biblical faith, was in a developmental process to a "better stage."[3] The "historical" part of criticism is the attempt to situate each biblical text in a particular historical context, albeit often a constructed historical context, so that the argument is at times circular. What must be stressed is the notion of "historical evolution" about every facet of creation, so that no moment in the text can be assigned an absolute status.

As a consequence of this academic (*Wissenschaftliche*) challenge to Church authority, the context for faith in Europe and the United States eventually came to a quarrel that persists to this day among:

- The *orthodox*, who continued to traffic in absolutist dogmatic claims that manifestly stood some distance from the biblical text itself;
- The *rationalists*, who prized autonomous reason and who held the Bible accountable to modern rationality that fit their own intellectual conviction (these are the practitioners of historical criticism);
- The *pietists* (my own tradition), who tried to duck the battle by an affective approach to the gospel and who looked askance at both the orthodox and the rationalists.

Insofar as the battle was between the orthodox and the rationalists, it is clear that the terms of engagement concerned ideas that had only passing connection to the claims of the Bible itself, for the orthodox were caught in seventeenth-century reductionism, and the rationalists were committed to nineteenth-century developmentalism, neither of which lived very close to the claims of the Bible.

It is clear that the struggle between the orthodox and the rationalists continues to our own time. From the retrenchment of Roman Catholicism in the First Vatican Council of 1870 with papal infallibility and the Syllabus of Errors, to the famous liberal-fundamentalists conflict of the 1920s that culminated with Harry Emerson Fosdick, to the current rearguard action among Baptists and Missouri Synod Lutherans with occasional Presbyterian flourishes, to the current popularity of Marcus Borg, Dominic Crossan, and John Spong—contemporary rationalists keep the issue before us. And all the while the pietists, whom we now call "folks into spirituality," stand on the side and wish for a peaceableness.

II

This war may continue. But I suppose we are at this time and place and topic because we have, in on our unarticulated way, arrived at a weariness of the battle and concluded that it is not in any case worth arguing about. I submit that it is a nineteenth century battle that is ill-suited to the twenty-first century, even though it may still evoke adrenaline from time to time on all sides. The battle becomes not worth waging:

- because *the developmental scheme* is persuasive only to those who have been wounded by or are suspicious of an authoritarian church but is otherwise without energizing force;
- because the offer of *a static package of truth* is too remote and without dynamism for a humanity that yearns for a generous, lively relationship of mutual fidelity that is reliable;
- because the disorder of the world and the manifest power of evil press us to think again *about dialogic engagement*, and the ancient theodic legacy of Leibniz is no longer adequate.

Beyond the old categories and the old quarrels, there is a general wonderment among us (and among our young) about what can be claimed in this tradition and whether it can offer a credible place in which to live that is outside of and in tension (if not contradiction) with the power of nation-states, the reductionisms of scientism, and the capricious hunger of the market. The failure of nation-states, the emptiness of scientism, and the exploitative injustice of the market (all seductions faced by the Church) create an environment in which the old quarrel no longer compels.

III

In what follows I will line out, as best I can, three perspectives that I have found useful in my attempt to move past the stalemate of the old quarrels. I should say that my sense of this is not theoretical, but lives very close to my recent experience with seminary students who simply have no energy for the old battles or even for the old critical consensus. There was a time when JEDP aroused great excitement or great resistance. But no more; now only a yawn. Because the enigma of a world at risk makes such a quarrel a luxury that does not deserve our energy.

1. Paul Ricoeur, in many of his writings, has proposed a hermeneutic that moves from precritical to critical to postcritical.[4] By "precritical,"

he means to take the text at face value. With reference to the Bible, this means most often, to take it as "the Word of God" in a direct way, a way that characteristically leads to an authoritarian view of an undifferentiated mass. The first task of interpretation is to problematize the text, to notice how complex and differentiated it is. In Old Testament study this task has been well accomplished by two centuries of criticism, and is the primary task in Scripture accepted by most mainline seminaries. This present company is fully aware of the problematic character of the biblical text that precludes taking it at face value as the Word of God. A critical perspective situates texts historically and moves powerfully against any attempt at absolutism; everything is relative to specific context and, as it happened, could be situated along the evolutionary track of "developing" human perception.

But Ricoeur's primary interest is in a postcritical move, one that concerns us here, and the one that now must, of necessity, preoccupy seminaries and churches. Indeed the critical project, I suggest, is mostly of interest only to those who have been wounded by the Church in its absolutism or are embarrassed by the Church's lack of intellectual rigor. That same critical task, in another idiom, is the undertaking of Dawkins and Hitchens, who have no sensibility for the postcritical work to be done in religion or in social theory more generally.[5]

By "postcritical" Ricoeur means continued serious theological interpretation that takes into account the significant gains of critical scholarship, but continues beyond. This move he terms a "second naïveté," that is, a willing suspension of disbelief, thus "naïveté," that is quite contrasted with the "first naïveté" of precritical, flat innocence.[6] In this "second naïveté," the interpreter knows better, knows about the two creation stories of P and J, knows about the two visions of monarchy in Samuel that are in tension, knows about the rewrite by the Chronicler of the Deuteronomist, knows about the tension between justice in Jeremiah and holiness in Ezekiel, knows that none of this fits together in a neat package of a seamless affirmation.

The postcritical interpreter has enough patience and imagination to watch how the canonizers have reconstrued the text, and has the courage as an interpreter to continue that reconstrual. Whereas the critical perspective is an act in history to ask, "What happened when?" the postcritical task is one of imagination, to ask, "What is being offered? What is being proposed? What is being imagined out beyond the givens of historical 'facticity'?" Thus, for example, a postcritical read of the book of Jeremiah notices the ("fictive?") role of Baruch, the scribe, to see that the book of Jeremiah is now designed as an act of scribal hope after the work of prophetic denunciation. It is clear in such a work of imaginative reconstrual—the ancient work and the contemporary work—that there are not the same methodological controls as criticism has enjoyed, so that the risks are greater. While such imaginative reperformance lacks "historical" appeal, what counts postcritically is the text-based articulation of another reality that depends neither upon the scholastic reductionism of the Church nor upon Enlightenment rationality, because neither scholastic reductionism nor Enlightenment rationality can bear the reality given in the text.

The character of God is now being reimagined in new circumstance and the world is being redescribed according to the rule of God. What becomes clear in postcritical "second naïveté" is that the theological offer of the text-*cum*-interpretation is an act of counter-imagination that moves beyond the critical and that contradicts the dominant imagination of culture that we generally take as a given. In the end, the pastoral declaration, "Christ is risen," is an invitation for the congregation to engage in a construal of reality out beyond the perceivable "facts" at hand. And one does not ask, in such an instance of reperformance, (a) "Is this a historical claim?" or (b) "Is this only a mere metaphor?" What counts is the naiveté that is not dumb or uninformed, but is willing to host a text-based world that lives on the lips of the interpreting community. And baptism, I propose, is an assent to enter into this particular "second naïveté."

I best understand the interpretive drama proposed by Ricoeur by the analogue of what happens to a candidate for ministry in the process of Clinical Pastoral Education (C.P.E.). Many such candidates enter seminary in a kind of precritical innocence about self and family: everyone is nice, moral, and churchgoing. In C.P.E., the work of critical analysis is an invitation to sometimes painful reflection on often unacknowledged hurt about self and family that often eventuates in an "authority problem" or some other dimension of alienation. As one discovers that Moses did not write the whole thing, so one may discover that one's life is more vexed and complex than one had suspected. But if one stays at the task long enough, one may arrive at a postcritical differentiation that, for all I now know about "me" and about "us," in fact my mother did love me as best she could.

I suggest that not only is the textual grid of precritical → critical → postcritical analogous to the personal dimensions of precritical → critical → postcritical work, but that in fact the two are intimately related to each other. By this I mean that a person with a precritical sense of self will not likely go very far with a critical sense of the text, or one with a critical sense of the text likely will not move to a postcritical sense of self. It is my judgment that pastoral leadership, in the crucible of text and person-hood, works at both of these tasks at the same time. A postcritical sense of self, engaged in a postcritical reading of the texts, yields freedom and energy for mission. Conversely, excessive lingering over the critical does very little except to nurse the wounds generated in precritical innocence. Thus I propose, following Ricoeur, that scribal critical work is a moment along the way. We in mainline culture have tended to make it an end point with the text rather than a step along the way. What we are now considering is the step beyond the critical that has rarely been on our horizon in any sustained way.

2. A second perspective I have found helpful in moving past the old quarrel between faith and criticism is to observe that in the last gen-eration there has been an explosion of newer criticisms that have moved away from old-fashioned historical criticism. The historical issues never disappear, but they do not need to be handled through the narrow cat-egories of Enlightenment historicity. The ground for moving beyond such criticism is the recognition that "tradition" cannot be reduced to "history" and in any case "memory" pertains when scientifically verifi-able history no longer suffices.[7] In Old Testament study, my impression is that historical questions preoccupy either detractors of the Bible who want to show that it is "not true" or conservatives who want to fight a rearguard action for precritical historicality. Neither of these, so it seems to me, carries us very far concerning the urgent tasks of faith and minis-try. I will mention two emergent habits of criticism that take us beyond lean historicity.

(a) Rhetorical criticism, a notion formulated by my teacher, James Mui-lenburg, attempts to bracket out historical questions and to go "inside the text" to see how the words work and how a "world" is proposed out of a configuration of words.[8] It is surely the case that when historical ques-tions are posed, we read books about the Bible rather than the Bible. Rhetorical criticism proposes that we put those books aside for an instant and read the text, and notice the twists and turns of the artistry of the text, and take the text as an imagined, artistically offered proposal of a world that we would not have, except for the utterance of this text. Such a focus on a particular text to generate a world implies (1) an acknowledgment that the world depends on utterance and not "factuality," and (2) that what the text and its interpreters offer is not a universal truth about the world for all times and places, but rather a hint, a trace, and a glimpse for this particular moment of speaking and hearing in this assemblage.

The outcomes are modest. Such a read yields not a great cosmic truth, but an empowered body of "text-creatures" who live by utterance. Every preacher knows, after church, about those who live by such utterance, because they tell us so. Rhetorical criticism proceeds in the conviction that the text itself, in its network of detail and nuance, is more interesting than extraneous anecdotes we might add on, more interesting than our reasoned self-confidence, and more interesting than the settled dogmatic claims of the Church.

Thus, for example, a scanning of the familiar text of Psalm 103 lets us notice that the psalm revolves around the fourfold usage of the term *hesed*—covenantal fidelity:

- In verse 4, the term occurs in a recital of God's good deeds:

  > who forgives all your iniquity,
  >> who heals all your diseases,
  > who redeems your life from the Pit,
  >> who crowns you with *steadfast love* and mercy (vv. 3–4, italics added).

- In verse 8 (italics added), we find a doxology about the character of God:

  > The Lord is merciful and gracious,
  >> slow to anger and abounding in *steadfast love*.

- In verse 11, the term concerns the forgiveness of sins:

  > He does not deal with us according to our sins,
  >> nor repay us according to our iniquities.
  > For as the heavens are high above the earth,
  >> so great is his *steadfast love* toward those who fear him (vv. 10–11, italics added).

- In verse 17, the term offers assurance in the face of mortality:

  > As for mortals, their days are like grass;
  >> they flourish like a flower of the field;
  > for the wind passes over it, and it is gone,
  >> and its place knows it no more.

But the *steadfast love* of the LORD is from everlasting to everlasting . . . (vv. 15–17, italics added).

The outcome in this psalm is the constant of a world grounded by God's reliable loyalty. That world clearly contradicts the world we mostly inhabit. We are invited to trust the text more than our worldly judgment. The focus on *hesed* is even more appreciated when we notice the fourfold use of the same term in Psalm 109, a great song of vengeance:

- The quality is lacking in the one condemned by the psalmist:

   For he did not remember to show *kindness*,
    but pursued the poor and needy
    and the brokenhearted to their death (v. 16, italics added).

- In verse 12 (italics added), in response, there is a wish that he will receive no *hesed*:

   May there be no one to do him a *kindness*,
    nor anyone to pity his orphaned children.

- An urgent appeal is made, apart from him, to the God of *hesed*:

   But you, O LORD my Lord,
    act on my behalf for your name's sake;
    because your *steadfast love* is good, deliver me (v. 21, italics added).

   Help me, O LORD my God!
    Save me according to your *steadfast love* (v. 26, italics added).

No historical judgments are required in order to see how the rhetorical repetitions focus us on the elemental issue of trust that subverts and transcends all Enlightenment notions of what "happened." Of course that is an easy case to make in the Psalms. But the case is the same elsewhere. My impression is that such freedom with rhetoric as a generator of worlds is more available to those who are less inured to Enlightenment notions of historicity, as for example, in much of the black church. This does not mean that pastors in the black church tradition do not know about Enlightenment criticism; it means only that it has not become defining there as in many of our white establishment venues.

(b) A second cluster of emerging methods goes under the name of "social scientific methods" that includes sociology and political economy; these methods see that the text is embedded in power relationships, even if we cannot identify specific historical contexts. The facet of this I wish to identify is "ideology criticism" that has been variously taken up in liberation theology, feminist hermeneutics, and, more recently, in postcolonial interpretation.[9] Indeed Schüssler Fiorenza has proposed that the insignia of empire is so deeply inscribed in our way of interpretation that to interpret outside the claims of empire is exceedingly difficult if not impossible.[10] "Ideology critique" is the critical awareness that our interpretation is never disinterested, but characteristically we occupy a field of power in which we have a stake. The text itself is likewise never disinterested for the same reason. From that it follows that here are no innocent texts and no text that stands outside vigorous contestation. One can readily contrast that awareness with older historical criticism that could claim, in good Enlightenment fashion, that it offered an "objective" read of texts, a common assumption of Enlightenment autonomy. In the Church, moreover, there is a common assumption that the texts are innocent and that the readers close at hand (preachers) are also innocent. To be sure, every serious interpreter (including present company) is clear that one's own work is not so contaminated. Most assuredly, moreover, good rational liberals who have been wounded by precriticism imagine they have a better angle.

Thus in Old Testament study it is possible to trace trajectories of interpretation, whether of the Jerusalem elites or the Deuteronomic school or even the Shiloh priesthood.[11] In our reading habits moreover, it matters about our denominational location and even more acutely which seminary and who our defining teachers have been. Once we grasp this truth about our practice of the text, it is impossible any longer to pay much attention to the old claims of "objectivity," for it turns out that the old "objective" consensus was simply arrived at by limiting the voices in the room.

It is possible, even in a local congregation, to reflect on the vested interest that is evident in the text, what dispute is engaged in the text, and what the advocacies are that operate in the utterance that very often go unnoticed and unacknowledged. Beyond Ricoeur's notion of "second naïveté," Jason Byassee has pled for a "third naiveté" that exposes the stance of the interpreter as well as the stance of the text.[12] It turns out, not surprisingly, that every local congregation is a venue of textual advocacy that lives among many rival advocacies; we find the texts that advance our particular advocacy, even when our finding of the right text is called "a lectionary." A pastor's experience of this reality of advocacy occurs when adult children help to plan the funeral for an aged parent. Clearly there is no "interpretation" of the life of the parent that even pretends to be disinterested, for every entry into the planning process is one of great emotional force rooted in ancient experience. So it is with texts as well.

What may happen in ideology critique is that anyone can ponder the question, "What vested interest is being championed in this text?" In the end, the best postcritical truth comes to us filtered through our interests, some of which can be recognized and of which we may repent.

The movement beyond historical criticism (in which most of us are schooled) to rhetorical and ideological criticism makes possible a greater possibility for postcritical affirmation that is rich and thick. It may be rich and thick because we ourselves are now implicated in the process of interpretation, whereas in thin Enlightenment rationality we had thought we stood outside the text as objective observers, judges, and critics.

3. A third perspective I have found useful in moving beyond the quarrel of faith and criticism is the prospect of learning more from characteristic Jewish modes of interpretation that do not move so urgently toward closure. As you know, in rabbinic practice, one is offered a story or an old rabbinic saying by way of interpretation. And if one asks about that response, one evokes yet another rabbinic saying or story, because the supply is limitless and each one carries interpretation to another angle of possibility.

One helpful way into such Jewish modes that refuse closure is to pay attention to Freud's theory and practice of psychoanalysis, for it is clear enough that Freud's way of "reading" repressed personhood was taken from rabbinic ways of reading the hiddenness of texts. As you know, the psychotherapeutic conversation can walk endlessly around a memory, an event, a dream, a phrase, because the memory, event, dream, or phrase has a rich capacity for multiple meanings, any of which may be censored, but all of which may be emancipatory.

Freud's great insight is that the human self, never more than partially brought to awareness, is thick, layered, and conflicted:

> *The self is thick* in the sense that word and image and memory are freighted with more meaning and force than any single saying of it can ever unpack.
>
> *The self is layered* because, in our fearful repression, we have stacked experience upon experience, hurt upon hurt, rage upon rage, and sometimes even joy upon joy.

> *The self is conflicted* because of the inescapable friction between the felt self and the socially expected self, a friction that we spend our lives negotiating.[13]

And of course what we present (even to ourselves) of such a complex self is most often only in bits and pieces, only some of which come to our awareness.

If, as I believe following Susan Handelman, Freud learned this approach from rabbinic ways of reading texts to watch for their thickness, layered quality, and conflictedness, we may take his great insight about the modern self back into our reading of biblical texts that are also thick, layered, and conflicted.[14] At its best, criticism has seen exactly that about the text:

- *The text is thick*; that is what keeps preachers going. The text, in rich artistry, cannot be flatly explained or reduced to single meaning, even though precritical innocence and critical rationality tried to do so. You can check this by reading the old historical critical commentaries. What strikes one about them is how thin they are; when the text is taken thinly, there is almost nothing to be said about texts.
- *The text is layered* most broadly in the JEDP hypothesis, so that the text, like the self, is an assemblage of many voices over time, each of which has struggled to be the last word.
- *The text is conflicted*, so that it is not difficult to discern tensions and contradictions in the text. When honored, those tensions and contradictions are not to be explained away; rather they are the matrix of generative interpretation as with the work of pastoral therapy.

A precritical certainty wants to deny this quality of the text. A critical understanding wants to explain and resolve and sort it out. But in good psychotherapy, after the work of "explanation" has been attempted, there comes a time of pause for wonderment, silence, and respect for the rich dimensions of the self in front of us, "the many selves of the self."[15] So it is with the text. There comes a time for a pause in wonderment, silence, and respect for a text than refuses thinness. We dare to say, moreover, that it is precisely this text, in its thickness, layeredness, and conflictedness, that bears witness to the true God, this Jewish God who refuses the old Greek rationality and who continues to refuse our modernist thinness, this triune God who refuses the old deistic flatness of monarchy.

We dare say, beyond that as we move from the text to the God witnessed there, that we are in the image of that God, thick, layered, and conflicted. So we can imagine that any congregation, met around this thick, layered, conflicted text, bears witness to this God in whom we live and move and have our being. We do so in resistance against the reductionism of precritical innocence, in refusal of Enlightenment rationality, and in defiance of the thin requirements of technological consumerism. The entire interpretive project is open and deep and emancipatory. We have, to be sure, often failed to recognize that in our long history of wound and reason; that process, moreover, continues to be largely entrusted to the pastors of the church.

Thus I propose that in the crisis of moving from the critical to the postcritical, we take the text with new seriousness as a revelatory disclosure of the character of God, world, and self that speaks powerfully against the reductionisms of contemporary society. The challenge for a pastoral hermeneutic, of course, is that one must minister, all at the same time, among those committed to precritical innocence, among those recovering from precritical wounds, and those eager to move on to the postcritical. The critical is an important step in that process, as the scribes have understood, one always again to be revisited. But to linger there excessively, as we have done, is a measure (a) of how much we have been wounded by the precritical, (b) of how embarrassed we are by the precritical, and (c) of how much our Church has been co-opted by Enlightenment rationality.

The Western church has gone through a critical phase of Enlightenment rationality and now moves to a postcritical perspective. It is not surprising that ministers of the gospel may now move to a new innocence, not denying the wounding of precritical absolutism but not yielding finally to the thin remedy of criticism.

IV

I draw the conclusion that the work of the scribes—in our case the critical scholars—is to help the Church read Scripture knowingly, responsibly, and, as a result, more faithfully:

- The scribes insist that text is problematic—thick, layered, and conflicted—when the Church is tempted to regard it as simple, direct, and straightforward.

- The scribes insist that there is always more work to be done in reading Scripture, when the Church is seduced to think it has arrived at a final reading, a final solution to the Scripture problem.
- The scribes insist that reading and listening to Scripture is, lifelong, a worthy, fully occupying vocation, when the Church is variously distracted into its several orthodoxies, its moralisms of the right or of the left, its liberal rationalism, or even its patronizing entertainment.

The work of the scribes is not, to be sure, the final word about the text. That word belongs to the Spirit to whom the Church must finally listen. But in anticipation of the Spirit, or even as a vehicle for what the Spirit may want to say to the Church, the scribes may make it possible for the Church to listen more attentively.

A. The ongoing dynamism of scribal activity is evidenced in the work of the two great scribes of the Old Testament. On the one hand, Baruch made the book of Jeremiah possible, and he is plausibly implicated in the formation and canonization of the book of Deuteronomy.[16] In Jeremiah 36, that narrative in which Baruch both writes and promulgates the book of Jeremiah at considerable personal risk, it is reported that when the scroll of Jeremiah had been shredded by royal anxiety, Jeremiah took another scroll. Baruch wrote on it the words of the previous scroll, "and many similar words were added to them" (Jer. 36:32). Baruch is the vehicle whereby the old prophetic utterances are kept alive and available for time to come.

On the other hand, Ezra, the great scribe, convened the Jews in order to reconstitute the community of Judaism. It is reported of that convocation held at the Water Gate in Jerusalem: "The Levites helped the people to understand the law, while the people remained in their places. So they read from the book, from the law of God, with interpretation. They gave the sense, so that the people understood the reading" (Neh. 8:7–8).

The Levites, the aides to Ezra, the early exegetes and preachers, "interpreted"; they "gave sense"; they helped the people to "understand." They extended the tradition by their exegesis. Scribalism, ancient and contemporary, is an engagement with the text not only to reiterate and treasure: Ezra knew, as all faithful scribes have known, that the text must be interpreted, made contemporary according to the best interpretive categories available, in order to exhibit its powerful, defiant force for renewal.

B. The dynamism of Baruch and Ezra extends to Jesus. He is the one who knew "of old" but who said, "But I say to you . . ." (Matt. 5:21–48).

That same generative interpretation is the work of contemporary scholarship when it is done at its best. The scribes keep learning. We must not imagine that critical scholars are still doing what they did in ancient days when we were in seminary. The scribes keep learning how to do their work:

- The scribes have learned in recent times how the old traditions have been put together in what we call the canonizing process. The scribes know about *redaction criticism* in the same way the therapist helps us to see how each of us has been complexly arranged.
- The scribes have learned in recent time how words matter and how texts are in fact a network of artistically arranged signs and symbols, what we call *rhetorical criticism*. The nuance and detail of such speech is as freighted as is when we recall the shaping utterances of our parents, who sometimes healed by words and sometimes wounded.
- The scribes have learned in recent time how they themselves are present in the text, what we call *ideology criticism*, or at least the force of context. The scribes have traduced the modernist assumption that we are objective observers, to see that both the text and they themselves are saturated with vested interest. Listen to this testimony from Mark S. Smith, a noted interpreter who wrote earlier this year:

  > Yet in our work, we rarely ask about the impact of life events or world events on our intellects. In this respect, we often operate on autopilot. For all the riches of our knowledge, even the best scholars among us are only human; if we academics cannot fathom our own place in our work, then at least we could express some humility about the limit of our interpretations.[17]

- The scribes have learned in recent time that the text sounds a large voice of truth, but with countless nooks and crannies for otherness, traces of variation and hints of imaginative defiance, the large awareness of canon criticism that cannot be reduced into a single seamless witness.
- The scribes have learned in recent time that the text is so thick, layered, and conflicted, because it is occupied by this elusive, sometimes irascible character of God who is the hope of the world. This is the God who moves through the text and comes

among us with freedom: "Am I a God near by, says the LORD, and not a God far off? Who can hide in secret places so that I cannot see them? says the LORD. Do I not fill heaven and earth? says the LORD" (Jer. 23:23–24).

Preoccupation with the text is what the scribes do. They set the table so that the Church can see and meet this Holy Character in all of God's own thickness, layeredness, and conflictedness. The scribes have learned to keep going, to read and listen yet again, precisely because "time makes ancient good uncouth."[18]

C. The scribes speak a penultimate word about Scripture, but it is a word without which we cannot do. In Matthew 13, Jesus tells a series of parables. The disciples ask him, in verse 10, "Why do you speak to them in parables?" He replies, "To you it has been given to know the secrets of the kingdom of heaven, but to them it has not been given" (Matt. 13:10–11).

When the series of parables is finished, Jesus says to his disciples, "Have you understood all this?" And they say, "Yes," not knowing what they did not understand. Oh my! And then he says to his disciples, "Therefore every scribe who has been trained for the kingdom of heaven is like the master of a household who brings out of his treasure what is new and what is old" (vv. 51, 52).

Scribes trained for the kingdom have two responsibilities: to treasure what is old and to offer what is new. A failed scribe may linger over what is old but offer nothing new. Or a failed scribe may scuttle what is old for the sake of what is new. But kingdom scribes, scholars who serve the secret of God, work at the artistic pivot point of old and new, of tradition and interpretation, of crucifixion and resurrection. At their best, scribes preclude the dumbing down to which the Church is deeply tempted in its effort to domesticate. They insist that what is familiar and comfortable must be recognized as strange.[19] He left them with the parables; and he left them with the heavy lifting to do.

Notes

1. Reprinted in *Anglican Theological Review* 93, no. 3 (Summer, 2011): 385–403.
2. See Patrick D. Miller, "Wellhausen and the History of Israel's Religion," in idem, *Israelite Religion and Biblical Theology: Collected Essays*, JSOTSup 267 (Sheffield: Sheffield Academic Press, 2000), 182–96. The reference "JEDP" is to a scholarly theory

that the Pentateuch is composed of four discrete literary documents, each with its own unique perspective on important aspects of ancient Israel's history, ritual, and communal identity. The four source documents are identified by sigla standing for their putative authors' names in scholarly parlance: "J" for "Yahwist," "E" for "Elohist," "D" for "Deuteronomist," and "P" for "Priestly source." The Documentary Hypothesis has come under devastating attack in recent years from a variety of directions in North American and European biblical scholarship. For a vigorous defense of the Documentary Hypothesis, see Joel S. Baden, *The Composition of the Pentateuch: Renewing the Documentary Hypothesis* (New Haven, CT: Yale University Press, 2012).

3. The evolutionary hypothesis reached an artistic acme with Teilhard de Chardin, *The Divine Milieu* (Brighton: Sussex Academic Press, 2004), with his notion of "the omega point."

4. Over time Ricoeur has used a variety of terms to characterize the process of moving from precritical to postcritical. In "Reply to Lewis S. Mudge," *Essays on Biblical Interpretation* (Philadelphia: Fortress Press 1980), 43–44, he has it "'naïve' understanding, objective explanation, and appropriation." In *Freud and Philosophy: An Essay on Interpretation* (New Haven, CT: Yale University Press, 1970), he speaks of "suspicion" and "retrieval." For variations on the terminology, see Mark I. Wallace, *The Second Naiveté: Barth, Ricoeur, and the New Yale Theology* (Macon: Mercer University Press, 1990), 5 n. 16. On suspicion, Ricoeur, *The Philosophy of Paul Ricoeur: An Anthology of His Work*, ed. by Charles E. Regain and David Stewart (Boston: Beacon Press, 1978), 219, writes, "In this sense one can say that *this* atheism concerning the gods of men, pertains hereafter to any possible faith. What we have therefore appropriated to ourselves is first, the critique of religion as a mask, a mask of fear, a mask of domination, a mask of hate. A Marxist critique of ideology, a Nietzschean critique of resentment, and a Freudian critique of infantile distress, are hereafter the views through which any kind of mediation of faith must pass." But then, beyond suspicion, he judges (ibid., 222), "This circle can only be broken by the believer in the hermeneutics when he is faithful to the community, and by the 'hermeneut' in the believer when he does his scientific work of exegesis. This is today the dual condition of modern man in whom struggles both a believer and an atheist; in the believer himself there confront one another an adult critic and a naïve child who listen to the Word." In this conference we are considering the move from "adult critic" to "naïve child."

5. See Richard Dawkins, *The God Delusion* (Boston: Houghton Mifflin, 2006) and Christopher Hitchens, *God Is Not Great: How Religion Poisons Everything* (New York: Warner Books, 2007). The best response I know to the strictures of Dawkins and Hitchens is by Terry Eagleton, *Reason, Faith, and Revolution: Reflections on the God Debate* (New Haven: Yale University Press, 2009). His response is not one of "ideas," but of "praxis."

6. Ricoeur uses the phrase in *The Symbolism of Evil* (Boston: Beacon Press, 1967), 351–52. More broadly see Mark I. Wallace, *The Second Naiveté*.

7. See Yosef Hayim Yerushalmi, *Zakhor: Jewish History and Jewish Memory* (Seattle: University of Washington Press, 1982).

8. The definitive study is Phyllis Trible, *Rhetorical Criticism: Context, Method, and the Book of Jonah* (Minneapolis: Fortress Press, 1994).

9. See *Ideological Criticism of Biblical Texts*, ed. David Jobling, *Semeia* 59 (1992) and James Barr, *History and Ideology in the Old Testament: Biblical Studies at the End of a*

Millennium (Oxford: Oxford University Press, 2000). Barr himself, given his commitment to Enlightenment "objectivity," fails to understand what is at issue in the discussion as it pertains to the Old Testament.

10. Elisabeth Schüssler Fiorenza, *The Power of the Word: Scripture and the Rhetoric of Empire* (Minneapolis: Fortress Press, 2007).

11. See, for example, Odil Hannes Steck, "Theological Streams of Tradition," in *Tradition and Theology in the Old Testament*, ed. Douglas A. Knight (Philadelphia: Fortress Press, 1977), 183–214; and Walter Brueggemann, "Trajectories in Old Testament Literature and the Sociology of Ancient Israel," *Journal of Biblical Literature* 98 (1979): 161–85.

12. Jason Byassee, *Praise Seeking Understanding: Reading the Psalms with Augustine* (Grand Rapids: Eerdmans, 2007), 272 and passim.

13. See D. W. Winnicott, *The Maturational Processes and the Facilitating Environment: Studies in the Theory of Emotional Development* (Madison: International Universities Press, Inc., 1965), 140–52.

14. Susan A. Handelman, *The Slayers of Moses: The Emergence of Rabbinic Interpretation in Modern Literary Theory* (Albany: SUNY Press, 1982).

15. See Roy Schaeffer, *Retelling a Life: Narration and Dialogue in Psychoanalysis* (New York: Basic Books, 1992), chap. 2 and passim.

16. On the cruciality of Baruch for the formation of the Bible, see Richard Elliott Friedman, *Who Wrote the Bible?* (New York: Harper & Row, 1987).

17. Mark S. Smith, *The Priestly Vision of Genesis 1* (Minneapolis: Fortress Press, 2010).

18. The phrase is taken from verse 3 of the hymn, "Once to every man and nation," the lyrics of which were penned by poet James Russell Lowell in 1845 and set to music by Thomas J. William in 1890. The full line reads, "New occasions teach new duties, time makes ancient good uncouth, / They must upward still and onward, who would keep abreast of truth."

19. See Karl Barth, "The Strange New World within the Bible," in idem, *The Word of God and the Word of Man* (New York: Harper & Brothers, 1957), 28–50. Ricoeur's term for "making strange" is "distanciation." See Dan R. Stiver, *Theology after Ricoeur: New Directions in Hermeneutical Theology* (Louisville, KY: Westminster John Knox Press, 2001), 89–97.

Chapter 6

"Hungry for This Word"

A Conversation with Roger S. Greene and Walter Brueggemann at St. Timothy's Episcopal Church, Cincinnati February 10, 2011

In August 2008, Brueggemann moved from Columbia Theological Seminary in Decatur, Georgia, to Cincinnati, Ohio, and found a new church home at St. Timothy's, an Episcopal congregation led by the Rev. Roger S. Greene. In this conversation, Brueggemann and Greene reflect on the deep need of the Church for Scripture study and the struggles that congregants have with the complexity of the Bible. Greene remembers a transformational early encounter with the Gospel of John; Brueggemann mulls further the problem of the violence of God in the Bible. The two men consider their shared compulsion to "perform," their distinctly different approaches to prayer, and the ever-present temptation to believe the accolades that can be lavished upon them in their respective positions of public leadership.

CJS

CAROLYN SHARP: Walter, you have said that St. Timothy's is one of the best things that has ever happened to you. And Roger, you have said that when Walter first came, people didn't really know who he was. Which is really a gift, in a certain way. When you have people coming up to you because you're famous, it's not that that's not an honor, but it's not the same kind of authentic connection as when you're just who you are.

WALTER BRUEGGEMANN: There's almost none of that celebrity stuff at St. Timothy's.

SHARP: It can be anxiety-producing for preachers. My rector knows that there's an Old Testament professor in the sanctuary. I've worshiped there for eight years, and he's still anxious about that, even though I never say

119

a negative word about anyone's sermon, ever! I would never do it. But there's a pressure that people can feel when they're around that sort of expertise.

ROGER GREENE: I guess what's happened with me is, it was clear that they [Brueggemann and his wife, Tia Foley] just wanted to be part of this community. The way I'd describe it is this: a real gift of Walter's presence is to have someone in my congregation who loves this stuff as much as I do. And as a preacher, what I am longing for is people who are hungry for this Word, who come longing for something. The worst thing is to feel like I'm talking to a brick wall.

BRUEGGEMANN: Right.

SHARP: Whether they agree or disagree, you want them to care.

GREENE: Yes. So I think that was the dominant kind of sense: he's looking forward to what the readings are, what I'm going to say, what the music's going to be.

SHARP: He raves about the music. You know that, right?

GREENE: Yes! So it's energizing as opposed to, you know, "Have I done my exegesis well enough?" [Brueggemann laughs] and "What if he doesn't agree?" and "What's he thinking?"

SHARP [to Brueggemann]: Have you ever harrumphed or folded your arms during a sermon?

BRUEGGEMANN: Not with Roger! Thank goodness. With some preachers, I guess they skipped seminary the day they taught Greek! Some of them just don't know what to do with the text.

SHARP: Using it solely as a jumping-off point for other reflections?

BRUEGGEMANN: Yep. But not Roger.

GREENE: In the end, Walter's presence is a positive circulation of energy, for me. I can't speak for Heather [Wiseman, the associate rector] or Christopher [Richardson, the youth director], of course. And the other gift is this. I've been here a long time, and one of the challenges when you've been in a place a long time is, how do you keep things fresh and new, and how do you keep feeding yourself in fresh, new ways, as well as the congregation? So I have some colleagues in this area, and I've tried to get them to do Bible study with me. Bible study—I don't want to just get together and bitch and moan or whatever. I cannot get them to do it. Now, they wouldn't say they're not into it—there's always something else that comes up. So what is so cool for me is to have someone in my congregation who will pop in and leave me a book or e-mail me and say, "Look at this article!" Walter's done some presentations in the fall that have been wonderful. For me it's the best continuing ed I could ever have dreamed of.

SHARP: A really enthusiastic dialogue partner!

GREENE: And at least the way I'm wired, my ministry is sustained in large measure by this ongoing encounter with these texts. Preaching is about discovering anew what I believe, getting new eyes to see after a week in which I've been blinded by whatever. So to have him in the mix of that is a real gift! My sense is that Walter prefers not to preach on Sunday morning. He'd rather just be a worshiping member, although he has preached once. But the things he's done on Wednesday nights have been, for me and many others, a real gift. Your book—this collection [*Disruptive Grace: Reflections on God, Scripture, and the Church*] is the kind of thing that feeds. Not only because of who Walter is—his vibrancy, his vitality, his love of the Church—but also for what is important to him, this just so feeds a preacher like me. When you're preaching most Sundays, year round, if you cannot keep engaged with the text, you're just gonna die, and then the congregation's gonna die. But when I have that spark, it's like, "Yeah! Okay!"

SHARP: And it would seem that the whole congregation is experiencing that under your leadership, Roger, because from what I understand, St. Timothy's has really grown.

GREENE: It has grown, and in recent years they have been getting some of this stuff.

SHARP: The room last night [for Brueggemann's Bible study on Isaiah 14, his second presentation in a four-part Lenten series] seemed more keenly aware about Scripture and more deeply engaged than one generally sees with adult ed groups. Not that they necessarily have more knowledge, but perhaps they have experienced a more sustained invitation into the text than some congregations do. I was very impressed with how engaged they were.

GREENE: Everybody says that they want to study the Bible, but . . .

BRUEGGEMANN: [laughing] They really don't!

GREENE: Few ever get around to it. More of that is happening, and it's very helpful to have another voice in the mix, a voice that has a lot of authority. It just reinforces things I am trying to do, and it's another voice. Some folks will show up just because someone has some credentials. They're not sure they're going to buy any of it, but they'll give it a shot.

SHARP: Including people from other churches, as we saw with the Presbyterian gentleman who came last night.

BRUEGGEMANN: I've figured out—and it took me a long time to understand this—that my first audience was clergy and laypeople. It took me a long time to figure out that I was not talking primarily to other members of the scholarly guild.

SHARP: Although both groups are your constituents. You've had a huge impact in the guild, and you know that. But that is a more uncertain relationship for you, in some ways.

BRUEGGEMANN: Right.

GREENE: And what the Church needs are people who can help not just the clergy but also the broader population to engage with this stuff. So I'm all for reading a wide variety of literature from different perspectives and some stuff that's pretty far up in the ivory tower, but I must say, there are times when I'm thinking, if this particular scholar is a member of the Church, are they thinking about what the hell this really will do?

SHARP: And it does so often matter, but we don't always think about how to say why it matters.

GREENE: Exactly! I'm not suggesting that scholars can't be rigorously academic and all the rest of it, but let's face it, this world we're living in is in need of a lot. And I think that people need to be thinking about what this doctoral dissertation has to do with anything.

SHARP: It reminds me of my first project. It was on Jeremiah and competing voices in the Jeremiah prose, which I do think are perceptible there. There was a lot at stake precisely on the issue Walter was discussing last night: submitting to imperial power or resisting it. Those are the two voices that I hear in Jeremiah. And I was really proud of myself when I finished the dissertation. It's fun, just like tennis. [Greene is an avid tennis player who was ranked nationally when he was 14; he continues to play in senior events at the local and national levels.] It's fun to exercise your brain in the technical aspects of interpretation, just like it's fun to master topspin or rifle an amazing backhand across the net. And I was thinking about why anyone should care about all this. I spent maybe six pages at the end of the book thinking about how it matters that in our sacred text, we have communities—fractured and broken, pressed down under the thumb of Babylon or trying urgently to figure out who they were after colonization—fighting over what this prophet Jeremiah meant in their history. Was he a prophet who said, "Pray for the *shalom* of Babylon"? Was he a prophet who said, "No, resist Babylon! Babylon too will be punished by God"? I think it matters for communities of faith to know that they can fight about this kind of stuff and still be faithful. There's not only one godly way to be.

GREENE: Right, right!

SHARP: But as I said, I spent only five or six pages in the book discussing this. That wasn't the project, to think about that. I do think there's a lot of relevance to these scholarly endeavors—maybe not every philological argument, sure, but there's a lot of relevance for contemporary life. And it's important not only to have the leisure to reflect on these matters, but to have the chops—the technical ability—to be eloquent about how this stuff matters for life today. That ability is somewhat unusual in our guild, and that's where Walter stands head and shoulders above so many of his colleagues.

GREENE: I was reading the pieces in your collection, and somebody asked me last night, "Could I read this?" And what I find is that for the most part, this stuff is accessible to people if they'll give it a shot. Whereas there are some books that are just never going to be accessible. And because the Church has people who want to take their journeys seriously, there have to be writers who can talk to them in a way that they can understand, who invite them to go deeper and who help them to do that.

SHARP: Yes—rather than just hand them "the answers," which first of all is not right, and second of all is mind-deadening. That's what I love about your way of engaging the text, Walter. You really open it up, helping people see what they can find for themselves. Who cares if I have "the answer" to something? Why is anyone going to care about that in their spiritual life? It's much more about equipping people for their own journeys.

BRUEGGEMANN: Yes.

GREENE: The other thing is that he has an extraordinary passion that comes through. And as we all know, sometimes what will happen with people is—I see this sometimes with sermons I give—I may not really know whether they "got" it, but they can see, "Man, the preacher really believes this! Maybe I should give it a shot too." The energy sounds authentic in Walter's preaching. And that's all so different from some deadly preaching. Our culture doesn't have much patience to begin with. And if you lose them in the first few minutes, it's all over. That doesn't mean you pander. But they've got to have a reason to believe it's worthwhile to spend time listening to you. Otherwise they'll be saying to themselves, "if this isn't going to make a difference in my life, why am I doing it?"

SHARP: Especially with the multitasking that goes on today. Electronic instant gratification dominates this age in which we live.

BRUEGGEMANN: That's right.

SHARP: Do you use electronic media at your church—blogging, projecting images, or anything like that?

GREENE: We don't use those in worship. We're trying to get more up-to-date in terms of the digital world, how we communicate who we are and how people connect to us. That's been a real step up. With Walter's presentations in the Bible study series, I've encouraged people to go to the St. Timothy's site on Facebook to share comments. A few did. I've got a woman in the congregation who would love more of that. She says, "I can't come to most of these things because I travel a lot. I would love to have some sort of online Bible study where I could be engaging people and reading Scripture."

SHARP: I led an online Bible study from 2006 to 2010. It came out of a sermon I was preaching on Isaiah—pretty much on the spur of the moment, which is not ideal because I didn't clear it with my rector beforehand, but let's just hope it was the Holy Spirit at work! I said from the pulpit, "Let's read Isaiah this year, one chapter a week." I set up an e-mail list on which people could respond to my posts about the biblical material. The group grew from about twenty-five people in the first year to about 150 people from all over the country by the time we quit. But the problem there is, if you have just one leader, it can get exhausting. At first I just sent a few spiritual questions to open up folks' engagement with the text.

But then I got all over-compensatory and started to feel like, "No, I've got to provide scholarship, I've got to research each text before I post on it," and it got exhausting.

But I will say this: there are people who would never come to a face-to-face Bible study—they're traveling, or they have young children; they can't do it on a Sunday morning, they can't get out on Wednesday nights—and people were very happy to have another kind of possibility. So it's a whole market that is usually not tapped, unless maybe in emergent-church contexts, where they do a lot with digital media. In traditional parishes, there is a whole lot more that could be done. It's just a matter of time and resources to develop the new means of communication.

BRUEGGEMANN: I want to ask you this, Roger: the woman who was sitting over on my right against the wall, who said, "We all failed"—is she a member of the church?

GREENE: She is. She's a science teacher at a local high school. Her great distinction is that she is married to my tennis buddy! She's a great lady, raised Episcopalian, and I'm just delighted that she's gotten into this. Coming from her science background, her whole thing is, "How do I know I've gotten this right?"

SHARP: For scientists, the humanities are so vague and nebulous, aren't they?

GREENE: What are we trying to do? The vision is that we might end up with four or five smaller groups that want to continue this Bible study. I see a good number of people there who have the energy and the will to stay with this.

SHARP: Say more about what St. Timothy's offers already.

GREENE: What we have now are different small group experiences that often have a lot of Bible in them, but there is not, right now, an ongoing weekly Bible study that's year-round. We might do a segment here or a segment there. What I'd like to see is a group of six to eight people who say, "Just like we work out regularly, we want to meet weekly and learn this method for reading Scripture, and we're going to stick with it."

SHARP: And train, as it were.

GREENE: And train. And we're asking, How, over time, can that grow and how can presentations at other times during the year feed into that?

SHARP: You've said that the deep learning in Christian education is cumulative, which is absolutely right. It is like developing strong muscles in athletic training.

GREENE: If people start working out in January, by January 15th they're done.

BRUEGGEMANN: [chuckles] Yes, indeed.

SHARP: Oh, you know me? I didn't realize you knew me as well as that. Go on.

GREENE: [laughs] But if they can stay with it, and say, "This is work, but I know that if I stop, it's a long road back. . . ." That's the thing about the Bible. People are so intimidated! Part of what Walter does for some people is to convince them that if they will just read the text, without any commentaries or other sources, something can happen.

SHARP: Yes! Walter, last night you focused on the words and were saying to people, "Tell me about the words in this passage." You keep them from getting too abstract, which is excellent. You say, "No, tell me what words you see on the page in front of you." It's great.

GREENE: At our table [during Brueggemann's Bible study], people were seeing all the important things in the passage. And of course what's going to happen is that they'll be reading a different passage three weeks later, and they'll say, "Oh, that's like the other thing I saw."

BRUEGGEMANN: Before dinner last night, Phil's sister showed me something in Isaiah 2 where there's a repeated phrase, "The LORD alone will be exalted," "The LORD alone will be exalted." And in between, it says, "The LORD . . . has a day against _____," "against _____," "against _____," and she said, "I saw the pattern! It's everywhere!"

SHARP: Excellent! And it's marvelous not just that she saw the pattern itself, but that she was so excited about her perception, about having new eyes for that.

BRUEGGEMANN: That's right! "I'm not making this up!" [laughs]

GREENE: It's fun to imagine that we could have these groups or that we could have, a couple of times of year, this kind of larger gathering. What a deal!

BRUEGGEMANN: If you get a critical mass of folks who stay at it for a while, it creates a different preaching requirement.

GREENE: I see it all the time: all this feeds the whole system. The hardest sell are the folks in their thirties and forties with small kids who just can't imagine having time for this—they're having trouble just getting up.

SHARP: Right. With small kids, getting through the day can be exhausting. I remember!

GREENE: It's so hard to get them involved. And yet in some ways, they're the ones who most need to be reminded that the Lord is king.

BRUEGGEMANN: Yes.

GREENE: But there may be other ways for them that will work better. The crowd last night was, for the most part, a crowd in which very few had small children. They may be infectious for the rest of the congregation, too. I'm amazed—and this is a credit to Walter—that with this and the presentations he made back in the fall, a broad cross-section of people came, with a whole variety of political and theological views. One of the things Walter does really well is this: without pulling any punches, he is able to keep them on board. I feel like some speakers are lying when they say that they think both the political left and the right have gotten it wrong—they're just trying to build a democracy among the crowd. But the way Walter has been able to address what might be the divisions in a group has been honest. He is honest about how he views the text and all the rest of it. He doesn't humiliate anybody, and he challenges them at the same time. And they are willing to stay with him on that! Last night, Walter, when you were talking about the dead—about the shades in Sheol—I thought, "I wonder where he's going with this." But you used Roosevelt and Reagan [as examples of leaders enamored of their own power who, ironically, end up in Sheol]. Had it been only Reagan or Bush, that would have been less balanced. But the way you did it, the conservative folks could stay on board. Folks wouldn't stay around long if they felt like they were being beat up.

BRUEGGEMANN: Yes. You never know when something is going to get through. But someone said to me, that was the first time anyone had helped him understand any of this. He said, "I have never understood a word of this stuff."

GREENE: Some folks say to me, "Roger, I just wish I could believe this like you believe it." And therefore they want me to convince them that they ought to believe this. My take on some of these folks—and I don't know whether this is true or not—is that they are pretty well defended [i.e., emotionally guarded]. It may be their way of not having to change. There's a protective side to it. But they keep coming! They're there every Sunday. It's a way for them to say, "I'm not sure I really want to buy into this, because if I did buy into this, it might mean that some of the ways I view the world would have to change." It would be pretty hard for such a person to come to me and say, "Okay. I give in." But with Walter, here's a new voice—a voice with authority—and this might be an avenue for him to engage.

SHARP: One of the things that's so important about your work with the text, Walter, is that you are all about the dialogical: the various voices and the different ways in which different texts witness. Some readers of Scripture reach too easily for the metanarrative: "It's all about salvation history. Period." Or, "it's all about grace." Or, "it's all about love." No, it's not! If you read the text, it isn't all about any one thing. So the skeptic— the person who has been able to get through suffering or seeing the world suffer by being an Ecclesiastes kind of person—needs to understand that there are ways into the conversation from all of those different vantage points within the text, as well as different interpretive vantage points.

BRUEGGEMANN: That's right.

SHARP: You make that available to them in a way that other interpreters don't. Do you remember Bernhard Anderson's *Understanding the Old Testament*?[1] That was a foundational text in the '80s when I was in college, and it's beautifully done. I don't want to take anything away from that excellent project. But that book made the Old Testament entirely coherent and positive—it ended up being all good news. And you know what? Scripture has bad news in it, too, and not just for emperors—for all of us, when we are creating our idols, when we are complicit in oppressive politics, or whatever else. So we have to concede that that kind of positive metanarrative is untrue—in our experience of violence, or when we see people dying in the streets of Calcutta. And then we have to find ways of believing that honor all the experiences that a thinking person can have in this world, including the traumatizing and destabilizing experiences.

GREENE: People's lives are not always good news, not always a seamless experience of joy. So quite frankly, what's often good news for someone is to be told, "I don't get it!" Sometimes the Bible is just all over the map, and there are what appear to be real contradictions in it. So maybe it's okay to have real contradictions in your life, as well. And maybe it's good news to be part of a community, like the Episcopal Church, or the Anglican approach: a big tent in which folks are tolerant of a lot of gray area on these questions and that's okay. As opposed to a lot of communities now where theological certainties are essential.

SHARP. Right. That's a bad word, in Walter's lexicon! Words like "certitude" and "surety"—Walter rails against the narcotic effects of certitude and surety, which we see in fundamentalist interpretation. Now, sometimes you do need something simple and sure. "I just need to know today that God loves me, and I don't give a fig about anything else." That's fair. We all need that. But life is normally so full of moments of darkness and confusion and conflict, you have to know that you're walking in that, instead of pretending that it's not real. He doesn't like any of this "settled" stuff. It's all about the unsettling nature of what Scripture does among us. I think that's very generative for people. They don't hear that very often.

BRUEGGEMANN: In George Steiner's book *No Passion Spent*,[2] he says that when he finished reading Job, he realized that the Bible, and particularly Job, is questioning us. About Anderson's book: you know, he's sold millions and millions of copies. He had a very nice summer place in Vermont, and he said it was built by *Understanding the Old Testament*!

SHARP: How nice for him! And it is a great book—he deserved every benefit that came from that kind of writing.

[At this point, we adjourned from the restaurant and reconvened in Roger Greene's spacious, sunny office at St. Timothy's for the rest of the conversation.]

GREENE: [Responding to a query about a colorfully decorated chair] One year we had our teenage group take a blank chair and paint it, decorate it in whatever way they wanted, in order to make it unique to them. So that one, reminiscent of Pollock, was my son Andrew's chair. Others put stickers on, and so forth.

SHARP: We had a marvelous time, back when we were demolishing a building at Yale Divinity School that had housed many faculty offices temporarily. We knew they were going to tear down the whole thing on Monday. So a friend and I—Wes Avram, who was in homiletics at the time—went in with our kids and magic markers and paints. We painted all over the walls, the doors, and so forth. You know, I put Bible verses all over the place. A favorite verse of mine, for no good reason, is Isaiah 14:23: "And I will make it a possession of the hedgehog." Is that supposed to be scary? They're so small, the little bristly darlings! Why is that scary? Anyway, I drew a hedgehog and, you know, threw a flamingo onto the wall and so forth. The kids were little at the time and really enjoyed it.

BRUEGGEMANN: Down on the River Road, where Tia commutes, there are a couple of trashed car lots where they sell parts, and there's a little grass strip along the road. She said that for many months there was one hedgehog that lived there. He had about four feet of grass to work with, surrounded by traffic! That's all I know about hedgehogs.

SHARP: Excellent! So, thank you for continuing this conversation. I would like to get a little more background from you, Roger: where you studied, who taught you Old Testament, whether it was helpful or not in preparing you for ministry, and so forth. Say a little about your seminary experience, if you would.

GREENE: Well, I was not raised in the Church—I was raised playing tennis. I worked all my life to go to college. If my family was into anything, it was, work hard and go to a good college. My sister went to Stanford, and I wanted to go to Stanford. I got into Stanford, and I arrived, and within two months I was miserable. I was lovesick for the hometown honey, I didn't know what I wanted to do with my life—all the existential questions.

SHARP: Where was home?

GREENE: Salt Lake City. I grew up in a Mormon community, but that wasn't what we did. Things got so bad after Christmas break, after I'd come back to Stanford, that I thought, "Why am I spending all this money to be miserable?" I was actually going to file a leave of absence and go home and figure it out. That night, I started having conversations with a woman in the dorm who was going through some physical stuff. Three nights in a row, we were up until the wee hours, just talking about life. She was a Christian, and she wasn't pushing that on me, but at one point said very diplomatically, "You might want to read the Bible." What the hell—I'd tried everything else! The next night, in the Common Room of my dorm, I had a Bible with me. I'd never read the Bible before, you understand. I opened it up, and I read the Gospel of John from beginning to end. In the Common Room, with music blasting, Ping-Pong going on, and so forth. And at the end of this, I just thought, "Oh my God!" I was completely blown away.

SHARP: What was it that touched you so deeply?

GREENE: The way I look at it now is, I grew up in a family that loved me deeply, but I discovered in the Gospel of John a love even better than that. Here I was, a freshman in college wondering, "What am I doing with my life? Is life just about one more degree to get a job, to get rich, and then you die? Is it just an endless series of accomplishments?" And I thought, "Wow, I can just be who I am, and maybe that would be okay." I knew nothing about any of these guys—this Jesus guy, I didn't know whether John was the guy who wrote the Gospel or anything like that.

SHARP: I think we still don't know!

BRUEGGEMANN: [laughs]

GREENE: But I do remember profoundly the imagery of the vine and the branches, the indwelling of God. So anyway, I went back to this woman and said, "We've gotta talk!" We talked, and she said, "You might want to go see the dean of the chapel." I went to talk with him and told him my story, and I said, "I don't know what to do. What do I do now? Do I get baptized? What's the next step?" Well, he was a pretty smart guy, and I think he was a little wary that I might be going from one emotional extreme to the next. So he said, "Keep praying, and keep reading, and come back." He was a New Testament scholar, as it turned out. I remember leaving that meeting and thinking, "He doesn't really believe that I had this experience, or at least he's suspicious." I came back to him and said, "I'm still reading and life is really good right now—I don't fully understand why." And he asked me, "So how do you know if someone has the Holy Spirit in them?" I think he was fishing for an answer like, "If they're speaking in tongues," or something like that, which might have confirmed his suspicion that I was primarily interested in ecstatic experiences. I remember saying, without flinching, "Well, they're just full of love."

SHARP: Good answer!

GREENE: At which, this South African, Cambridge-trained New Testament scholar who was not known for being the most emotional sort—his eyes welled up, and he said, "Well, when do you want to get baptized?"

BRUEGGEMANN: Wow!

GREENE: So March 13, 1977, I was baptized at Memorial Church. My freshman roommate, a Lutheran, and the woman, who's now my wife, were my sponsors.

SHARP: Very nice! Walter says that your wife is an Episcopal priest.

GREENE: Yes, she's a priest. Well, that just opened up the doors of my freshman experience and the rest of my undergraduate experience. I started learning more about the Church, its history, my faith, and pretty quickly into that, thought, "Wow, what if I could just do this for the rest of my life? That would be a cool career!" So that then led to needing to get connected to a denomination. I went on a church hunt, went to a wide variety of places, and then one day walked into an Episcopal church and thought, "This is it." Got married the day before Commencement. My bishop required that someone as young as I go off and do some real-life stuff for a while.

SHARP: Yes, bishops do tend to require that. It's a good idea.

GREENE: Then we decided I'd go to a seminary near where my wife got a job. Her company in Salt Lake City, where we lived for our first year of married life, had offices in the Bay area and in Boston, both of which have Episcopal seminaries. She got a job in the Bay area, and I went to CDSP [Church Divinity School of the Pacific, in Berkeley]. My first experience of seminary was somewhat discouraging. The great thing about Stanford was the energy and vitality of the student body. They're all into it—they want to be there! The discouraging thing when I arrived at the seminary was how many folks were still trying to figure out why they had to do this part of it. They were wondering, "Why don't I just go get ordained?"

SHARP: So they thought it was just a hoop to get through.

GREENE: It was so deflating! So I spent the better part of a year just being angry. People would just waste time in class—"let's just see if we can distract the professor long enough to spin out the rest of the time." You asked about Old Testament: I took a class with a professor named John Endres, who was on the faculty at the Jesuit School [the Jesuit School of Theology at Santa Clara University, one of the member schools of the Graduate Theological Union]. Donn Morgan was the guy on the CDSP faculty, and I remember taking a Psalms course, a course on Ecclesiastes, and learning Hebrew from him. Talk about the things you want to go back to in life: I'm really sad that I didn't keep up any disciplined reading of Hebrew. I've done that with the Greek, but not the Hebrew. I'd love to dedicate a year to really getting up to speed on that.

SHARP: Perhaps in that clergy study group that you want to get off the ground! Easier said than done, of course. I don't read Greek as regularly as I'd like, and I feel terrible about it.

GREENE: I don't think Old Testament was big on the seminary agenda. One of the things that's happened to me in the past couple of years because of this guy [indicates Brueggemann] is an invitation to engage that more in terms of my own preaching. Which has been a great thing.

SHARP: Do folks here at St. Timothy's preach on the Old Testament?

GREENE: Yes, but in the average Episcopal church, it really is just the reading before the psalm. The preacher might refer to it, but not much more than that. In my seminary days, the Old Testament stuff was not a big part of my formation.

SHARP: Thinking about the life of the Church, we've talked already a good bit about the richness of offerings here at St. Timothy's, and I have wondered whether the two of you have ever come close to disagreeing about something—whether it be a liturgical change or a matter of ecclesial polity. And if you haven't yet: do you suspect there's an area where you might really have a disagreement, if it came down to it?

BRUEGGEMANN: Well, I'm not into polity or liturgical change, so I'm not aware of anything like that where I'd disagree with Roger.

SHARP: Roger, did you move the altar when you first arrived here, or anything like that?

GREENE: The only thing I did—the first day, and maybe I'd do it differently now, in terms of informing people; maybe I was just scared to tell them ahead of time—was to remove the flag from the sanctuary.

SHARP: Good for you!

GREENE: The interesting thing about that was, nobody noticed until— this was 1995 or 1996—until President Clinton had ordered fighter jets to go and bomb Libya, or somewhere. It sparked me to muse, the following Sunday, on to whom we pledge our allegiance. Well! Right after that, I heard, "Where did the damned flag go?" But they didn't see it until something triggered their memory. That has been an ongoing source of irritation for some. I have a handful who will occasionally send me something about the flag and ask, "Why don't we have the flag?" It's all pretty respectful, but it's just a reminder that this stuff goes really deep.

SHARP: Especially in the heartland, although elsewhere too. In Morning Prayer there's a collect that says in part, "Grant that people everywhere may seek after you and find you; bring the nations into your fold."[3] And I just balk at nation-state ideology. From the very beginning, the Church was precisely not about nation-states and their power! So I keep wanting to change that, which I'm sure will not happen any time soon.

BRUEGGEMANN: During World War II, the German church community in which I later grew up sent Reinhold Niebuhr around to our churches to plant American flags, to make clear our common loyalty to the United States in its war against the "Fatherland." And they are still there, even though they now have a very different function than they did then.

SHARP: Wow. So, Roger, is there anything on which you'd disagree with Walter? Anything on which you'd contest his position?

GREENE: Over the last few years, I've read a lot of what Walter has written, and I've seen his presentations. What I'd like to do some-time—because this comes up pastorally a lot—has to do with Kathleen O'Connor's book on Lamentations.[4] At the end of that, she asks, what about this God who is often very violent in the Bible, and how do we make sense of that? If I remember correctly, she offers three differ-ent views, one of which is Walter's view, one of which is her own, and so on. I don't know if we'd end up disagreeing here or not, Walter, but I was certainly trained to believe that this God who was so violent along the way is, in Jesus, revealed to be boundless love and compas-sion. Now, I acknowledge that there are places in the Gospels that are scary. But I was certainly led to believe that the ancient Israelite view of a punitive, harsh God was a view that was in process. That's the way folks viewed that at the time. So if someone came up to you and asked about it, you could say, "Well, that's the way they viewed it then, that's mostly their interpretation." Walter has talked about "the God of violence who's in recovery." We need to take that seriously. And that's challenged me to look at whether the view I once held [about the historically conditioned limitations of Israelite theology] was simply convenient. And what do I do with that? I want to be faithful to this Word. I think I have the capacity to live with ambiguity and discomfort in this regard. So I'm trying to integrate that into my own experience and not let my own experience just be the dominant thing. It would be helpful for me to have an ongoing conversation with Walter about that. Because that's a big issue.

BRUEGGEMANN: It is! I've heard some readers say, "If Walter Bruegge-mann is right about this, I don't want any part of his God." What I think about that is that is not something about which you and I would disagree, Roger. We might disagree strategically on how to proceed about that. But it's so impossible to get at. It's not something that would lead to dis-agreement. We might just process it differently.

SHARP: I've seen in your work, Walter, what I think is a salutary resistance to supersessionist moves, to reaching too quickly for the New Testament. Now we do reach for it, as Christians, to be sure. We understand that the revelation that we have in Jesus Christ is new and world-defining. Nev-ertheless, I think you want to put the brakes on our reaching too quickly for that.

BRUEGGEMANN: What has dawned on me is, the whole evolutionary hypothesis that God is getting better is really a Marcionite view. Folks just pick out the parts they like! And I do too, but I want to resist that.

SHARP: So say more about how recovery works. How does recovery work as a metaphor for this violent God, if it's not that God is "getting better and better" as our own sensibilities become more enlightened?

BRUEGGEMANN: Well, God repents. God is instructed by Moses: "You ought to be a better God than the way You are performing here" (Exod. 32:11-14).

SHARP: "Live up to Yourself!"

BRUEGGEMANN: You're going to do a commentary on Joshua—well, I'm giving a paper on Joshua at the SBL this fall. What I think I'm going to argue is, the violence in the book of Joshua is because Joshua refused to do his work with God the way that Moses did. Moses called God on it. But Joshua doesn't offer a peep. I do think that issue of the violence of God is a huge problem.

SHARP: It's certainly a major problem for Christian appropriation of the Old Testament. I'm so grateful that in Hebrews 10 we have the line, "It is a fearful thing to fall into the hands of the living God" (Heb. 10:31), because it is the same God, but the dictions and embodied experiences of these communities change over time.

BRUEGGEMANN: Roger, part of my resistance to explaining the problem away is that I tend to get invited to speak in liberal churches, among pro-gressives. And progressives are so condescending about this primitivism:

"We certainly know better than that!" So that just spurs me to try to say it differently!

GREENE: This raises an interesting issue. I don't want Walter to feel that as a member of the congregation and because of his credentials and his authority, he is somehow responsible for keeping us all honest about Scripture.

SHARP: That would be a big job!

GREENE: But as a preacher, I would hope he would feel free to challenge me in ways that would help me grow, if he felt that I were ducking an issue. And I would want him to know, just because he says it doesn't mean I will necessarily say, "Oh, okay—fine!"

SHARP: "Yes, sir, Mr. Famous Old Testament Scholar, sir!" Walter, do you feel free to challenge Roger in that regard?

BRUEGGEMANN: Oh, I suppose I do. But I'm not inclined to. When I come to church on Sunday morning, I don't abandon my critical capacity, but for the most part, I'm a guy who needs to hear the gospel. [to Greene] You witness to the gospel, and I'll take it!

GREENE: And that's what I wouldn't want him to lose. I wouldn't want him to feel like, "Oh, gosh, I need to be 'on' during worship." On the other hand, what I want from all the members of the congregation is for them to feel free to respond out of their own encounters with God and their own experiences. The worst thing is to get no response.

SHARP: Experience including, then, one's vulnerability. Which leads me to one of my favorite questions for anyone in any time or place. Walter, what kind of vulnerability do you think you might have been hiding here in this church that you might be willing to share with Roger now? Is there something that Roger doesn't yet know?

BRUEGGEMANN: My defining vulnerability is my—I don't know whether to say shame or embarrassment—about my family upbringing and my inadequate education, which leads me to want to overcompensate for that.

SHARP: [laughing] So for someone who has three advanced degrees, nevertheless a feeling of inadequacy about your education! I do honor that it feels that way to you—can you say more about that?

BRUEGGEMANN: Well, I came out of an ethnic background that wasn't intellectually equipped. And I think way down deep, I have been running scared all my life from the intimidation of the guild. I have no doubt that scholarship is a kind of escape from all that. I think it's a pretty good escape!

SHARP: It's an adaptive mechanism on your part that has enriched very many people. Roger, did you know that about Walter?

GREENE: Yes, he's shared some of that in the past. I think one of the gifts of this place for him can be that we will just love Walter as he is. Whether we know anything about what he has done or not. And that is what my conversion was all about. Roger Greene did not need to do anything more. I am a child of God, priceless treasure, as is. So my sense is that part of what he might be able to do here is just tap into that Good News. Nobody really gives a fig how many books he has published. And what I think would be a real gift to him is, they got to love him before they knew about all that. "Hey, this new guy in the congregation is cool!" The first time Tia came, she was wondering whether the congregation was loving them because of all Walter had done. What she didn't realize is, nobody knew or cared! And now they would care about that, because he's done things here. But that's a different dynamic.

SHARP: Walter, has there been healing for you here?

BRUEGGEMANN: Yes. I couldn't have said it that way, but that's exactly what has been going on.

GREENE: Clearly, a lot of what Walter grapples with in the text is, God has the answer to our anxiety, and we are in a very anxiety-producing world. And then we've got all of our own s***, to boot. That speaks to my own journey. I was one of four children, a late "mistake" for not only my parents but three other siblings, and they all just adored me. That's a great thing, but somewhere along the way, the enemy of my human nature said, "Okay, well, you'd better damned well show them that you appreciate all that. You'd better perform for them." They weren't demanding this of me—it's just what we do. And so Roger the tennis player, and Roger the student. The moment for me in freshman year was, "I don't need to do that anymore. Isn't that cool!" Now, that doesn't mean that those [internal emotional] tapes don't still play sometimes. You get ordained one day, and you're rector for the first time, and everybody loves you, and they're excited, and you want to do it well. This is such a great place for me. But you want to deliver! One of the things that has happened for me in the last several years is that I felt less the need to do any of that. Those places in me are slowly getting healed.

SHARP: And when you understand, even just for a moment, that you're loved just for who you are, you can then show other people that they are too.

BRUEGGEMANN: Which is what Roger does.

SHARP: That's what I'm gathering, from having known you just for a little while and spending time with your community, which seems to be such a warm, welcoming, and loving community. On the flip side of this, those of us who are driven perfectionists do not mean to transmit that set of high expectations to others—usually we intend to direct it only at ourselves—but we still do. When I am hard on myself but want to be pastoral and nurturing with others, even if I don't intend for that message of perfectionism to be directed at them, others will still pick up on it. That's where the guild is a very hard place to be. It takes a lot of energy to resist that.

BRUEGGEMANN: That's right.

GREENE: The same could be said of clergy gatherings. There's nothing more deadly than that kind of clergy gathering where everybody is trying to prove that they matter and what they are doing is important. But what may be happening, at least in the Episcopal Church during this time of decline in numbers, is that not many of us can boast about those things about which we are most fond of boasting. [in a faux boastful tone] "Oh, yes, I've gotten a remarkable increase in pledges!" Maybe the boasting now will be about the nature of the ministry.

SHARP: That's funny, because ever since Paul, we've known that we're supposed to boast only in Christ, but we still don't get it!

GREENE: We don't! We don't get it.

SHARP: Here's a Christian praxis question for each of you. If you ever feel down—you both have a ton of energy, but maybe you have moments when you are down or overwhelmed (I have those moments daily): what Christian practice sustains you the most? This could be prayer, worship, or whatever. And which practice irks you or seems least helpful to you, out of the panoply of Christian options that are available to us?

BRUEGGEMANN: I'm energized most by exegesis. I go to the text. On your other question: I wouldn't say I'm irked by this, but I find regular prayer very difficult to sustain as a daily practice or discipline.

SHARP: What does it feel like when you try it? Where does the resistance come from?

BRUEGGEMANN: Well, it's not resistance, but it's just negligence. So that's a place where *I know* much better than *I do*.

SHARP: That's interesting, because, of course, you're famous for your prayers in the classroom.

BRUEGGEMANN: Prayer means a lot to me when I do it, but then I puzzle, "Well, if that's true . . ."

GREENE: [laughing] ". . . why don't I do it more often?!"

SHARP: How about you, Roger?

GREENE: Well, I'm an early-morning person, and I love nothing more than getting up early—Nancy's still asleep, the kids are asleep. I go downstairs, pull out *Disruptive Grace*, and think, "Oh, fantastic—I get to read the next one!" I'm having my coffee, and then I have some time for prayer, whether that's just silent prayer for twenty minutes or so, or Morning Prayer. It varies a bit. If I don't get that time in the morning, I really feel dislocated. So when the kids were little, I had to change that all around, and that wasn't easy. Also, it's never good when my mind is so busy with so many things to do that I leave that prayer practice behind in the morning. "Oh, I'd better just go get the kids' lunches ready." But for the most part, that's been a regular pattern for me, and it's only frustrating for me when I don't have a book to read. The other thing that's bedrock for me is Sunday morning. I've got something to do, and when you're "on" it's a different thing, but I get so much out of the worship and the interaction with people. I love to preach! It's where the sparks fly for me. So I'll go in on Sunday morning with some dread and foreboding, because I have so much to do and don't know how I'll get it all done. But I come out with new eyes, and I'm reminded why I exist and how much I love these folks. That is a regular experience for me, and I couldn't survive without it.

SHARP: Wonderful. So what leaves you cold?

GREENE: That's a good question. I don't know whether you'd call this a Christian practice, but . . . I don't have a confessor, and I deplore fasting, although I do it on Ash Wednesday and Good Friday.

SHARP: You don't like it, or you think it's not good?

GREENE: I love to eat!

SHARP: Don't we all! Let's just get that on the record for all of us here.

GREENE: So I do that [fasting], but . . . you read some of the masters in this stuff and they talk about how alive they feel, and all I'm thinking about is, "Oh, God, I need more food!" And here's another thing I'll tell you. I've talked about my frustration in not being able to get a small group of colleagues together for Bible study. I've found over time that I've become more disengaged from my colleagues, because I just don't find that interaction helpful to me. Which is too bad. It would be great if it were there, but it's not there.

BRUEGGEMANN: What's so clear about Roger is, Sunday is Game Day!

GREENE: I love the game, and it's good for me as well as for the people who come here to worship. It's interesting, what Walter said about his own prayer life. That's where most of us are, most of the time. It's hard to sustain, even though we know that when we go there, it's a good thing. I guess I would wonder, Walter, whether your exegesis is a prayerful endeavor . . . a hovering over the text.

BRUEGGEMANN: I think that's right. It's possible that I engage in self-deception by understanding it that way, but I think that's right. When I am working with the text in a close and sustained way, I sense a deep connection to ancient voices that mediate the voice of God. I do not have any magical notion about that, but the confrontation often gives me goose bumps when I imagine that I am being given access to this conversation that has been going on for a long time, with a participant from "elsewhere."

SHARP: I have one more question—a question about temptation. Speaking of things that have irked me in the life of the Church: I was in an ordination process in the early '90s, and then discerned the call to scholarship and cheerfully left that process, only to be brought back into it, amusingly enough, years later. But what I have always deeply disliked about the Church is the politics and careerism. You have clergy trying to jockey for plum positions, and folks at the diocesan convention trying to organize and lobby each other around politics. I'm an idealist by temperament—Myers-Briggs NF—and I really dislike it when the ways of the world distort church relationships.

So here's one temptation for me (this is background for the question I'm going to pose for you). I do believe, and I think we have ample warrant in the Gospels for believing, that we are called to be servants. Each one of us. Each Christian leader, every single Christian is called to serve the world in Christ's name. One of the temptations for me is that I love to believe the press about myself. When students rave to me about how pastoral I am in the classroom, or someone says that my book is brilliant or whatever, it is so deeply tempting to me to believe that, and to not be focused on true servanthood, which is not about grabbing for fame or affirmation—even grabbing for love. True service might mean that you have to serve in a way where people won't like you, because maybe the gospel is calling you to do something that's unpopular. So one of my main spiritual goals in life is to try to figure out what servanthood is really about. Otherwise, I could be distracted literally for the rest of my life by the affirmations that I get. So here's the question for you: what do you think is your own deepest or most profound spiritual temptation?

BRUEGGEMANN: I think there is that for me. I get a lot of accolades, and I remember particularly this one statement that someone made in a review once: "he is the leading Old Testament scholar of his generation."

SHARP: Well, it's kind of true. . . .

BRUEGGEMANN: I don't think it's true! What I consider the "hard men" of the discipline[5]—the Harvard-trained guys—I know that my scholarship is weak. But I have to say, given that temptation, my deepest temptation is in the other direction. Which is to over-believe my inadequacy. This is a delicate thing to say, but it is a temptation not to take the validity of those affirmations seriously.

SHARP: The affirmations show that people perceive giftedness in you—giftedness that is from God, and real.

BRUEGGEMANN: And I incline, at a deeper level, to pass it off. I was with the son of a famous Baptist writer the other day. He works with poor people here, and he was talking about his dad. He said, "My father needs a standing ovation every third day."

SHARP: [laughing] What happens if he doesn't get it?

BRUEGGEMANN: What I have noticed about standing ovations is, you only need two people to get up at the right time, and then the whole room gets up. So I think I'm wise enough to sit lightly to those accolades. That is a temptation, but I'm also aware of the temptation in the other direction, and I think that one probably runs deeper, for me.

GREENE: At one point in my life, I knew some folks at a prestigious Episcopal church that had a very high regard for itself. One of the gifts of that time was to see what I didn't want to become, which was the rector. The guy had his gifts. But he was a tortured man. For him, life was all about how you could work the system and please the folks and get ahead. It was an ugly thing to watch. That was an important thing for me to see. Later, when I came to St. Timothy's, things took off in lots of wonderful new directions. And I don't ever remember this being a conscious decision so much as, after about five or six years here, former bishops started saying to me, "Roger, you really need to start thinking about the next step in your career."

SHARP: The episcopacy.

GREENE: Yeah. Every time I talked about it with someone, it just didn't feel right. Something inside me did not connect. I would say, "I'm always open to wherever God calls me, blah blah blah," but . . . I remember early on I got a phone call from a church in San Francisco. I went to visit—I love the Bay area—and talked to the folks there. I said, "It's my policy to be open to whatever God calls me to." I got back to the guy the next day and said, "You know, this doesn't need to go any further. You've got a great community here, and this would be a wonderful opportunity. But the only way I can say this is,"—at that point, I had a four-year-old and a six-year-old—"I want to see my kids get on the bus in the morning for the next five, six years. I know myself well enough that if I were to come there, or anywhere else for that matter, I'd get caught up in the newness and the establishing of my ministry, and I think I'd wake up four years later and say, 'What happened? I missed it.' "

SHARP: "How did my kids become teenagers without my noticing?"

GREENE: I think the temptation all along the way has been to listen to other voices rather than the voice inside. And I don't know when this happened, but with this place, I felt like I'm here for better, for worse, for richer, for poorer, 'til death do us part. Who knows where things might go? But I think what rears its ugly head every so often—and this really relates to what Walter just said—is that there are those voices inside that say, "Do you mean to tell me that you're just going to stay there for the rest of your ministry? Do you mean to tell me that when that diocese contacted you about being their bishop, you wouldn't want to do that? Don't you know that the Church needs that? Are you really going to be content when you're sitting on a couch somewhere when you're 80, that you were just the rector of St. Timothy's?" But I have to say that those voices don't come as often as they used to. The other temptation, I would say, is that we are all so trained to evaluate our communities and our ministries quantitatively.

SHARP: Church growth, budget. . . .

GREENE: For the first time in seventeen years, we've gone through a financial challenge in the past few months. Which is a whole new thing for me.

SHARP: How nice that it hasn't come up before now!

GREENE: I know, and we've been very grateful for that. But I'm aware that that's new territory for me. You're at a diocesan gathering, and someone asks, "How's it going at St. Timothy's?" and how honest will you be? Or do you want to keep pretending? Is that okay, really? Will telling the truth reflect badly on me? I guess the temptation has to do with how honest will you be about everything that's going on?

SHARP: That question faces all of us every day, in so many dimensions and capacities. "Can I be real?" That might free up the person to whom I'm talking, so that person can be real in return. Or do we keep up the facade?

GREENE: And can I trust that that will take me to the gold? Playing the other game really does not deliver. The end result of that is the guy I knew at that prestigious church, for whom every Sunday service had to be bigger and more spectacular than the last. It had to have seventeen trombones and fifteen timpani, and he was addicted to this. Lots of other people had to work to make him look good.

SHARP: How exhausting for the whole system!

GREENE: Talk about expending energy!

SHARP: "Where two or three are gathered in my name": seriously, where two or three nobodies are gathered in Jesus' name, Jesus is present. I'm using the term "nobodies" ironically, of course. We're all equally precious and equally "nobodies" before the throne of God! But it's hard to remember that in this world—even in the Church.

In closing I'd like to ask, Walter, whether there is anything you want Roger to know about how you value him, and Roger, is there anything you want to make sure Walter knows?

BRUEGGEMANN: Well, I've said this before to Roger, but I think it is providential that I fell into St. Timothy's. There are many, many wonderful things about St. Timothy's, but elementally, it's Roger. He is an embodiment of God's gracious goodness, as I experience him. And for the first time in my adult life, I look forward to going to church! You asked earlier whether there could be disagreements where I would challenge Roger. In the church I belonged to in Atlanta, I had one conversation with my pastor, because I was going home angry every Sunday. I disagreed with him so much, theologically, and I was so upset by that, that's what finally drove me to the Episcopal cathedral. I'm not a fighter—I'm not going to quarrel with anybody.

SHARP: But you might withdraw.

BRUEGGEMANN: Yes. But I have supreme confidence that that's not going to happen at St. Tim's, because it's such an embracive place. It's wonderful to have a priest who is on the same wavelength about so many things.

GREENE: Thanks for saying that. It's funny that you used the word "providential," because not long before Walter came—one of the challenges in a long-term pastorate has been to find what keeps me fresh and new and fed. Over the years, I've had things I've done regularly that do that. But I was going through a time where I wasn't quite sure what the next thing ought to be. Walter's arrival was the arrival of a kindred spirit. Someone who gets what makes me tick, appreciates what makes me tick, and feeds me with what he's up to, what he's thinking. That's huge. Walter had sent me an e-mail about a sermon of mine, and I shared it with Nancy. It wasn't long. And she said, "You need to save that." And I remember wondering, am I letting the authority that Walter carries—and rightly so—am I letting that in enough in a way that's good for me? In the providence of God, could the Old Master be coming along and saying, "Well done, good and faithful servant" (Matt. 25:23 NIV)? Maybe in my own prayer, I need to enjoy that as a gift from God. I steadfastly try to avoid—with colleagues and others—talking about Walter, for obvious reasons. But I'm grateful that God sent you, Walter!

Maybe I'll end this conversation more fully appreciating what this might mean for my own sense of who I am. We all have moments where we work really, really hard and it doesn't pan out. I find it a bit of a paradox, or interesting, that last year for me was far and away the most demanding year of my ministry. Mostly from a pastoral perspective—with so many deaths of people who were significant to me—and then the economy tanking. The year demanded all my spiritual resources. What you most need to hear when you're going through a time like that is,

"Well done, good and faithful servant!" Especially if at the end of that year, you find yourself in a budget crunch. Part of us is always naive: "If I just work hard enough, everything will come out rosy in the end." But it doesn't always happen that way. So those words mean a lot.

BRUEGGEMANN: I'm aware that with the three worship services and the youth group and all that, I know only a slice of St. Tim's and what you face. So I'm conscious of not wanting to crowd in or to take too much space or to claim too much attention. I'm mindful of that all the time. I want to be in a proper, responsible place with you.

SHARP: It's true, I think, that ten percent of the parishioners take up most of the energy of the clergy! But most of those folks aren't aware of it, so I'm guessing you're safe, Walter.

I'm grateful to both of you for your candor and your willingness to be in conversation with me about your life and your ministries here in this place. Thank you.

Notes

1. Bernhard W. Anderson's *Understanding the Old Testament* is now in its fifth edition (2006) with Prentice-Hall.
2. George Steiner, *No Passion Spent: Essays 1978–1995* (London: Faber; New Haven: Yale University Press, 1996). In his piece, "A Preface to the Hebrew Bible," from the Everyman Library edition (1996), Steiner writes, " 'Who is it that darkeneth counsel by words without knowledge?' I am unable to account wholly rationally for the ways of the man or woman who put the question and who asks me where I was when 'the morning stars sang together' or whether 'the rain hath a father?' Perhaps this is as it should be. It is the Hebrew Bible, of all books, which most questions man" (87).
3. One of the prayers for mission in the Morning Prayer service in the Episcopal *Book of Common Prayer* (New York: Church Publishing, orig. pub. 1979), 100: "O God, you have made of one blood all the peoples of the earth, and sent your blessed Son to preach peace to those who are far off and to those who are near: Grant that people everywhere may seek after you and find you; bring the nations into your fold; pour out your Spirit upon all flesh; and hasten the coming of your kingdom; through Jesus Christ our Lord. Amen."
4. Kathleen M. O'Connor, *Lamentations and the Tears of the World* (Maryknoll: Orbis, 2002).
5. The term "hard men" comes from the semantic arena of the military. It has been used for decades to denote Irish Republican Army militants committed to the perpetuation of violence. By analogy, it has also been used to characterize British troops deployed to Northern Ireland, armed forces in other conflicts, gangsters more generally, and notoriously tough athletes.

Chapter 7

"On the Road Again!"

Sermon by Walter Brueggemann for
Trinity Church, Copley Square, Boston
March 20, 2011

YEAR A, SECOND SUNDAY IN LENT
PSALM 121; ROMANS 4:1–5, 13–17; JOHN 3:1–17

We are on the road again! As followers of Jesus, we are on the road again in Lent, walking the way of obedience to Jerusalem for the big showdown with the authorities of Church and state. It turns out, every time, to be a hazardous journey, full of toils and snares, potholes and adversaries, ending in a rigged trial. But women and men of faith are always on the road again, departing safe places, running risks, and hoping for well-being on the journey. So here are some thoughts about our travel, where we go, how we go, and with whom we travel.

WB

I

The defining journey of biblical faith begins in the departure of Abraham and Sarah back in the book of Genesis. They were dispatched by God to leave their safe place, to go to a new land yet to be given, to get a new name, to be blessed by God, and to be a blessing to the others around them. They went! And their family, generation after generation, has gone. And we, finally in their wake, must also travel beyond safe places to the gifted end that God intends, hopefully to be blessed and a blessing on the way.

Paul, in our Romans reading, casts the entire life of faith in terms of Abraham's travel. Abraham did not stay in a place he could manage or control or have on his own terms. Abraham trusted himself to God so completely that he acted in great freedom. As he went he found that the

147

God he trusted was indeed totally reliable. Paul turns our attention from Abraham, who trusted, to the God who traveled with him, whom Paul characterizes in the most stunning doxological language: ". . . who gives life to the dead and calls into existence the things that do not exist" (v. 17).

This God is the only self-starter and can make newness for us as the God who presides over Easter and makes newness for the whole world. Faith, like that of Abraham, consists in moving into the generative newness given by God.

II

Jesus, in his instruction to Nicodemus, makes the summons to a journey as radical as can be. He says to this well-established intellectual in the Jewish tradition that we can and may journey to a new self, to a new life. He uses the language of "born again," or better, "born from above," born of God, birthed by God's goodness, re-created with a new identity by God's generous mercy. Of course Nicodemus does not get it. Unlike Father Abraham, Nicodemus does not want to go. As a result, by the time Jesus gets to verse 16, the famous John 3:16, Nicodemus has disappeared from the narrative. He is a dropout, suggesting that if we linger with our old self, our old identity, our old world, we drop out of the narrative of God's merciful governance.

III

So here we are, children of Abraham and Sarah, addressed by the God of all travel, companions of Nicodemus who was interrupted by Jesus who says that a new self and a new life are offered, grounded in the God who loves the world so much that God gives God's own self for the world. As children of Abraham and Sarah and companion of Nicodemus, accompanied by the God of all mercy, we may consider where we are summoned to go on our Lenten journey. The matter is in dispute among us. But if we think that a journey in God's love and mercy away from the world we know and love and control—the world that Abraham left and that Nicodemus could not leave—then it may be that our departure concerns the world of privilege, entitlement, power, and wealth that we simply take for granted in our conventional Euro-Caucasian chosenness. And if we ponder our destination, perhaps it is to be to the neighborhood of *shalom*, the neighborhood of shared resources, of inclusive politics, of random acts of hospitality and intentional acts of justice, of fearless neighborliness that is not propelled by greed or anxiety or excessive self-preoccupation. The big departure now required for the faithful in the United States and the big arrival for the faithful in the United States is an evangelical wake-up call that moves past our usual Lenten pieties to the ways in which our society and our world political economy are at a life-or-death stage of development. The issue before us is not partisan or liberal or conservative. It is rather an awareness that our conventional way of life in the United States is organized so that we do not love the neighbor whom we have seen, and can hardly come to love God whom we have not seen. Thus we are situated, I suggest, for our Lenten journey between the willingness of Abraham and the stubborn refusal of Nicodemus, and we are left to decide to stay or to go, for participation or for dropping out, eventually for life or for death.

IV

So here is a good word: Psalm 121 is designed exactly for travelers who face a demanding, risky journey. It is a psalm that has been used over and over by travelers and now is available for us.

- This traveler in the psalm knows about being exposed and thinks cosmically about being safe:

> The LORD is your keeper;
>   the LORD is your shade at your right hand.
> The sun shall not strike you by day,
>   nor the moon by night (vv. 5-6).

- This traveler knows about stumbling on the way:

> He will not let your foot be moved (v. 3a).

- This traveler knows about being weary and being afraid to fall asleep and not on guard, and then remembers we can rest safely on the way, because:

> he who keeps you will not slumber.
> He who keeps Israel
>   will neither slumber nor sleep (vv. 3b–4).

- This traveler does not sense so much risk in a world that threatens, but is kept safe by the guardian of life:

> The LORD will keep you from all evil;
>   he will keep your life.

> The LORD will keep
> your going out and your coming in
> from this time on and forevermore (vv. 7–8).

- This traveler knows about being self-sufficient and wonders about assistance from elsewhere. The traveler asks:

> from where will my help come? (v. 1)

And then promptly answers:

> My help comes from the LORD,
> who made heaven and earth (v. 2).

This psalm is an assurance and an affirmation that the journey we now undertake is not by ourselves alone. We are surrounded on the way by the God of all trust, the God who kept Abraham and Sarah safely, the one who walked all the way to Jerusalem with Jesus, all the way to Friday and on through to Sunday.

I imagine Lent for you and for me as a great departure from the greedy, anxious anti-neighborliness of our economy, a great departure from our exclusionary politics that fears the other, a great departure from self-indulgent consumerism that devours creation. And then an arrival in a new neighborhood, because it is a gift to be simple, it is a gift to be free, it is a gift to come down where we ought to be.[1]

Imagine the journey staged by the self-giving God who calls into existence the things that do not exist, a new you and me, a new society, a new world, one neighbor at time. At the table today, we will receive gestures of that self-giving God. We will be given the daily provision for the journey. It is an old Scottish blessing, "May you have traveling mercies," all the days of Lent.

Notes

1. Brueggemann here draws on the hymn "Simple Gifts," written by Shaker elder Joseph Brackett Jr. (1797–1882) and represented in the Episcopal *Hymnal 1982* as #554. The lyrics are in the public domain: "'Tis the gift to be simple, 'tis the gift to be free, / 'tis the gift to come down where we ought to be, / and when we find ourselves in the place just right, / 'twill be in the valley of love and delight. When true simplicity is gain'd, / to bow and to bend we shan't be asham'd, / to turn, turn will be our delight / till by turning, turning we come 'round right."

Chapter 8

Biblical Theology in Dialogue

Reflections of Terence E. Fretheim, May 2011,
with a Response by Walter Brueggemann, July 2011

Walter Brueggemann and Terence E. Fretheim have known each other for decades as colleagues and friends. Brueggemann served as editor for the Fortress Press series Overtures to Biblical Theology and in that capacity helped prepare Fretheim's book *The Suffering of God: An Old Testament Perspective* for publication in the series in 1984. The two scholars have much in common theologically, for, as Brueggemann notes, both were "nurtured in the dramatic moment of revival of Old Testament studies" generated by the work of Gerhard von Rad in Germany. Differences of emphasis in their scholarship have contributed to a lively intellectual engagement between Brueggemann and Fretheim over the years. Brueggemann observes that while he himself tends to emphasize justice, Fretheim has focused on creation, as can be seen in his *Exodus* commentary (Westminster John Knox Press, 1988; new edition, 2010) and other works, including his *Creation Untamed: The Bible, God, and Natural Disasters* (Baker Academic, 2010). While the two agree on much that lies at the heart of Old Testament theology, they differ in how they frame the agency of God. Acknowledgment of the untrammeled sovereignty of God is vital to Brueggemann's exegesis. Fretheim prefers to emphasize the intimate connection of God with humanity; he worries that Brueggemann's focus on God's power may eclipse the relationality of covenant in these sacred texts. The conversation between Fretheim and Carolyn Sharp recorded here, followed by a written response from Walter Brueggemann, explores dimensions of an intellectual dialogue that has unfolded over many years between two of the guild's preeminent biblical theologians.

CJS

151

CAROLYN SHARP: When did you first encounter Walter's work? What was your first impression of what he was attempting to do?

TERENCE FRETHEIM: Though I have no memory of a specific time, no doubt his theological interests initially attracted me. His 1972 book, *In Man We Trust: The Neglected Side of Biblical Faith*, was the first I remember specifically. Theological issues were evidently at the center of his concern early on in his research and writing.

SHARP: When did you two first meet in person? Over the years, have you had any tussles on SBL panels or moments of bonding over a particular biblical passage?

FRETHEIM: I have no memory of a first encounter. I do remember some interaction at an SBL meeting in 1977, where we did tussle over interpretation of creation issues in a paper I had given. To this day, issues regarding creation are revealing of differences between us. At the same time, Walter has often referenced my work on creation and often in positive terms. To have carried on a conversation with Walter for over thirty years, including conversations and written notes, has been a privilege and a blessing.

SHARP: Have you assigned any of Walter's books and articles in your own classes? What is the best aspect of teaching from Walter's work, pedagogically speaking? What makes it challenging?

FRETHEIM: I have assigned one or more of Walter's books in at least one of my courses every year for the last quarter century or so. The two most frequent assignments have been his commentary on *Genesis*, for a Pentateuch course, and his *Prophetic Imagination*, for a prophets course.

Students have appreciated Walter's theological angle of vision and his concern to weave contemporary issues into his exposition—with respect to both Church and culture. They have often found his work to be "homiletically useful," addressing issues in language that moves rather easily into preaching and teaching. Moreover, while students have not always been comfortable with his perspectives regarding texts—particularly regarding his Calvinistic centering in the sovereignty of God and, more generally, his theological views that challenge the tradition—they have appreciated that encounter.

Viewing the Old Testament from a Reformed perspective has been the dominant theological angle of vision in American Hebrew Bible scholarship over much of the last century. Walter has continued that perspective, though in ways that challenge some traditional Reformed perspectives—especially "unsettling" issues regarding God. One early example is his cut against the grain of the tradition regarding divine omniscience. In his commentary on Genesis 22 (*Genesis*, p. 187), he says that the test of Abraham "is not a game with God; God genuinely does not know. . . . The flow of the narrative accomplishes something in the awareness of God. He did not know. Now he knows." Or, in the same book he challenges traditional formulations regarding divine temporality and divine affectability by the claim: ". . . God is not timeless and immune to the flow of human events" (p. 85).

Though these comments were undeveloped, they continued a conversation regarding God-talk that would pervade his writings. In a more recent article, he suggests that "the most difficult and interesting issue in the new discussion [regarding Old Testament theology] is the relation between Old Testament attestations for God, that is, 'God talk' . . . and the more or less strong claims of the dominant theological tradition" (*The Book That Breathes New Life: Scriptural Authority and Biblical Theology*, p. 119). The issues regarding the God of the Old Testament remain an important agenda for the discipline and for his own work. Marcion never dies.

SHARP: How has Walter supported, engaged, or contested what you've written?

FRETHEIM: Generally speaking, I have appreciated Walter's support of my work over the years. This support, I suspect, is rooted in our common concern to address texts theologically. Probably the most common works he has referenced are my studies in the book of Exodus and my books, *The Suffering of God* and *God and World in the Old Testament: A Relational Theology of Creation*. The points where we have differed have largely centered in matters relating to the God of the texts. This disagreement has perhaps been most evident in the interpretation of images of divine sovereignty.

SHARP: In what ways do you think Walter is misunderstood?

FRETHEIM: Perhaps most commonly such misunderstanding is rooted in Walter's "untamed" language about the texts. His language is passionate; indeed, his work often parallels the rhetorical force of the texts and the unsettling metaphors within them. There is a kind of "in your face" or "get under your skin" dimension to his work that serves to confront his readers more directly with texts. His emotional use of language has a way of confronting us directly with important textual issues and moving us past a solely "academic" perspective (where many do not want to go, indeed think we should not go). His refusal to back away from such disturbing language and troubling images is very important for both Church and academy, forcing us to take more seriously the often deeply emotional dimension of many texts.

At the same time, speaking as a Christian interpreter, Walter is suspicious of churchly traditions of theological interpretation, not least because they often seek to control the text in the interest of supporting ecclesial commitments. Walter resists an easy closure with respect to the interpretation of any text or theme. The text for him always challenges preconceived categories and breaks them open. The God of the Bible will not be domesticated and neither will Walter's exposition of the texts that witness to this God. For Walter, theological pluralism has been canonized. The Old Testament does not offer a finished portrayal of God and neither should contemporary readers. But, even if we recognize this reality, many of us will slip quickly past the theologically awkward texts on our way to a more "sensible," traditional interpretation.

For Walter, the Bible must be given its own voice, even if it means undercutting traditional ways of thinking and doing. While he recognizes that all interpretations are laden with special interests, including his own, he may be insufficiently critical with respect to his own commitments. The dominance of royal language for God (e.g., sovereignty) is revealing of a strong impact of the Reformed tradition in his theological reflection. As I have said, "The Reformed centering in the sovereignty of God is always near at hand, and in it he seems to rest when his theological back is up against the wall."[1] Though he breaks out of traditional understandings of sovereignty in many ways (e.g., impassibility and immutability), his not uncommon appeals to divine "intervention," divine "irresistibility," and "unlimited" divine sovereignty show that this tradition about God still centers his reflections. In fact, I wonder whether his emphasis on an unsettled and unsettling God is "a postmodern restatement of sovereignty"[2] that comes back around the theological bend and threatens his own pluralistic agenda.

One is given to wonder whether these moves by Walter do not at times threaten his own effort to get the Old Testament more pervasively into the lives of Christian individuals and communities. With his emphasis on divine instability, capriciousness, irrationality, violence, etc., he may be feeding the Marcionite tendencies in the Church. Such an imaging of

God is one of the key factors for rejecting the Old Testament these days; his presentation of God may be in danger of reinforcing that perspective and in the process contributing to the marginalization of the Old Testament in the life of the Church.

From another angle, Walter is rightfully concerned about the ways in which the God of the Bible can be co-opted by the establishment (in both Church and academy) and imaged in ways that are maximally supportive of that very establishment (a "settled 'establishment' Yahweh"). The better to maintain control of people's life and thought! At the same time (to my knowledge), he seems insufficiently concerned about another theological establishment for whom an unsettling God is precisely the trump card to keep matters settled. Such a portrayal of "God on the loose" is designed to keep people on edge, always looking over their shoulders wondering what God is going to do next if they do not toe the mark. This is a troubling form of sovereignty, for it has few of the restraints and constraints that genuine relationship entails.

What counts for Brueggemann as "unsettling" with respect to God? Certainly many of the statements about God in the Old Testament are unsettling. But are they always appropriately unsettling? What about the Bible's patriarchy? Unsettling, yes. But not appropriately so. What about violence language for God in the Bible? Unsettling, yes. But is all the Bible's violent language for God appropriate? If not, on what grounds does one sort the issues out? Criteria must be developed to sort out these testimonies, to make distinctions regarding appropriateness among images of God. That the Bible itself is self-critical regarding the imaging of God (e.g., Gen. 18:25), indeed provides an inner-biblical warrant for such critical reflection, needs closer attention.

SHARP: Is there something about your own work—exegetically, hermeneutically, theologically—that you think Walter has misunderstood?

FRETHEIM: It is difficult to say that Walter has "misunderstood" anything that I have written. We certainly have some differences of opinion, particularly regarding matters theological. Given our many common interests, I wish he had grappled with my *Suffering of God* book more directly than what I've seen. Our views regarding the God of the Old Testament have many similarities, but there are significant differences that might be helpfully worked through at some point.

SHARP: On what might you disagree with Walter? On which interpretive issues would you like to hear more from him?

FRETHEIM: I have not read everything that Walter has written(!), but in my reading, the following issues centering on the imaging of God have come to the surface for me:

1. The category of relationality is insufficiently central for Walter's work, perhaps because of his strong emphasis on divine sovereignty. Relationship language is present in his work, but it tends to be considered in bits and pieces, rather than being the groundwork out of which talk about God is developed in the Hebrew Bible. While he will speak of "sovereignty in relationship," I wonder whether that formulation continues to stress sovereignty at the expense of relationship (see his sections on sovereignty in his *Old Testament Theology: An Introduction*, pp. 75–120).

2. Issues of divine freedom and faithfulness are also raised. Walter speaks of "God's freedom, even from God's partner," of "something wild, dangerous, unfettered, and free in the character of Yahweh" (*Jeremiah*, p. 138), particularly in matters regarding divine judgment. For example, he speaks of God's *"failure to adhere to covenant"* (*Theology of the Old Testament* [hereafter abbreviated *TOT*], p. 373; emphasis his). Or, "God has withdrawn fidelity"; God "has ceased to care"; "a complete absence of fidelity on God's part" (*Jeremiah*, pp. 121, 142, 152). God can be abusive in abandoning fidelity (*TOT*, p. 359). It seems to me that images of divine freedom and sovereignty have tended to "trump" images of divine faithfulness. "One never knows whether Yahweh will turn out to be a loose cannon, or whether Yahweh's commitment to Israel will make a difference" (p. 296).

3. Walter claims that God's actions in judgment bring faithfulness into question, but judgmental action may be the only way that God can be faithful in such situations. The immense agony of God in, say, Jeremiah is a demonstration that God is *not* truly free of the relationship with Israel. Otherwise, he would not agonize so; he would just get up and leave! God agonizes because God has chosen not to be free of these people; he loves them with an "everlasting love" and "continues his faithfulness" to them, come what may (Jer. 31:3). Judgment is necessary if God is going to "continue faithfulness" (31:3), do justice to relationships established (9:23–24), and move toward a new world (29:10–11, "only when . . .").

4. Another direction in need of attention is Walter's claims regarding God's actions in the world and the issue of agency. For example, in Jeremiah, God is the only "real agent"; there is "no mediating agent" or "the army may be Babylonian, but the real agent is Yahweh" (*Jeremiah*, pp. 54, 176, 193, 430, 439). From another angle, in his article on "Presence of God",[3] "There is no interest in any *form* of appearance." His lack of interest in the divine form in theophanies is also evident in his *TOT* (pp. 567–77). Remarkably, he considers some theophanies to be unmediated, "direct and immediate" (p. 570), even in texts such as Genesis 18:1–2. It needs to be considered whether God ever acts in an unmediated way in the Old Testament.

5. From a different angle, Walter speaks of some texts (e.g., Ezekiel 16; 23) in terms of the "profound irrationality" of Yahweh, a "Yahweh who is out of control with the violent, sexual rage of a husband who assaults his own beloved"; God "goes wholly overboard in passion" (*TOT*, pp. 383–84). God even has "delight in rage" (*TOT*, p. 276). Yet, in such texts God's wrath is clearly motivated by Israel's covenantal infidelity, so the language of divine "irrationality" seems off base. This kind of reflection suggests that the "yes" and "no" of the metaphor have been insufficiently considered.

6. Or, Walter speaks of the will of God as "irresistible" (*Jeremiah*, p. 222) or of the "irresistible sovereignty of Yahweh" (*Divine Presence and Violence*, p. 41). I wonder, if God's will is irresistible, why would God ever be angry?

7. The word "intervention" is also often present in Walter's reflections about God. Such language opens up key issues regarding divine presence. It is as if God's presence is more occasional than the texts suggest, intervening now and again with a "goodie" or a "baddie." It needs to be considered whether the language of "intervention" is ever appropriate when considering Old Testament texts.

8. Divine "self-praise" or "excessive self-regard" is a recurrent theme in Walter's theological work (see *TOT*, pp. 272–79), or "uncompromising self-regard" (p. 298), "passionate, perhaps out-of-control self-regard" (p. 309; see pp. 268–76). Or, "Yahweh's self-regard is massive in its claim, strident in its expectation, and ominous in its potential" (p. 296; cf. p. 282). God has a "singular preoccupation with self," which is "massive, savage,

and seemingly insatiable" (pp. 293, 556). In the exercise of wrath, God seems really focused on God's own self. To ascribe such self-centeredness to God seems to go beyond the God presented in these texts. Again, the "yes" and the "no" of the metaphoric language seem insufficiently considered.

I've previously listed some of the descriptors for God in Walter's work as he seeks to describe Yahweh as both settled and unsettling: savage, odd, abusive, mean-spirited, wild, self-indulgent, unreliable, unstable, capricious, irascible, irrational, sulky, and more ("Brueggemann's God"). Once again, one wonders whether such language is not finally defeating of Walter's legitimate concerns about Marcionism in Church and academy.

SHARP: What crucial issues matter most for Old Testament interpretation today, in your view? How do you seek to engage those issues? How has Walter engaged or avoided them?

FRETHEIM: My focus has been on hermeneutical and theological issues. Within that, I have centered on issues regarding God, creation, and the God–world relationship. God's will for a genuine relationship with all creatures is grounded in the relational life of God, evidenced initially in the dialogical way in which God created humankind (Gen. 1:26) and henceforth in God's interrelational and interdependent way of interacting with the world. Relationality is fundamental to God's way of being and doing in, with, and under the world. The Old Testament uses language for God that is fundamentally relational (the vast majority of metaphors for God are relational, e.g., Exod. 19:4; Deut. 32:18). How one works out what it means for God to be in a genuine relationship with the world will need continuing attention (see my *God and World*, pp. 13–22, for an initial statement). God's relationship with this people constitutes a genuine story, in which the journey of both God and people are lived out in dynamic interrelationship. God is not unaffected by this ongoing relationship with human and nonhuman creatures.

Generally, God's relationship with the world is such that God is present on every occasion and active in every event (though not in a controlling way), no matter how heroic or Hitlerian. In every such moment God is at work on behalf of the best possible future for all creation, whether in judgment or salvation. At the same time, God does not have a solitary will in place from the beginning regarding every aspect of the created order. In view of the ongoing story of the world, God makes adjustments in the divine will (evident in the ongoing revision of law).

The power of God is a related theme. I would affirm that, again and again, God chooses to exercise constraint and restraint in the exercise of power in the life of the world. This is decisively shaped by God's promises at the end of the flood story, where God chooses to limit the divine options in working in the world. God chooses to entrust creatures, human and nonhuman, with creaturely responsibilities and does not manage their work. God honors and values such work on the part of the agents (though does not always positively assess it; see Zech. 1:15). This is a risky move for God, for God's work through such less-than-perfect instruments will always have mixed results (e.g., Assyrian and Babylonian armies). The divine sovereignty in creation is understood, not in terms of divine control, but as a sovereignty that gives power over to the created for the sake of a relationship of integrity.

This understanding of relationship should not be collapsed into talk about the covenant. Relationship is a much more basic theme than covenant. Covenants are made with individuals (Noah, Abraham, David) and Israel, with whom God has already established a relationship. Covenants formalize an already existing relationship. The Sinaitic covenant, for example, is a vocational covenant with those who are already God's people. The Sinai covenant is a matter, not of the people's status (they are already God's people!), but of their vocation within relationship.

Finally, I take two examples from Walter's *Introduction to the Old Testament* as a way of lifting up some key differences in our work.

First, creation accounts. Walter claims that Genesis 1:1–2 constitutes a premise for creation: namely, that "disordered chaos" was already there when God began to create. I do not dispute that, but I do dispute the idea that this chaos is an evil force, "operating destructively against the will of the creator." From another angle, the serpent, interpreted as anti-God, belongs among God's creatures, and this means "that the seductive voice of evil is intrinsic to the creation; that is, the creation in principle is under siege from evil that contradicts the intention of the Creator" (p. 36). Walter then goes on to speak of this "intrinsic contradiction to God's will that is present in the 'stuff' of creation itself" (p. 34). On the contrary, disorder is integral to God's ongoing creative work; God created the world good, not perfect, precisely in the interests of the creativity of human and nonhuman creatures.

While Walter denies that Genesis 3 speaks of a fall ("nothing could be more remote from the narrative" [Genesis, p. 41]), it seems to me that his language regarding the evil forces of chaos is his replacement for the fall story, only cast in terms of either an eternal dualism or evil as God's creation, at least in effect. To opt for the first is to claim that something comes into being without God, and the claim that God is the Creator of all is then a compromised confession. To opt for the second, evil is God's creation. This compromises the claim that sin and evil always stand against God, for God would be their ultimate author, the one responsible for the introduction of evil into the life of the world. In either case, the place of moral evil is diminished, indeed human responsibility for evil. We can, in effect, say, either that the devil made me do it or God did. That God is responsible for the possibility of moral evil is another matter and more consistent with the text.

Second, Job 38–41—The God-speeches. For Walter, God "pays no attention to Job's defiant demands and exhibits no interest in Job's troubles. Indeed, Job is, in fact, a profound irrelevance in the large vista of Yahweh's rule." Or, "the earlier dispute is about nothing important, so that a quibble about suffering and guilt or innocence is of no significance to the inscrutable mystery of life with God" (p. 298). This is a huge conversation. But suffice it to say: I simply cannot get anywhere close to this reading of the God speeches. I wonder whether this reading does not stand in considerable tension with Walter's general welcoming of the place of the lament in life. I'm thinking not only of his excellent "The Costly Loss of Lament," but, generally, that human questions are welcomed by God and of immense importance to the life of faith. It seems to me that his interpretation of the God speeches stops the questions and could fall into the category he later criticizes: namely, to make the book of Job conform to ready-made theological packages (p. 302). I worry that a God so portrayed is but an echo of the views of Job's friends.

I want to commend Walter in his concern that Old Testament theological scholarship is not be pursued for its own sake, but most basically on behalf of the preaching, teaching, and pastoral care of the Church. I hope that my work can join his work in seeking to pursue this goal.

A Response from Walter Brueggemann, July 2011

I am grateful to Terry for his thoughtful comments. As is usual with him, he manages here, all at the same time, to be judicious, critical, and generous. For a very long time I have regarded Terry as my closest and most important conversation partner in Old Testament studies, besides being a good friend. There is just enough distance and tension between our perspectives to keep the exchange going, while I am sure we are on common ground for the big and important issues.

I am never so much aware of being "Reformed" as when I am in Terry's presence with his greatly self-conscious Lutheranism. Indeed, "some of my best friends" in Reformed circles would surely doubt that I am all that reliably "Reformed," but in Terry's presence it turns out that way. I have no doubt that a Reformed accent on "sovereignty" operates for me, though it is not as conscious and as dominant in my thinking as Fretheim imagines. I am attempting, as far as I can, to let the Bible speak in its own voice. It follows that the Bible has a great deal of rhetoric about God's sovereignty, and I do not flinch from that. That claim of sovereignty is to some extent deconstructed by lament and complaint to which I have given great attention. In more recent work I have accented dialogic matters that condition sovereignty. I suspect that it is not simply sovereignty but also "agency" to which Fretheim objects. And on that point, he and I simply disagree, because I believe that without divine agency, there is no gospel.

For a long time, we have been at the question together about the character and agency of YHWH. My propensity, which Terry takes as Reformed in its assumption, is to take seriously the rhetoric of YHWH's direct agency; whereas Terry, through appeal to "process" categories, tends to accommodate to a much more acceptable "reasonable" reading so that such rhetoric of divine agency regularly is transposed into or points toward human initiative. Thus, for example, in Exodus 3:7–10, a text both of us have studied closely, YHWH resolves to do all sorts of things for the emancipation of Israel with first-person verbs; but then that rhetoric turns into a mandate for Moses to go to Pharaoh. Or in Judges 5:10–11, the "triumphs" (*tsidqoth*) are at the same time, in poetic parallelism, the work of YHWH and of the "peasants."

It is awesome to think that Terry and I are simply living out and expositing interpretive decisions made in the sixteenth century in Wittenberg and Geneva, decisions that have been mediated to us through liturgical formation, our own theological education with deeply grounded teachers, and most especially the deep and shaping presence of our fathers, each of whom was strongly grounded in a particular faith tradition. I think, however, that too much should not be made of the contrast of Lutheran and Reformed lenses, because my own "bloodline" runs more from and toward pietism with its practical accent on social compassion than on any doctrinal commitment of a Reformed kind. I believe that the space that separates us is not space simply generated by belated theological trajectories, but it is contested space or unresolved tension that is in the biblical text itself.

It is clear that the biblical tradition struggled with and toyed with the way in which to attest YHWH; the rhetorical outcome of that struggle and toying reaches all the way from direct divine action to mediated human agency. Thus I believe that we cannot ever arrive at a settlement of that issue but always must revisit it again, living at the interface of divine agency and the amazement of human capacity. It is that *both/and* that makes the biblical testimony endlessly interesting and beyond resolve, a *both/and* that evokes our continuing interpretive effort.

Agency is very difficult, especially when it collides with Enlightenment rationality. I think the text in Judges 5, for example, allows that divine agency is enacted through human agents (here the peasants). And Terry accepts that. But the rhetoric does not completely concede the point. And of course there are many divine actions in the text not taken by human agents. I don't think the rhetoric can be made to conform to our dominant rationality. It is indeed God's otherness who refuses our explanatory categories who is the ground of hope.

I think we need to recover our nerve about divine agency that cannot be explained away. There is no doubt that divine agency calls human agents to act, as with Moses or the servant in Isaiah 61. There is clearly a need in the world for lavish compassion, both divine compassion and human compassion that will be enacted as neighborly care and in public policy. I think relationality features agency, the very point about which we disagree. In my recent book on *The Unsettled God*, my first chapter represents fresh thinking for me about the dialogical character of God. I am likely influenced by Terry about that, though I have also found Jewish interpreters to be the most helpful on this issue.

Terry is a most responsible interpreter. I think in some ways his Lutheran location matters. But more than that, he has a long-term preference for "process" categories with which he works very well. His categories from process theology are not as compelling for me as they are for him, because process categories dispose of "agency." But if we think about such core claims as "love" and "forgive," these also require an agent. Without an agent we have nothing to say that is theologically serious.

Terry suggests that my emphasis on divine irrationality or violence may be a cause for the "marginalization of the Old Testament in the life of the Church." I have not found that to be the case. In my teaching, I have found people interested in and ready to work on these aspects of God's character. The reason, I think, that people will readily engage this is that it is a match for and illumination of their own complexity about which they know very well. I do not find a hunger for a God who will fit all our settled categories. I am not sure what Terry wants to do with the witness of the text. One can of course skip over it as we do, or assign it to "human projection." But finally one cannot deny what is there in the text, even if we prefer not to notice. After we honestly acknowledge the text and its claims, we can do a lot of explanatory interpretation that is often "explaining away." But we have to start with the text and what it gives us. Otherwise we are in fact reading some other text and imposing it here.

Terry asks, "What counts as 'unsettling' with respect to God?" and I respond, "Unsettling for whom?" I think that perhaps Terry would like God to be closer to the traditional confessions. But of course God in the Old Testament is endlessly surprising in freedom. And in the same way, the Jesus given us in the New Testament is filled with surprise. I find it more likely that we might have on our hands a God who is not so boxed in as to be predictable. Serious fidelity requires that kind of freedom. I think God's freedom and God's faithfulness are in deep tension, just as they are with every other "character" who has a complex interior life. Of course fidelity may show up as judgment. But in such divine rants as Ezekiel 16, the voice of God goes beyond any credible fidelity. I think this is an endless problem. Terry will settle it differently from the way I try to, but one cannot just impose preferable categories on the claims of the text.

I do not think the texts all speak with one voice. There are texts in which God is irresistible, as in Job and Isaiah 14. But there are other texts to the contrary. That is exactly the freedom of God that is expressed in the freedom taken by different texts. But the word "God," even when passed through the relational categories of covenant, still means something. We may want to make it softer, but the text often tells otherwise. The challenge is to let the text speak in all its variations and not to reduce it to our best categories. And if irresistible is required some times, then so be it, . . . but not always.

I am much influenced by Jon Levenson in his thesis that chaos (evil) is an untamed force in the world. It is promised that God will prevail, but not yet. I think that our lived experience testifies to the fact that evil remains untamed among us. The Kingdom has not yet fully come. That is as good as I can do, but no one really knows what to say theologically about evil.

Beyond that, I continue to learn from Terry. His accent on creation (and the creator) is a deep counterpoint to my own accent on the "historical" traditions. I have in recent time articulated the dialogical character of YHWH in a way that I think is not remote from Terry's preference for process categories, which is to say that if I live long enough and pay sufficient attention to Terry's work, I may in time get it right. In the meantime, I live with a contented gratitude for Terry as a lively colleague and a generous friend.

Notes

1. Terence E. Fretheim, "Some Reflections on Brueggemann's God," in *God in the Fray: A Tribute to Walter Brueggemann*, ed. Tod Linafelt and Timothy K. Beal (Minneapolis: Fortress, 1998), 25.
2. Ibid.
3. Walter Brueggemann, "Presence of God," in *Interpreter's Dictionary of the Bible: Supplementary Volume*, ed. Keith Crim (Nashville: Abingdon, 1976), 681, my emphasis.

Bibliography of Published Works by Walter Brueggemann

Books

1968–1975

Confronting the Bible: A Resource and Discussion Book for Youth. Boston: United Church Press, 1968.

The Renewing Word. Edited by Elmer J. F. Arndt. Boston: United Church Press, 1968.

Tradition for Crisis: A Study in Hosea. Atlanta: John Knox Press, 1968.

What Are Christians For? An Inquiry into Obedience and Dissent. Dayton, OH: Pflaum-Standard, 1971.

The Evangelical Catechism Revisited, 1847–1972. St. Louis: Eden Publishing House, 1972.

In Man We Trust: The Neglected Side of Biblical Faith. Atlanta: John Knox Press, 1972.

Ethos and Ecumenism: The History of Eden Theological Seminary, 1925–1970. St. Louis: Eden Publishing House, 1975.

The Vitality of Old Testament Traditions. With Hans Walter Wolff. Atlanta: John Knox Press, 1975. 2nd edition, 1982.

1976-1985

Living toward a Vision: Biblical Reflections on Shalom. Philadelphia: United Church Press, 1976. Reprint, 1982.

The Bible Makes Sense. Winona, MN: St. Mary's College Press, 1977.

The Land: Place as Gift, Promise, and Challenge in Biblical Faith. Philadelphia: Fortress Press, 1977.

The Prophetic Imagination. Philadelphia: Fortress Press, 1978.

Belonging and Growing in the Christian Community. Edited by Elizabeth McWhorter. Atlanta: General Assembly Mission Board, The Presbyterian Church in the United States, 1979.

Confirming Our Faith. With Eugene Wehrli. Edited by Larry E. Kalp. New York: United Church Press, 1980.

The Creative Word: Canon as a Model for Biblical Education. Philadelphia: Fortress Press, 1982.

I Kings. Knox Preaching Guides. Edited by John H. Hayes. Atlanta: John Knox Press, 1982.
II Kings. Knox Preaching Guides. Edited by John H. Hayes. Atlanta: John Knox Press, 1982.
Genesis. Interpretation: A Bible Commentary for Teaching and Preaching. Edited by James
    Luther Mays. Atlanta: John Knox Press, 1982.
Praying the Psalms. Winona, MN: St. Mary's College Press, 1982.
A Imaginação Profética. Sao Paulo: Edicoes Paulinas, 1983. Originally published as *The Pro-
    phetic Imagination.*
Advent/Christmas. Proclamation 3: Aids for Interpreting the Lessons of the Church Year,
    Series B. Edited by Elizabeth Achtemeier. Philadelphia: Fortress Press, 1984.
The Message of the Psalms: A Theological Commentary. Augsburg Old Testament Studies.
    Edited by Terence E. Fretheim. Minneapolis: Augsburg Publishing House, 1984.
David's Truth: In Israel's Imagination and Memory. Philadelphia: Fortress Press, 1985.
O Dinamismo das Tradições do Antigo Testamento. Sao Paulo: Edicoes Paulenas, 1985. Transla-
    tion of *The Vitality of Old Testament Traditions.*
The Vitality of Old Testament Traditions. With Hans Walter Wolff. 2nd ed. Louisville, KY:
    Westminster John Knox Press, 1985.

1986–1995

Hopeful Imagination. Minneapolis: Fortress Press, 1986.
Revelation and Violence: A Study in Contextualization: 1986 Pere Marquette Theology Lecture.
    Milwaukee, WI: Marquette University Press, 1986.
A Terra Na Bíblia: dom, Promessa y desafio. Sao Paulo: Edicois Paulinas, 1986. Originally pub-
    lished as *The Land: Place as Gift, Promise, and Challenge in Biblical Faith.*
To Act Justly, Love Tenderly, Walk Humbly. With Sharon Parks and Thomas H. Groome.
    New York: Paulist Press, 1986.
Hope within History. Atlanta: John Knox Press, 1987.
Israel's Praise: Doxology against Idolatry and Ideology. Philadelphia: Fortress Press, 1988.
To Pluck Up, to Tear Down: A Commentary on the Book of Jeremiah 1–25. International Theo-
    logical Commentary Series. Grand Rapids, MI: Eerdmans, 1988.
Easter. Proclamation 4, Series A. Minneapolis: Fortress Press, 1989.
Finally Comes the Poet: Daring Speech for Proclamation. Minneapolis: Fortress Press, 1989.
First and Second Samuel. Interpretation: A Bible Commentary for Teaching and Preaching.
    Edited by James Luther Mays. Louisville, KY: Westminster/John Knox Press, 1990.
Power, Providence, and Personality: Biblical Insight into Life and Ministry. Louisville, KY: West-
    minster/John Knox Press, 1990.
Abiding Astonishment: Psalms, Modernity, and the Making of History. Literary Currents in Bibli-
    cal Interpretation. Louisville, KY: Westminster/John Knox Press, 1991.
Interpretation and Obedience: From Faithful Reading to Faithful Living. Minneapolis: Fortress
    Press, 1991.
To Build, to Plant: A Commentary on Jeremiah 26–52 . International Theological Commentary
    Series. Grand Rapids, MI: Eerdmans, 1991.
Old Testament Theology: Essays on Structure, Theme, and Text. Edited by Patrick D. Miller.
    Minneapolis: Fortress Press, 1992.
Biblical Perspectives on Evangelism: Living in a Three-Storied Universe. Nashville: Abingdon
    Press, 1993.
From Despair to Hope: Peacemaking in Isaiah. With Vera K. White. Louisville, KY: Presby-

terian Peacemaking Program of the Social Justice and Peacemaking Ministry Unit, Presbyterian Church (U.S.A.), 1993.

Il primo libro dei Re: Guida alla lettura. Torino: Claudiana, 1993. Translation of *I Kings.*

Texts for Preaching: A Lectionary Commentary Based on the NRSV–Year B. With Charles B. Cousar, et al. Louisville, KY: Westminster/John Knox Press, 1993.

Texts under Negotiation: The Bible and Postmodern Imagination. Minneapolis: Fortress Press, 1993. Also published as *The Bible and Postmodern Imagination: Texts under Negotiation.* London: SCM Press, 1993.

Using God's Resources Wisely: Isaiah and Urban Possibility. Louisville, KY: Westminster/John Knox Press, 1993.

A Social Reading of the Old Testament: Prophetic Approaches to Israel's Communal Life. Edited by Patrick D. Miller. Minneapolis: Fortress Press, 1994.

The Psalms and the Life of Faith. Edited by Patrick D. Miller. Minneapolis: Fortress Press, 1995.

Texts for Preaching: A Lectionary Commentary Based on the NRSV–Year A. With Charles B. Cousar, et al. Louisville, KY: Westminster John Knox Press, 1995.

1996–2005

The Threat of Life: Sermons on Pain, Power, and Weakness. Edited by Charles L. Campbell. Minneapolis: Fortress Press, 1996.

Cadences of Home: Preaching among Exiles. Louisville, KY: Westminster John Knox Press, 1997.

Theology of the Old Testament: Testimony, Dispute, Advocacy. Minneapolis: Fortress Press, 1997.

Isaiah 1–39. Westminster Bible Companion. Louisville, KY: Westminster John Knox Press, 1998.

Isaiah 40–66. Westminster Bible Companion. Louisville, KY: Westminster John Knox Press, 1998.

To Act Justly, Love Tenderly, Walk Humbly. With Sharon Parks and Thomas H. Groome. New York: Paulist Press, 1986. Reprint, Eugene, OR: Wipf & Stock Publishers, 1997.

A Commentary on Jeremiah: Exile and Homecoming. Grand Rapids, MI: Eerdmans, 1998.

El mensaje de los Salmos. Ciudad de México: Universidad Iberoamericana, 1998. Translation of *The Message of the Psalms.*

The Covenanted Self: Explorations in Law and Covenant. Edited by Patrick D. Miller. Minneapolis: Fortress Press, 1999.

1 and 2 Kings. Macon, GA: Smyth & Helwys, 2000.

Deep Memory, Exuberant Hope: Contested Truth in a Post-Christian World. Edited by Patrick D. Miller. Minneapolis: Fortress Press, 2000.

I de rotlösas land: Att predika om hemkomst och hopp. Örebro, Sweden: Bokförlaget Libris, 2000. Translation of *Cadences of Home: Preaching among Exiles.*

Practicar la equidad, amar la ternura, caminar humildemente. Bilbao, Spain: Editorial Desclée de Brouwer, S.A., 2000. Translation of *To Act Justly, Love Tenderly, Walk Humbly.*

Texts That Linger, Words That Explode: Listening to Prophetic Voices. Edited by Patrick D. Miller. Minneapolis: Fortress Press, 2000.

The Bible Makes Sense. 2nd rev. ed. Louisville, KY: Westminster John Knox Press, 2001.

Peace. Understanding Biblical Themes. St. Louis: Chalice Press, 2001. Rev. ed. of *Living toward a Vision.* Philadelphia: United Church Press, 1976.

The Prophetic Imagination. 2nd ed. Minneapolis: Fortress Press, 2001.

Testimony to Otherwise: The Witness of Elijah and Elisha. St. Louis: Chalice Press, 2001.

Deuteronomy. Nashville: Abingdon Press, 2002.

Ichabod toward Home: The Journey of God's Glory. Grand Rapids, MI: Eerdmans, 2002.

The Land: Place as Gift, Promise, and Challenge in Biblical Faith. 2nd ed. Minneapolis: Fortress Press, 2002.

Reverberations of Faith. Louisville, KY: Westminster John Knox Press, 2002.

Spirituality of the Psalms. Minneapolis: Fortress Press, 2002.

Struggling with Scripture. With Brian K. Blount and William C. Placher. Louisville, KY: Westminster John Knox Press, 2002.

Teologia dell'Antico Testamento: Testimonianza, dibattimento, perorazione. Brescia, Italy: Editrice Queriniana, 2002. Translation of *Theology of the Old Testament: Testimony, Dispute, Advocacy*.

Awed to Heaven, Rooted in Earth: Prayers of Walter Brueggemann. Edited by Edwin Searcy. Minneapolis: Fortress Press, 2003.

The Bible Makes Sense. 3rd rev. ed. Cincinnati: St. Anthony Messenger Press, 2003.

Hope for the World: Mission in a Global Context. Louisville, KY: Westminster John Knox Press, 2003.

An Introduction to the Old Testament: The Canon and Christian Imagination. Louisville, KY: Westminster John Knox Press, 2003. 2nd ed. to be published in 2012.

Kuyak sinhak: chǔngŏn, nonjaeng, ongho. Translation of *Theology of the Old Testament: Testimony, Dispute, Advocacy*. Seoul: Christian Literature Crusade, 2003.

The Book That Breathes New Life: Scriptural Authority and Biblical Theology. Edited by Patrick Miller. Minneapolis: Fortress Press, 2004.

Immaginazione profetica: La voce dei profeti nella Bibbia e nella Chiesa. Bologna, Italy: Editrice Missionaria Italiana, 2004. Translation of *The Prophetic Imagination*.

Inscribing the Text: Sermons and Prayers of Walter Brueggemann. Edited by Anna Carter Florence. Minneapolis: Fortress Press, 2004.

La spiritualità dei Salmi. Brescia: Editrice Queriniana, 2004. Translation of *Spirituality of the Psalms*.

Polyphonie und Einbildungskraft: Aufsätze zur Theologie des Alten Testaments. Frankfurt: Peter Lang, 2004.

I e II Samuele. Torino, Italy: Claudiana, 2005. Translation of *First and Second Samuel*.

Introduzione all'Antico Testamento. Torino, Italy: Claudiana, 2005. Translation of *Introduction to the Old Testament: The Canon and Christian Imagination*.

Solomon: Israel's Ironic Icon of Human Achievement. Columbia, SC: University of South Carolina Press, 2005.

A Theological Introduction to the Old Testament. With Bruce C. Birch, Terence E. Fretheim, and David L. Petersen. 2nd ed. Nashville: Abingdon Press, 2005.

Theology of the Old Testament: Testimony, Dispute, Advocacy. Minneapolis: Fortress Press, 2005.

Worship in Ancient Israel: An Essential Guide. Nashville: Abingdon Press, 2005.

2006–2011

In Man We Trust: The Neglected Side of Biblical Faith. Atlanta: John Knox Press, 1972. Reprint, Eugene, OR: Wipf & Stock Publishers, 2006.

Like Fire in the Bones: Listening for the Prophetic Word in Jeremiah. Minneapolis: Fortress Press, 2006.

The Word That Redescribes the World: The Bible and Discipleship. Minneapolis: Fortress Press, 2006.

Mandate to Difference: An Invitation to the Contemporary Church. Louisville, KY: Westminster John Knox Press, 2007.

Praying the Psalms: Engaging Scripture and the Life of the Spirit. 2nd ed. Eugene, OR: Cascade Books, 2007.

Teología del Antiguo Testamento: Un juicio a Yahvé Testimonio. Disputa. Defensa. Salamanca, Spain: Ediciones Sígueme, 2007. Translation of *Theology of the Old Testament: Testimony, Dispute, Advocacy.*

The Theology of the Book of Jeremiah. Old Testament Theology. New York: Cambridge University Press, 2007.

The Word Militant: Preaching a Decentering Word. Minneapolis: Fortress Press, 2007.

A hit: A Zsoltárok Könyvében. Budapest, Hungary: Kálvin János Kiadója, 2008. Translation of *Spirituality of the Psalms.*

Great Prayers of the Old Testament. Louisville, KY: Westminster John Knox Press, 2008.

Old Testament Theology: An Introduction. Nashville: Abingdon Press, 2008.

A Pathway of Interpretation: The Old Testament for Pastors and Students. Eugene, OR: Cascade Books, 2008.

Prayers for a Privileged People. Nashville: Abingdon Press, 2008.

Entrare nella Parola di Dio. Milan, Italy: San Paolo Press, 2009. Translation of *The Bible Makes Sense.*

Great Prayers of the Old Testament. Russian translation. Moscow: Eksmo, 2009.

An Introduction to the Old Testament: The Canon and Christian Imagination. Russian translation. Moscow: St. Andrews Press, 2009.

Divine Presence amid Violence: Contextualizing the Book of Joshua. Eugene, OR: Cascade Books, 2009 and Milton Keynes, U.K.: Paternoster, 2009.

An Unsettling God: The Heart of the Hebrew Bible. Minneapolis: Fortress Press, 2009.

Xian zhi shi de xiang xiang. Zhonghe City, Taiwan: Taiwan Christian Literature, 2009. Translation of *The Prophetic Imagination.*

Yeŏnjajŏk sangsangnyŏk. Seoul, South Korea: Pok innŭn Saram, 2009. Translation of *The Prophetic Imagination.*

Journey to the Common Good. Louisville, KY: Westminster John Knox Press, 2010.

Out of Babylon. Nashville: Abingdon Press, 2010.

Psalmist's Cry: Scripts for Embracing Lament. With Steve Frost. Kansas City, MO: House Studio, 2010.

The Collected Sermons of Walter Brueggemann. Louisville, KY: Westminster John Knox Press, 2011.

Disruptive Grace: Reflections on God, Scripture, and the Church. Edited by Carolyn J. Sharp. Minneapolis: Fortress Press, 2011.

Du jiu yue xue dao gao. Xianggang, China: Heaven Book House Company, 2011. Translation of *Great Prayers of the Old Testament.*

Articles

1965–1975

"Amos 4:4–13 and Israel's Covenant Worship." *Vetus Testamentum* 15, no. 1 (Jan. 1965): 1–15.

"Tradition Engaged with Crisis." *Theology and Life* 9, no. 2 (June 1966): 118–30.

"David and His Theologian." *Catholic Biblical Quarterly* 30, no. 2 (April 1968): 156–81.

"Isaiah 55 and Deuteronomic Theology." *Zeitschrift für die alttestamentliche Wissenschaft* 80, no. 2 (Jan. 1968): 191–203.

"Kerygma of the Deuteronomistic Historian." *Interpretation* 22, no. 4 (Oct. 1968): 387–402.

"Amos' Intercessory Formula." *Vetus Testamentum* 19, no. 4 (Oct. 1969): 385–99.

"King in the Kingdom of Things." *Christian Century* 86 (1969): 1165–66.

"Trusted Creature." *Catholic Biblical Quarterly* 31, no. 4 (Oct. 1969): 484–98.

"Of the Same Flesh and Bone, Gn 2:23a." *Catholic Biblical Quarterly* 32, no. 4 (Oct. 1970): 532–42.

"Scripture and an Ecumenical Life-Style: A Study in Wisdom Theology." *Interpretation* 24, no. 1 (Jan. 1970): 3–19.

"Triumphalist Tendency in Exegetical History." *Journal of the American Academy of Religion* 38, no. 4 (Dec. 1970): 367–80.

"Kingship and Chaos: A Study in Tenth Century Theology." *Catholic Biblical Quarterly* 33, no. 3 (July 1971): 317–32.

"From Dust to Kingship." *Zeitschrift für die alttestamentliche Wissenschaft* 84, no. 1 (Jan. 1972): 1–18.

"Kerygma of the Priestly Writers." *Zeitschrift für die alttestamentliche Wissenschaft* 84, no. 4 (Jan. 1972): 397–414.

"Life and Death in Tenth Century Israel." *Journal of the American Academy of Religion* 40, no. 1 (March 1972): 96–109.

"On Trust and Freedom: A Study of Faith in the Succession Narrative." *Interpretation* 26, no. 1 (Jan. 1972): 3–19.

"Weariness, Exile and Chaos: A Motif in Royal Theology." *Catholic Biblical Quarterly* 34, no. 1 (Jan. 1972): 19–38.

"Jeremiah's Use of Rhetorical Questions." *Journal of Biblical Literature* 92, no. 3 (1973): 358–74.

"Transforming Order into Justice." *Engage/Social Action* 1 (Nov. 1973): 33–43.

"From Hurt to Joy, from Death to Life." *Interpretation* 28, no. 1 (Jan. 1974): 3–19.

"Healing and Caring: Health Care Is an Affirmation about Dignity, Worth and Hope." *Engage/Social Action* 2 (July 1974): 14–24.

"Israel's Sense of Place in Jeremiah." In *Rhetorical Criticism: Essays in Honor of James Muilenburg*, edited by Jared J. Jackson and Martin Kessler, 149–65. Pittsburgh: Pickwick Press, 1974.

"On Coping with Curse: A Study of 2 Sam 16:5–14." *Catholic Biblical Quarterly* 36, no. 2 (April 1974): 175–92.

"Reflections on Biblical Understandings of Property." *International Review of Mission* 64, no. 256 (Oct. 1975): 354–61.

1976-1985

"Luke 3:1–4." *Interpretation* 30, no. 4 (Oct. 1976): 404–9.

"An Attempt at an Interdisciplinary M.Div. Curriculum." *Theological Education* 13, no. 3 (March 1977): 137–45.

"Biblical Perspective on the Problem of Hunger." *Christian Century* 94 (1977): 1136–41.

"Formfulness of Grief." *Interpretation* 31, no. 3 (July 1977): 263–75.

"Israel's Social Criticism and Yahweh's Sexuality," *Journal of the American Academy of Religion* 45 (1977): 739-72.

"Neglected Sapiential Word Pair." *Zeitschrift für die alttestamentliche Wissenschaft* 89, no. 2 (Jan. 1977): 234–58.

"Blessed Are the Hungry." *Thesis Theological Cassettes* 9, no. 3 (April 1978).

"The Epistemological Crisis of Israel's Two Histories (Jer 9:22–23)." In *Israelite Wisdom: Theological and Literary Essays in Honor of Samuel Terrien*, edited by John G. Gammie, 85–105. Missoula, MT: Scholars Press, 1978.

"Our Heritage and Our Commitment." In *Festival of the Church: Celebrating the Legacy of the Evangelical Synod of North America*, edited by Walter Brueggemann, 3–21. St Louis: Office for Church Life and Leadership, 1978.

"Covenanting as Human Vocation: A Discussion of the Relation of Bible and Pastoral Care." *Interpretation* 33, no. 2 (April 1979): 115–29.

"Trajectories in Old Testament Literature and the Sociology of Ancient Israel." *Journal of Biblical Literature* 98, no. 2 (June 1979): 161–85.

"Canon and Dialectic." In *God and His Temple: Reflections on Professor Samuel Terrien's* The Elusive Presence: Toward a New Biblical Theology, edited by Lawrence Frizzell, 20–29. South Orange, NJ: Institute of the Judaeo-Christian Studies, Seton Hall University, 1980.

"A Convergence in Recent Old Testament Theologies." *Journal for the Study of the Old Testament*, no. 18 (Oct. 1980): 2–18.

"Covenant as a Subversive Paradigm: The Move God Has Made in Heaven Opened Up for Us a New Agenda; What Is Possible on Earth?" *Christian Century* 97 (1980): 1094–99.

"The Crisis and Promise of Presence in Israel." *Horizons in Biblical Theology* 1 (1980): 47–86.

"On Land-Losing and Land-Receiving." *Dialog* 19, no. 3 (June 1980): 166–73.

"Psalms and the Life of Faith: A Suggested Typology of Function." *Journal for the Study of the Old Testament* 17 (June 1980): 3–32.

"The Tribes of Yahweh: An Essay Review." *Journal of the American Academy of Religion* 48, no. 3 (1980): 441–51.

"Why Study the Bible." With Douglas A. Knight. *Bulletin—Council on the Study of Religion* 11, no. 3 (June 1980): 76–81.

"The Childs Proposal: A Symposium." With Ralph W. Klein and Gary Stansell. *Word & World* 1, no. 2 (March 1981): 105–15.

"Social Criticism and Social Vision in the Deuteronomic Formula of the Judges." In *Botschaft und die Boten*, edited by Hans Walter Wolff, Jörg Jeremias, and Lothar Perlitt, 101–14. Neukirchen-Vluyn, Germany: Neukirchener Verlag, 1981.

"'Vine and fig tree': A Case Study in Imagination and Criticism." *Catholic Biblical Quarterly* 43, no. 2 (April 1981): 188–204.

"The Bible and Mission: Some Interdisciplinary Implications for Teaching." *Missiology* 10, no. 4 (Oct. 1982): 397–412.

"'Impossibility' and Epistemology in the Faith Tradition of Abraham and Sarah (Gen 18:1–15)." *Zeitschrift für die alttestamentliche Wissenschaft* 94, no. 4 (Jan. 1982): 615–34.

"Response to John Goldingay's 'The Dynamic Cycle of Praise and Prayer' (20, 85-90 1981)." *Journal for the Study of the Old Testament*, no. 22 (1982): 141–42.

"As the Text 'Makes Sense': Keep the Methods of Exposition as Lean and Uncomplicated as Possible." *Christian Ministry* 14, no. 6 (Nov. 1983): 7–10.

"A Better Governance: Meditations for Advent." *Sojourners* 12, no. 10 (Nov. 1983): 28–29.

"The Book of Jeremiah: Portrait of the Prophet." *Interpretation* 37, no. 2 (April 1983): 130–45.

"Psalm 77—The 'Turn' from Self to God." *Journal for Preachers* 6, no. 2 (Jan. 1983): 8–14.

"Reservoirs of Unreason." *Reformed Liturgy and Music* 17, no. 3 (June 1983): 99–104.

"Toward the Breakpoint—and Beyond." In *Social Themes of the Christian Year: A Commentary on the Lectionary*, edited by Dieter T. Hessel, 149–58. Philadelphia: Geneva Press, 1983.

"Trajectories in Old Testament Literature and the Sociology of Ancient Israel." In *Bible and Liberation: Political and Social Hermeneutics*, edited by Norman K. Gottwald, 307–33. Maryknoll, NY: Orbis Books, 1983.

"Will Our Faith Have Children." *Word and World* 3, no. 3 (June 1983): 272–83.

"A World in Jeopardy: Meditations for Advent." *Sojourners* 12, no. 11 (Dec. 1983): 28–29.

"Advent/Christmas." *Proclamation* 3: Aids for Interpreting the Lessons of the Church Year, Series B. Edited by Elizabeth Achtemeier. Philadelphia: Fortress Press, 1984.

"A Cosmic Sigh of Relinquishment." *Currents in Theology and Mission* 11, no. 1 (Feb. 1984): 5–20.

"Futures in Old Testament Theology." *Horizons in Biblical Theology* 6, no. 1 (June 1984): 1–11.

"A New Creation—After the Sigh." *Currents in Theology and Mission* 11, no. 2 (April 1984): 83–100.

"Unity and Dynamic in the Isaiah Tradition." *Journal for the Study of the Old Testament* 29 (June 1984): 89–107.

"Biblical Faith as Cosmic Hurt." In *Bulletin of the Moravian Theological Seminary, 1977–1985*, 83–92. Bethlehem, PA: Moravian Theological Seminary, 1985.

"Biblical Faith as Structured Legitimacy." In *Bulletin of the Moravian Theological Seminary, 1977–1985*, 71–81. Bethlehem, PA: Moravian Theological Seminary, 1985.

"The Family as World-Maker." *Journal for Preachers* 8, no. 3 (Jan. 1985): 8–15.

"Genesis 1:15–21: A Theological Exploration." In *Congress Volume 1983*, edited by John Adney Emerton, 40–53. Supplements to Vetus Testamentum Supplements, vol. 36. Leiden: E. J. Brill, 1985.

"Imagination as a Mode of Fidelity." In *Understanding the Word: Essays in Honor of Bernhard W. Anderson*, edited by James T. Butler, Edgar W. Conrad, and Ben C. Ollenburger, 13–36. Sheffield, England: JSOT Press, 1985.

"'Is There No Balm in Gilead?' The Hope and Despair of Jeremiah." *Sojourners* 14, no. 9 (Oct. 1985): 26–29.

"Passion and Perspective: Two Dimensions of Education in the Bible." *Theology Today* 42, no. 2 (July 1985): 172–80.

"Psalm 100." *Interpretation* 39, no. 1 (Jan. 1985): 65–69.

"Psalm 109: Three Times 'Steadfast Love,'" *Word and World* 5, no. 2 (March 1985): 144–54.

"The Prophet as a Destabilizing Presence." In *Pastor as Prophet*, edited by Earl E. Shelp and Ronald H. Sunderland, 49–77. New York: Pilgrim Press, 1985.

"2 Kings 18–19: The Legitimacy of a Sectarian Hermeneutic." *Horizons in Biblical Theology* 7, no. 1 (June 1985): 1–42.

"A Second Reading of Jeremiah after the Dismantling." *Ex auditu* 1 (Jan. 1985): 156–68.

"A Shape for Old Testament Theology: 1, Structure Legitimation; 2, Embrace of Pain." *Catholic Biblical Quarterly* 47, no. 1 (April 1985): 28–46.

"A Subversive Memory in a Sacramental Container (Ex 16:31–35)." *Reformed Liturgy and Music* 19, no. 1 (Dec. 1985): 34–38.

"Theodicy in a Social Dimension." *Journal for the Study of the Old Testament*, no. 33 (Oct. 1985): 3–25.

"The 'Uncared for' Now Cared For (Jer 30:12–17): A Methodological Consideration." *Journal of Biblical Literature* 104, no. 3 (1985): 419–28.

"We Cried Out, the Lord Heard, the Lord Saw, the Lord Knew, the Lord Remembered, the Lord Came Down and Saved." *Engage/Social Action* 13 (Dec. 1985): 26–31.

1986–1995

"The Costly Loss of Lament." *Journal for the Study of the Old Testament*, no. 36 (Oct. 1986): 57–71.

"The Earth Is the Lord's: A Theology of Earth and Land." *Sojourners* 15, no. 9 (Oct. 1986): 28–32.

"Hunger, Food, and the Land in the Biblical Witness: The 1986 Zimmerman Lecture." *Lutheran Theological Seminary Bulletin* 66, no. 4 (Fall 1986): 48–61.

"Making History: Jeremiah's Guide for Christians Who Know How to Blush." *Other Side* 22, no. 8 (Oct. 1986): 21–25.

"Newness Mediated by Worship." *Reformed Liturgy and Music* 20, no. 2 (March 1986): 55–60.

"Prayer as an Act of Daring Dance: Four Biblical Examples." *Reformed Liturgy and Music* 20, no. 1 (Dec. 1986): 31–37.

"Proclamation of Resurrection in the Old Testament." *Journal for Preachers* 9, no. 3 (Jan. 1986): 2–9.

"Theological Education: Healing the Blind Beggar." *Christian Century* 103, no. 5 (1986): 114–16.

"The Third World of Evangelical Imagination." *Horizons in Biblical Theology* 8, no. 2 (Dec. 1986): 61–84.

"Before the Giant: Surrounded by Mother." *Princeton Seminary Bulletin* 8, no. 3 (Jan. 1987): 1–13.

"The Case for an Alternative Reading." *Theological Education* 23, no. 2 (March 1987): 89–107.

"The Commandments and Liberated, Liberating Bonding." *Journal for Preachers* 10, no. 2 (January 1987): 15–24.

"Dreaming, Being Home, Finding Strangers, and the Seminaries." *Mid-Stream* 26, no. 1 (Jan. 1987): 62–76.

"The Embarrassing Footnote." *Theology Today* 44, no. 1 (April 1987): 5–14.

"Land: Fertility and Justice." In *Theology of the Land*, edited by Bernard F. Evans and Gregory D. Cusack, 41–68. Collegeville, MN: Liturgical Press, 1987.

"A Response to 'The Song of Miriam' by Bernhard Anderson." In *Directions in Biblical Hebrew Poetry*, edited by Elaine R. Follis, 297–302. Sheffield, England: Journal for the Study of the Old Testament Press, 1987.

"Embracing the Transformation: A Comment on Missionary Preaching." *Journal for Preachers* 11, no. 2 (Jan. 1988): 8–18.

"Isaiah 37:21–29: The Transformative Potential of a Public Metaphor." *Horizons in Biblical Theology* 10, no. 1 (June 1988): 1–32.

"Jeremiah: Intense Criticism/Thin Interpretation." *Interpretation* 42, no. 3 (July 1, 1988): 268–80.

"Practical Aids to Lectionary Use: First Sunday of Advent (C)—Last Sunday after the Epiphany (C)." With Kenneth E. Williams and Robert Fort. *Reformed Liturgy and Music* 22, no. 3 (June 1988): 167–73.

"Second Isaiah: An Evangelical Rereading of Communal Experience." In *Reading and Preaching the Book of Isaiah*, edited by Christopher R. Seitz, 71–90. Philadelphia: Fortress Press, 1988.

"2 Samuel 21–24: An Appendix of Deconstruction?" *Catholic Biblical Quarterly* 50, no. 3 (July 1988): 383–97.
"The Social Nature of the Biblical Text for Preaching." In *Preaching as a Social Act: Theology and Practice*, edited by Arthur Van Seters, 127–65. Nashville: Abingdon Press, 1988.
"Truth-Telling and Peacemaking: A Reflection on Ezekiel." *Christian Century* 105 (1988): 1096–98.
"A World Available for Peace: Images of Hope from Jeremiah and Isaiah." *Sojourners* 17 (Jan. 1988): 22–26.
"The Legitimacy of a Sectarian Hermeneutic: 2 Kings 18–19." In *Education for Citizenship and Discipleship*, edited by Mary C. Boys, 3–34. New York: Pilgrim Press, 1989.
"Narrative Intentionality in 1 Samuel 29." *Journal for the Study of the Old Testament*, no. 43 (Feb. 1989): 21–35.
"A Poem of Summons (Is 55:1–3) / A Narrative of Resistance (Dan 1:1–21)." In *Schöpfung und Befreiung: für Claus Westermann zum 80. Geburtstag*, edited by Rainer Albertz, Friedemann W. Golka, and Jürgen Kegler, 126–36. Stuttgart: Calwer Verlag, 1989.
"Praise to God Is the End of Wisdom: What Is the Beginning?" *Journal for Preachers* 12, no. 3 (Jan. 1989): 30–40.
"Prophetic Ministry: A Sustainable Alternative Community." *Horizons in Biblical Theology* 11, no. 1 (June 1989): 1–33.
"The Psalms as Prayer." *Reformed Liturgy and Music* 23, no. 1 (Dec. 1989): 13–26.
"The Rhetoric of Hurt and Hope: Ethics Odd and Crucial." *Annual of the Society of Christian Ethics* (Jan. 1989): 73–92.
"Teaching as Witness: Forming an Intentional Community." In *The Pastor as Teacher*, edited by Earl E. Shelp and Ronald H. Sunderland, 28–64. New York: Pilgrim Press, 1989.
"Advent in Scripture and Contemporary Life." *Journal for Preachers* 14, no. 1 (Jan. 1990): 3–18.
"An Artistic Disclosure in Three Dimensions." *Cumberland Seminarian* 28 (March 1990): 1–8.
"The Call to Resistance." *Other Side* 26, no. 6 (Nov. 1990): 44–46.
"I Samuel 1: A Sense of a Beginning." *Zeitschrift für die alttestamentliche Wissenschaft* 102, no. 1 (Jan. 1990): 33–48.
"Peacemaking: An Evangelical Possibility." *Church and Society* 81, no. 1 (1990): 8–20.
"The Preacher, the Text, and the People." *Theology Today* 47, no. 3 (Oct. 1990): 237–47.
"The Social Significance of Solomon as a Patron of Wisdom." In *Sage in Israel and the Ancient Near East*, edited by John G. Gammie and Leo G. Perdue, 117–32. Winona Lake, IN: Eisenbrauns, 1990.
"Some Missing Prerequisites." *Journal for Preachers* 13, no. 2 (Jan. 1990): 23–30.
"Sport of Nature." *Cumberland Seminarian* 28 (March 1990): 9–25.
"When Jerusalem Gloats over Shiloh." *Sojourners* 19 (July 1990): 25–27.
"At the Mercy of Babylon: A Subversive Rereading of the Empire." *Journal of Biblical Literature* 110, no. 1 (March 1991): 3–22.
"Bounded by Obedience and Praise: The Psalms as Canon." *Journal for the Study of the Old Testament*, no. 50 (June 1991): 63–92.
"Genesis 17:1–22." *Interpretation* 45, no. 1 (Jan. 1991): 55–59.
"A Gospel Language of Pain and Possibility." *Horizons in Biblical Theology* 13, no. 2 (Dec. 1991): 95–133.
"Haunting Book—Haunted People." *Word and World* 11, no. 1 (Dec. 1991): 62–68.
"History on the Margins." *Sojourners* 20 (1991): 18–19.
"Poetry in a Prose-Flattened World." *Preaching* 6, no. 5 (March 1991): 28–34.

"Powered by the Spirit." *Sojourners* 20 (May 1991): 11–15.

"Psalms 9–10: A Counter to Conventional Social Reality." In *The Bible and the Politics of Exegesis: Essays in Honor of Norman K. Gottwald on His Sixty-Fifth Birthday*, edited by David Jobling, Peggy L. Day, and Gerald T. Sheppard, 3–15. Cleveland, OH: Pilgrim Press, 1991.

"Remember, You Are Dust." *Journal for Preachers* 14, no. 2 (Jan. 1991): 3–10.

"Rethinking Church Models through Scripture." *Theology Today* 48, no. 2 (July 1991): 128–38.

"2 Samuel 6." In *Telling Queen Michal's Story: An Experiment in Comparative Interpretation*, edited by David J. A. Clines and Tamara Cohn Eskenazi, 121–23. Sheffield, England: JSOT Press, 1991.

"Afterward . . . After George . . . After Bill . . . Newness." *United Church News, CONNact Edition* 8, no. 10 (Dec. 1992): 1, 18.

"A Chance for the Center to Hold." Living by the Word. *Christian Century* 109, no. 23 (1992): 710.

"A Choice amid Doxologies." Living by the Word. *Christian Century* 109, no. 25 (1992): 772.

"Disputed Present, Assured Future." Living by the Word. *Christian Century* 109, no. 27 (1992): 841.

"An 'Eastered' Alternative." In *From Deep Night to Bright Dawn: Theological Reflections*, edited by James Halfaker. Cleveland: United Church of Christ, 1992.

"Exegesis, Psalm 23." *No Other Foundation* 13, no. 2 (Winter 1992–93): 21–25.

"Foreword." *Journal for Preachers* 15, no. 3 (Easter 1992): 1.

"Foreword." *Journal for Preachers* 15, no. 4 (Pentecost 1992): 1.

"God's Relentless 'If.'" *Lexington Theological Quarterly* 27, no. 4 (Oct. 1992): 124–31.

"A New King and a New Order." Living by the Word. *Christian Century* 109, no. 31 (1992): 963.

"The Old One Takes Notice." Living by the Word. *Christian Century* 109, no. 28 (1992): 867.

"On Writing a Commentary . . . An Emergency?" *ATS Colloquy* (Sept.–Oct. 1992): 10–11.

"Pain Turned to Newness." *Cathedral Age* 68, no. 2 (Summer 1992): 18–19.

"The Practice of Homefulness." *Journal for Preachers* 15, no. 4 (Pentecost 1992): 7–22.

"Praise and the Psalms: A Politics of Glad Abandonment, Part I." *The Hymn: A Journal of Congregational Song* 43, no. 3 (July 1992): 14–19.

"A Prayer That Availeth Much." Living by the Word. *Christian Century* 109, no. 22 (1992): 677.

"The Psalms as Prayer." Reprinted in *Hymnology Annual: An International Forum on the Hymn and Worship*, vol. 2, edited by Vernon Wicker, 64–85. Berrien Springs, MI: Vande Vere Publishing Ltd., 1992.

"Pushing Past into Present." Living by the Word. *Christian Century* 109, no. 24 (1992): 741.

"Rude Interruptions to Faith." Living by the Word. *Christian Century* 109, no. 29 (1992): 899.

"Samuel, Book of 1–2: Narrative and Theology." In *The Anchor Bible Dictionary*, vol. 5, edited by David Noel Freedman, 965–73. New York: Doubleday, 1992.

"Scriptural Authority; Biblical Authority in the Post-Critical Period." In *The Anchor Bible Dictionary*, vol. 5, edited by David Noel Freedman, 1049–56. New York: Doubleday, 1992.

"The Terrible Ungluing." Living by the Word. *Christian Century* 109, no. 30 (1992): 931.

"Transforming the Imagination." *Books and Religion* 19 (March 1992): 9–10.

"Wrangling over Words." Living by the Word. *Christian Century* 109, no. 26 (1992): 804.

"Against the Stream: Brevard Childs's Biblical Theology." *Theology Today* 50 (1993): 279–84.

"A Case Study in Daring Prayer." *Living Pulpit* 2, no. 3 (July–Sept. 1993): 12–13.

Foreword to *The Globalization of Theological Education*, edited by Alice Frazer Evans, Robert A. Evans, and David A. Roozen, xi–xii. Maryknoll, NY: Orbis, 1993.

"Foreword." *Journal for Preachers* 16, no. 2 (Lent 1993): 1.

"Foreword." *Journal for Preachers* 16, no. 3 (Easter 1993): 1.

"The Friday Voice of Faith." *Reformed Worship* 30 (Dec. 1993): 2–5. Adapted from a lecture delivered at Calvin Theological Seminary, Grand Rapids, MI, April 22, 1993.

"Jeremiah: Faithfulness in the Midst of Fickleness." In *The Newell Lectureships*, vol. 2, edited by Timothy Dwyer. Anderson, IN: Warner Press, Inc., 1993.

"Narrative Coherence and Theological Intentionality in I Samuel 18." *Catholic Biblical Quarterly* 55 (1993): 225–43.

"The Peace Dividend." *Pulpit Digest* 74, no. 524 (Nov.–Dec. 1993): 5–11.

"Preaching to Exiles." *Journal for Preachers* 16, no. 4 (Pentecost 1993): 3–15.

"Psalm 37: Conflict of Interpretation." In *Of Prophets' Visions and the Wisdom of Sages: Essays in Honour of R. Norman Whybray*, edited by Heather A. McKay and David J. A. Clines, 229–56. Journal for the Study of the Old Testament: Supplement Series 162. Sheffield, England: Sheffield Academic Press, 1993.

"Response to James L. Mays, 'The Question of Context.'" In *The Shape and Shaping of the Psalter*, edited by J. Clinton McCann, 29–41. Journal for the Study of the Old Testament: Supplement Series 159. Sheffield, England: Sheffield Academic Press, 1993.

"Why Prophets Won't Leave Well Enough Alone." *U.S. Catholic* 58 (Jan. 1993): 6–13.

"The Baruch Connection: Reflections on Jeremiah 43:1–7." *Journal of Biblical Literature* 113 (1994): 405–20.

"Biblical Perspectives on Evangelism." *PACE: Professional Approaches for Christian Educators* 24 (Oct. 1994): 14–27.

"The Book of Exodus, Introduction, Commentary, and Reflections." In *The New Interpreter's Bible*, vol. 1, edited by Leander E. Keck et al., 675–981. Nashville: Abingdon Press, 1994.

"Brueggemann Sees Boogaart." *Perspectives* 9, no. 4 (April 1994): 7.

"Cadences which Redescribe: Speech among Exiles." *Journal for Preachers* 17, no. 3 (Easter 1994): 10–17.

"Crisis-Evoked, Crisis-Resolving Speech." *Biblical Theology Bulletin* 24 (1994): 95–105.

"The Daily Voice of Faith: The Covenanted Self." *Sewanee Theological Review* 37, no. 2 (Easter 1994): 123–43.

"The Density of Conflict: God and Sibling." *Living Pulpit* 3, no. 3 (July–Sept. 1994): 16–17.

"Disrupting the Hegemony in God and in Us." *Witness* 77, no. 4 (April 1994): 16–19.

"Duty as Delight and Desire." *Journal for Preachers* 18, no. 1 (Advent 1994): 2–14.

"Engedelmesség És Istendicséret: Zsoltár És Kánon," In *Mert örökké tart szeretete*, edited by Karasszon István, 5–34. Budapest, Hungary: Budapest Református Teológiai Akadémia Bibliai és Fudaisztikai kutatócsoportja, 1994.

"I Will Do It . . . but *You* Go." *Journal for Preachers* 17, no. 4 (Pentecost 1994): 27–30.

"James L. Crenshaw: Faith Lingering at the Edges." *Religious Studies Review* 20, no. 2 (April 1994): 103–10.

"Justice: The Earthly Form of God's Holiness." *Reformed World* 44, no. 1 (March 1994): 13–27.

"'Othering' with Grace and Courage." *Anglican* 23, no. 3 and 4 (Fall–Winter 1993–94): 11–21.

"Six Questions." *Presbyterian Outlook* 176, no. 20 (May 23, 1994): 6–7.
"Exodus 11:1–10, a Night for Crying/Weeping." In *Preaching Biblical Texts: Expositions by Jewish and Christian Scholars*, edited by Fredrick C. Holmgren and Herman E. Schaalman, 76–89. Grand Rapids, MI: Eerdmans, 1995.
"Five Strong Rereadings of the Book of Isaiah." In *The Bible in Human Society, Essays in Honour of John Rogerson*, edited by M. Daniel Carroll R., David J. A. Clines, and Philip R. Davies, 87–104. Journal for the Study of the Old Testament: Supplement Series 200. Sheffield, England: Sheffield Academic Press, 1995.
"Foreword." In *Psalms of Lament*, by Ann Weems, ix–xiv. Louisville, KY: Westminster John Knox Press, 1995.
"Gathering the Church in the Spirit: Reflections on Exile and the Inscrutable Wind of God." Adapted from the speech "New Issues and Challenges for the Faithful." Nanjing Theological Seminary, Nanjing, China, June 3, 1994. Decatur, GA: CTS Press, 1995.
"'In the Image of God' . . . Pluralism." *Modern Theology* 11 (1995): 455–69.
"Pharaoh as Vassal: A Study of a Political Metaphor." *Catholic Biblical Quarterly* 57 (1995): 27–51.
"Preaching as Reimagination." *Theology Today* 52 (1995): 313–29.
"The Prophets, Old Testament." In *Concise Encyclopedia of Preaching*, edited by William H. Willimon and Richard Lischer, 389–91. Louisville, KY: Westminster John Knox Press, 1995.
"A Shattered Transcendence? Exile and Restoration." In *Biblical Theology: Problems and Perspectives, in Honor of J. Christiaan Beker*, edited by Steven J. Kraftchick, Charles D. Myers Jr., and Ben C. Ollenburger, 169–82. Nashville: Abingdon, 1995.
"Two Narratives of 'The Flash Point' (Mark 9:2–8)." *Peacemaker* (Sept. 1995): 4.
"The Uninflected *Therefore* of Hosea 4:1–3." In *Reading from This Place Vol. 1: Social Location and Biblical Interpretation in the United States*, edited by Fernando F. Segovia and Mary Ann Tolbert, 231–49. Minneapolis: Fortress Press, 1995.

1996–2005

"A 'Characteristic' Reflection on What Comes Next (Jeremiah 32.16–44)." In *Prophets and Paradigms: Essays in Honor of Gene M. Tucker*, edited by Stephen Breck Reid, 16–32. Journal for the Study of the Old Testament: Supplement Series 229. Sheffield, England: Sheffield Academic Press, 1996.
"Exegesis, Isaiah 6:1–8." *No Other Foundation* 17, no. 2 (Winter 1996–97): 5–9.
"Foreword." *Journal for Preachers* 20, no. 1 (Advent 1996): 1–2.
Foreword to *Proclaim Jubilee! Spirituality for the Twenty-First Century*, by Maria Harris, ix–xii. Louisville, KY: Westminster John Knox Press, 1996.
"Hope and Despair as Seasons of Faith." In *The Landscape of Praise: Readings in Liturgical Renewal*, edited by Blair Gilmer Meeks, 172–79. Valley Forge, PA: Trinity Press International, 1996.
"James Muilenburg as Theologian." *Union Seminary Quarterly Review* 50 (1996): 71–82. Paper was presented at the Society of Biblical Literature, New Orleans, November 23, 1996, in commemoration of the centennial of Professor Muilenburg's birth.
"The Loss and Recovery of Creation in Old Testament Theology." *Theology Today* 53 (1996): 177–90.

«La Palabra Profética de Dios en La Historia.» Reprint and Spanish translation of "The Prophetic Word of God and History" in *Selecciones de Teologia* 35, no. 140 (Barcelona, Spain: Institute of Fundamental Theology of the Facultat de Teologia de Catalunya, 1996): 257–64.

"Passion and Perspective." Reprinted in *Theological Perspectives on Christian Formation: A Reader on Theology and Christian Education*, edited by Jeff Astley et al., 71–79. Grand Rapids, MI: Eerdmans, 1996.

"'Placed' between Promise and Command." In *Rooted in the Land: Essays on Community and Place*, edited by William Vitek and Wes Jackson, 124–31. New Haven, CT: Yale University Press, 1996.

"Psalm 73 as a Canonical Marker." With Patrick D. Miller. *Journal for the Study of the Old Testament* 72 (1996): 45–56.

"A Shifting Paradigm: From 'Mighty Deeds' to 'Horizon.'" In *The Papers of the Henry Luce III Fellows in Theology*, vol. 1, edited by Gary Gilbert, 7–47. Atlanta: Scholars Press, 1996.

"The Struggle toward Reconciliation." In *Talking about Genesis: A Resource Guide*, introduced by Bill Moyers, Public Affairs Television, 132–34. New York: Doubleday, 1996.

"What Christians Are Saying about the Need for Community." *Green Cross* 2, no. 3 (1996): 24.

"Why Read the Bible? The Possibility of a Fresh Perspective." Reprinted in *Keeping PACE*, edited by Padraic O'Hare, 131–37. Dubuque, IA: Brown-ROA, 1996.

"The Word of the Lord: Thanks Be to God," "A Hard Service (Job 7:1–7)." Reprinted in *Keeping PACE*, edited by Padraic O'Hare, 34–43. Dubuque, IA: Brown-ROA, 1996.

"Abuse of Command: Exploiting Power for Sexual Gratification." *Sojourners* 26, no. 4 (July–Aug. 1997): 22–25.

"Biblical Theology Appropriately Postmodern." *Biblical Theology Bulletin* 27 (1997): 4–9.

"Churches in a Changing Society." *Chinese Theological Review* 11 (1997): 36–53.

"Conversations among Exiles." *Christian Century* 114 (1997): 630–32.

"The Costly Loss of Lament." Reprinted in *The Poetical Books*, edited by David J. A. Clines, 84–97. Sheffield Reader. Sheffield, England: Sheffield Academic Press, 1997.

"The Cunning Little Secret of Certitude (On the First 'Great Commandment')." *Church and Society* 87, no. 6 (July–Aug. 1997): 63–80. Adapted from addresses to the Moderator's Pre-Assembly Conference, "Common Ground," Syracuse, June 13, 1997.

"Destroy . . . but Not Quite." *Caregiver Journal* 13 (1997): 25-27.

"The Exile Experience in Babylon and in America." Lifetime Scholar Course III. Inver Grove Heights, MN: Logos Productions Inc., 1997.

"Exodus 3: Summons to Holy Transformation." In *The Theological Interpretation of Scripture: Classic and Contemporary Readings*, edited by Stephen E. Fowl, 155–71. Blackwell Readings in Modern Theology. Oxford: Blackwell, 1997.

"Follow Your Thirst." *Journal of Stewardship* 49 (1997): 41–48.

"Foreword." *Journal for Preachers* 20, no. 4 (Pentecost 1997): 1–2.

"God's Gift of a Neighbouring Future." Theme Presentation II, *Reformed World*, 47, no. 3 and 4 (Sept. and Dec. 1997): 143–54. Address at the World Alliance of Reformed Churches 23rd general council, Debrecen, Hungary. Reprinted in *Debrecen 1997*, edited by Milan Opocensky, 90–101. Geneva: World Alliance of Reformed Churches, 1997.

"Holy One in Your Midst." *Living Pulpit* 6, no. 1 (Jan.–March 1997): 44–45.

"A Map for a Lost Church?" *Clergy Journal* 73, no. 6 (April 1997): 31–34.

"Neighborliness and the Limits of Power in God's Realm (On the Second 'Great Commandment')." *Church and Society* 87, no. 6 (July–Aug. 1997): 81–96. Adapted from addresses to the Moderator's Pre-Assembly Conference, "Common Ground," Syracuse, June 13, 1997.

"Pain Turned to Newness," appendix in *Preaching Jesus: New Directions for Homiletics in Hans Frei's Postliberal Theology*, Charles L. Campbell, 259–64. Grand Rapids, MI: Eerdmans, 1997.

"Planned People/Planned Book?" In *Writing and Reading the Scroll of Isaiah: Studies of an Interpretive Tradition*, vol. 1, edited by Craig C. Broyles and Craig A. Evans, 19–37. Leiden: Brill, 1997.

"Psalms and the Life of Faith: A Suggested Typology of Function." Reprinted in *The Poetical Books*, edited by David J. A. Clines, 35–66. Sheffield Reader. Sheffield, England: Sheffield Academic Press, 1997.

"A Response to 'Our Kind of Crowd.'" *Journal for Preachers* 20, no. 4 (Pentecost 1997): 25–26.

"Texts That Linger, Words That Explode." *Theology Today* 54 (1997): 180–99.

"Theodicy in a Social Dimension." Reprinted in *Social-Scientific Old Testament Criticism*, edited by David J. Chalcraft, 260–82. Sheffield, England: Sheffield Academic Press, 1997.

"Truth-Telling as Subversive Obedience." *Journal for Preachers* 20, no. 2 (Lent 1997): 2–3.

"Easter: Answer to Prayer." *Living Pulpit* 7, no. 1 (Jan.–March 1998): 37.

"Ecumenism as the Shared Practice of a Peculiar Identity." *Word and World* 18, no. 2 (Spring 1998): 122–35. Presented at the SBL consultation on character ethics and biblical interpretation in November 1996 with the title "The Scandal and Liberty of Particularity."

"'Exodus' in the Plural (Amos 9:7)." In *Many Voices, One God: Being Faithful in a Pluralistic World: In Honor of Shirley Guthrie*, edited by Walter Brueggemann and George W. Stroup, 15–34. Louisville, KY: Westminster John Knox Press, 1998.

"Faith with a Price." *Other Side* 34, no. 4 (July–Aug. 1998): 32–35.

"Foreword." *Journal for Preachers* 21, no. 3 (Easter 1998): 1–2.

"Foreword." *Journal for Preachers* 21, no. 4 (Pentecost 1998): 1–2.

Foreword to *Sing Justice! Do Justice! Alternatives for Simple Living*. Kingston, NY: Selah Publishing Co., Inc., 1998.

"Israel's Truth about Loss." *Living Pulpit* 7, no. 3 (July–Sept. 1998): 34–35.

"Life-or-Death, De-privileged Communication." *Journal for Preachers* 21, no. 4 (Pentecost 1998): 22–29.

"'Nourishing Spirit and Imagination': An Interview with Walter Brueggemann." *The Witness* 81, no. 4 (April 1998): 12–16.

"Preaching a Sub-Version." *Theology Today* 55 (1998): 195–212.

"Preaching to Exiles," "Cadences which Redescribe: Speech among Exiles," and "Duty as Delight and Desire: Preaching Obedience That Is Not Legalism." In *Exilic Preaching*, edited by Erskine Clarke, 9–61. Harrisburg, PA: Trinity Press International, 1998. Reprinted from *Journal for Preachers*.

"A Story of Loss and Hope." *Sojourners* 27, no. 6 (Nov–Dec. 1998): 44–48.

"Suffering Produces Hope." *Biblical Theology Bulletin* 28 (1998): 95–103.

"Theology of the Old Testament: A Prompt Retrospect." In *God in the Fray: A Tribute to Walter Brueggemann*, edited by Tod Linafelt and Timothy K. Beal, 307–20. Minneapolis: Fortress Press, 1998.

"Too Soon to Tell." *Prism* 13, no. 2 (Fall 1998): 58–64.

"The 'Baruch Connection': Reflections on Jeremiah 43.1–7." In *Troubling Jeremiah*, edited by A. R. Pete Diamond, Kathleen M. O'Connor, and Louis Stulman, 367–86. Journal for the Study of the Old Testament: Supplement Series 260. Sheffield, England: Sheffield Academic Press, 1999. Previously published as "The Baruch Connection." *Journal of Biblical Literature* 113 (1994): 405–20.

"The City: A Work in Progress." *The Bible Workbench* 6, no. 4 (April 11–May 30, 1999): 128–42.

"The City in Biblical Perspective: Failed and Possible." *Word and World* 19, no. 3 (Summer 1999): 236–50.

"Claus Westermann." In *Dictionary of Biblical Interpretation*, edited by John H. Hayes, 633–34. Nashville: Abingdon Press, 1999.

"Contemporary Old Testament Theology: A Contextual Prospectus." *Dialog* 38, no. 2 (Spring 1999): 108–16.

"Don't Let Government Abdicate Its Responsibilities." *Congregations*, no. 1 (Jan.–Feb. 1999): 15–16.

"Foreword." *Journal for Preachers* 22, no. 3 (Easter 1999): 1–2.

"Foreword." *Journal for Preachers* 22, no. 4 (Pentecost 1999): 1–2.

Foreword. In *The Old Testament and the Significance of Jesus: Embracing Change—Maintaining Christian Identity: The Emerging Center in Biblical Scholarship*, Fredrick C. Holmgren, ix–xii. Grand Rapids, MI: Eerdmans, 1999.

"Hope in the Face of Loss." *Other Side* 35, no. 2 (March–April 1999): 17-20, 49.

"The Hope of Heaven . . . on Earth." *Biblical Theology Bulletin* 29 (1999): 99–111.

"The Liturgy of Abundance, the Myth of Scarcity." *Christian Century* 116 (1999): 342–47.

"Ministry Among: The Power of Blessing." *Journal for Preachers* 22, no. 3 (Easter 1999): 21–29.

"Next Steps in Jeremiah Studies?" In *Troubling Jeremiah*, edited by A. R. Pete Diamond, Kathleen M. O'Connor, and Louis Stulman, 404–22. Journal for the Study of the Old Testament: Supplement Series 260. Sheffield, England: Sheffield Academic Press, 1999.

"The People of the Land"; "Collapse/Exile/Hope"; and "Wisdom, Order, Protest." In *A Theological Introduction to the Old Testament*, Bruce C. Birch, Walter Brueggemann, Terence E. Fretheim, and David L. Peterson, 175–213; 319–71; 373–415. Nashville: Abingdon Press, 1999.

"Preaching among Exiles." *Circuit Rider* 22, no. 4 (July–Aug. 1999): 22–24. Excerpted from *Cadences of Home*.

"The Psalms as Prayer." Reprinted in *Reformed Liturgy and Music* 33 (1999): 9–27.

Response to reviews of *Theology of the Old Testament* by Joel S. Kaminsky, Margaret S. Odell, and Rolf Rendtorff. *Review of Biblical Literature* (1999), http://www.bookreviews.org.

"The Role of Old Testament Theology in Old Testament Interpretation." In *In Search of True Wisdom: Essays in Old Testament Interpretation in Honour of Ronald E. Clements*, edited by Edward Ball, 70–88. Journal for the Study of the Old Testament: Supplement Series 300. Sheffield, England: Sheffield Academic Press, 1999.

"The Shrill Voice of the Wounded Party." *Horizons in Biblical Theology* 21 (1999): 1–25.

"Some Aspects of Theodicy in Old Testament Faith." *Perspectives in Religious Studies* 26 (1999): 253–68.

"Surprised beyond Ourselves." *United Church News* 15, no. 1 (Jan.–Feb. 1999): insert.

"Together in the Spirit, beyond Seductive Quarrels." *Theology Today* 56, no. 2 (July 1999): 152–63.

"Working on the Edge of Faith." Interview by Pauline Shelton. *Third Way* (Dec. 1999): 15.

"Always in the Shadow of the Empire." In *The Church as Counterculture*, edited by Michael L. Budde and Robert W. Brimlow, 39–58. Albany, NY: SUNY Press, 2000.

"Amos' Intercessory Formula." Reprinted in *Prophecy in the Hebrew Bible: Selected Studies from Vetus Testamentum*, compiled by David E. Orton, 41–55. Leiden: Brill, 2000.

"Ben Johnson after 19 Years." *Vantage* (Summer 2000): 3.

"Biblical Theology Appropriately Postmodern." In *Jews, Christians, and the Theology of the Hebrew Scriptures*, edited by Alice Ogden Bellis and Joel S. Kaminsky, 97–108. Atlanta: Society of Biblical Literature, 2000. Reprinted from *Biblical Theology Bulletin* 27 (1997): 4–9,

"Faith at the Nullpunkt." In *The End of the World and the Ends of God*, edited by John Polkinghorne and Michael Welker, 143–54. Theology for the Twenty-first Century. Harrisburg, PA: Trinity Press International, 2000.

"A First Retrospect on the Consultation." In *Renewing Biblical Interpretation*, edited by Craig Bartholomew, Colin Greene, and Karl Möller, 342–47. Scripture and Hermeneutics Series, vol. 1. Chester, UK: Paternoster Press, and Grand Rapids, MI: Zondervan, 2000.

"A Fissure Always Uncontained." In *Strange Fire: Reading the Bible after the Holocaust*, edited by Tod Linafelt, 62–75. The Biblical Seminar 71. Sheffield, England: Sheffield Academic Press, 2000.

"Foreword." *Journal for Preachers* 23, no. 3 (Easter 2000): 1–2.

"Foreword." *Journal for Preachers* 23, no. 4 (Pentecost 2000): 1–2.

"Foreword." *Journal for Preachers* 24, no. 1 (Advent 2000): 1–2.

Foreword. In *The Molten Soul: Dangers and Opportunities in Religious Conversation*, by Gray Temple, viii–x. New York: Church Publishing Inc., 2000.

Foreword. In *The Word on the Street*, Stanley P. Saunders and Charles L. Campbell, x–xvi. Grand Rapids, MI: Eerdmans, 2000.

"An Imaginative 'Or.'" *Journal for Preachers* 23, no. 3 (Easter 2000): 3–17.

"Journey: Attending to the Abyss." Bible Society, *TransMission* (Spring 2000): 6–8.

"Jubilee." *Apostle* 85, no. 3 (March 2000): 6.

"Psalms and Wrestling." *Lutheran Woman Today* 13, no. 2 (March 2000): 5–8.

"Psalms of Seduction." *Other Side* 36, no. 1 (Jan.–Feb. 2000): 10–15.

"The Public Practice of Faith." *APCE Advocate* 24, no. 4 (2000): 8, 12.

"A Response to Professor Childs." *Scottish Journal of Theology* 53, no. 2 (2000): 234–38.

"Social Criticism in the Old Testament." *First Evangelical Church Association Bulletin* 10 (Dec. 2000): 27–29.

"Texts That Linger, Not Yet Overcome." In *Shall Not the Judge of All the Earth Do What Is Right? Studies on the Nature of God in Tribute to James L. Crenshaw*, edited by David Penchansky and Paul L. Redditt, 21–41. Winona Lake, IN: Eisenbrauns, 2000.

"Twentieth-Century Old Testament Studies: A Quick Survey." *Word and World* 20, no. 1 (Winter 2000): 61–71.

"Vision for a New Church and a New Century; Part I: Homework against Scarcity." *Union Seminary Quarterly Review* 54, no. 1–2 (2000): 21–39.

"Vision for a New Church and a New Century; Part II: Holiness Become Generosity." *Union Seminary Quarterly Review* 54, no. 1–2 (2000): 45–64.

"The Bible as Scripture Canon Fire." *Christian Century* 118 (2001): 22–26.

"Biblical Authority: A Personal Reflection." *Christian Century* 118 (2001): 14–20.

"A Brief Moment for a One-Person Remnant (2 Kings 5:2–3)." *Biblical Theology Bulletin* 31, no. 2 (Summer 2001): 53–59.

"A Christian Counterpoint." *Tikkun* 16, no. 3 (May–June 2001): 73.

"Comments on the Prayer of Jabez." *Religion and Ethics Newsweekly.* Nov. 2, 2001. http://www .pbs.org/wnet/religionandethics/week509/wbrueggemann.html.

"Communities of Hope midst Engines for Despair." In *Hope for the World*, edited by Walter Brueggemann, 151–58. Louisville, KY: Westminster John Knox Press, 2001.

"A Defining Utterance on the Lips of the Tishbite: Pondering 'The Centrality of the Word.'" In *In Essentials Unity: Reflections on the Nature and Purpose of the Church: In Honor of Frederick R. Trost*, edited by M. Douglas Meeks and Robert D. Mutton, 141–50. Minneapolis: Kirk House Publishers, 2001.

"Dialogue between Incommensurate Partners: Prospects for Common Testimony." *Journal of Ecumenical Studies* 38, no. 4 (Fall 2001): 383–98.

"An Ending That Does Not End: The Book of Jeremiah." In *Postmodern Interpretations of the Bible—A Reader*, edited by A. K. M. Adam, 117–28. St. Louis: Chalice Press, 2001.

"Enough Is Enough." *Other Side* 37, no. 6 (Nov.–Dec. 2001): 10–13.

Epilogue. *The Bible on Suffering: Social and Political Implications*, edited by Anthony J. Tambasco, 211–15. Mahwah, NJ: Paulist Press, 2001.

"Foreword." *Journal for Preachers* 24, no. 3 (Easter 2001): 1–2.

"Foreword." *Journal for Preachers* 24, no. 4 (Pentecost 2001): 1–2.

"The Friday Voice of Faith." *Calvin Theological Journal* 36 (2001): 12–21. Revision of lecture delivered at Calvin Theological Seminary, Grand Rapids, MI, April 22, 1993. Appeared in *Reformed Worship* 30 (Dec. 1993): 3–5.

"Gospeling beyond Our Preferred Agendas." *Church and Society* 92, no. 2 (Nov.–Dec. 2001): 7–13.

"(I)chabod Departed." *Princeton Seminary Bulletin* 22, no. 2 (2001): 115–33.

Introduction. *Old Testament Theology*, vol. I, Gerhard von Rad, ix–xxxi. Louisville, KY: Westminster John Knox Press, 2001.

"Law as Response to Thou." In *Taking Responsibility: Comparative Perspectives*, edited by Winston Davis, 87–105. Charlottesville: University of Virginia Press, 2001.

"Living with a Different Set of Signals." *Living Pulpit* 10, no. 2 (April–June 2001): 20–21.

"The Matrix of Groan." *Journal for Preachers* 24, no. 3 (Easter 2001): 41–47.

"Mission as Hope in Action." *Journal for Preachers* 24, no. 2 (Lent 2001): 17–23.

"Missional Questions in a Fresh Context." In *Hope for the World*, edited by Walter Brueggemann, 3–12. Louisville, KY: Westminster John Knox Press, 2001.

"Off by Nine Miles." *Christian Century* 118 (2001): 15.

"Options for Creatureliness: Consumer or Citizen." *Horizons in Biblical Theology* 23 (2001): 25–50.

"The Permanence of Power and Thin Traces of Truth." The Houchen Lecture, Hamilton, New Zealand, 2001.

"The Practice of Homefulness." *Church and Society* 91, no. 5 (May–June 2001): 10–16.

"Preaching among Exiles." *Talk* 1, no. 1 (Summer 2001): 10–11. Excerpted from *Cadences of Home*. Appeared in *Circuit Rider* 22, no. 4 (July–Aug. 1999): 22–24.

"Prerequisites for Genuine Obedience: Theses and Conclusions." *Calvin Theological Journal* 36 (2001): 34–41.

"Rescripting for a Fresh Performance midst a Failed Script." *Reformed Review* 55, no. 1 (Autumn 2001): 5–17.

"The Stunning Outcome of a One-Person Search Committee." *Journal for Preachers* 25, no. 1 (Advent 2001): 36–40.
"Symmetry and Extremity in the Images of YHWH." In *The Blackwell Companion to the Hebrew Bible*, edited by Leo G. Perdue, 241–57. Malden, MA: Blackwell Publishers Inc., 2001.
"The Totalizing Context of Production and Consumption." In *Hope for the World*, edited by Walter Brueggemann, 55–56. Louisville, KY: Westminster John Knox Press, 2001.
"Truth-Telling Comfort." *Journal for Preachers* 25, no. 1 (Advent 2001): 46–48.
"Unmasking the Inevitable." *Other Side* 37, no. 4 (July–Aug. 2001): 20–24.
"Voice as Counter to Violence." *Calvin Theological Journal* 36 (2001): 22–33. Lecture delivered at Calvin Theological Seminary, Grand Rapids, MI, April 22, 1993.
"The ABC's of Old Testament Theology in the US." *Zeitschrift für die alttestamentlich Wissenschaft* 114 (2002): 412–32.
"A Biblical Perspective on Living Wage." *Witness* 85, no. 5 (May 2002): 18–20.
"The Creator, the Creation, and 'Us.'" Booklet insert to *Presbyterian Church (U.S.A.) 2003 Mission Yearbook* (Nov. 2002): 1–13.
"Ecumenism as the Shared Practice of a Peculiar Identity." In *Character and Scripture: Moral Formation, Community, and Biblical Interpretation*, edited by William P. Brown, 231–47. Grand Rapids, MI: Eerdmans, 2002. (The essay is reprinted [with slight editing] with permission from *Word and World* 18, no. 2 [Spring 1998]: 122–35. Its original form was presented at the SBL consultation on character ethics and biblical interpretation in November 1996 with the title "The Scandal and Liberty of Particularity.")
"The Endless Task of Interpretation." Mercer Law Review (in conjunction with Mercer University Commons and the Lilly Endowment), *A Symposium: The Theology of the Practice of Law* 53, no. 3 (Spring 2002): 1019–34.
"Exegesis: Jeremiah 31:7–14." *Lectionary Homiletics* 13, no. 2 (Jan. 2002): 1–2.
"Favorite Poems." *Christian Century* 119 (2002): 10.
"Foreword." *Journal for Preachers* 25, no. 2 (Lent 2002): 1–2.
"A Fourth-Generation Sell-Out." *Preaching Great Texts: The Unlectionary Journal* 1, no. 2 (Jan.–Feb.–March 2002): 2–4.
"Lament as Antidote to Silence." *Living Pulpit* 11, no. 4 (Oct.–Dec. 2002): 24–25.
"Meditation upon the Abyss: The Book of Jeremiah." *Word and World* 22 (2002): 340–50.
"Prophetic Energizing." In *The Company of Preachers: Wisdom on Preaching*, edited by Richard Lischer, 156–66. Grand Rapids, MI: Eerdmans, 2002. Excerpted from *The Prophetic Imagination*.
"Reading from the Day 'In Between.'" In *A Shadow of Glory: Reading the New Testament after the Holocaust*, edited by Tod Linafelt, 105–16. New York: Routledge, 2002.
"Sabbath as Active Faith." *Journeyers* 1 (2002): 1–3.
"Secretary of Woe." *Sojourners* 31, no. 4 (July–Aug. 2002): 30–33.
"The Tearing of the Curtain (Matt. 27:51)." In *Faithful Witness: A Festschrift Honoring Ronald Goetz*, edited by Michael J. Bell, H. Scott Matheney, and Dean Peerman, 77–83. Elmhurst, IL: Elmhurst College, 2002.
"A Text That Redescribes." *Theology Today* 58 (2002): 526–40.
"That the World May Be Redescribed." *Interpretation* 56 (2002): 359–67.
"Truth-Telling Comfort." Reprinted in *Strike Terror No More: Theology, Ethics, and the New War*, edited by Jon L. Berquist, 138–41. St. Louis: Chalice Press, 2002.

"A Voice beyond Our Own." *Cry* 8, no. 2 (Summer 2002): 14–15.

"The Voices behind the Text." *Christian Century* 119 (2002): 18–19.

"Ancient Utterance and Contemporary Hearing." In *Just Preaching: Prophetic Voices for Economic Justice*, edited by André Resner Jr., 67–75. St. Louis: Chalice Press, 2003.

"Foreword." *Journal for Preachers* 26, no. 3 (Easter 2003): 1–2.

"Foreword." *Journal for Preachers* 26, no. 4 (Pentecost 2003): 1–3.

"Four Proclamatory Confrontations in Scribal Refraction." *Scottish Journal of Theology* 56, no. 4 (2003): 404–26.

"Inventing the Poor." *Christian Century* 120 (2003): 30–31.

"Necessary Conditions of a Good Loud Lament." *Horizons in Biblical Theology* 25, no. 1 (June 2003): 19–49.

"The Need for Neighbor." *Other Side* 39, no. 4 (July–Aug. 2003): 32–36.

"On Scroll-Making in Ancient Jerusalem." *Biblical Theology Bulletin* 33, no. 1 (Spring 2003): 5–11.

"Patriotism for Citizens of the Penultimate Superpower." *Dialog* 42, no. 4 (Winter 2003): 336–43.

"Prayers for a New Day." *Christian Century* 120 (2003): 20–22.

"*Theme* Revisited: Bread Again!" In *Reading from Right to Left: Essays on the Hebrew Bible in Honour of David J. A. Clines*, edited by J. Cheryl Exum and H. G. M. Williamson, 76–89. London: Sheffield Academic Press Ltd., 2003.

"The Travail of Pardon: Reflections on *slh*." In *A God So Near: Essays on Old Testament Theology in Honor of Patrick D. Miller*, edited by Brent A. Strawn and Nancy R. Bowen, 283–97. Winona Lake, IN: Eisenbrauns, 2003.

"'Until' . . . Endlessly Enacted, Now Urgent." *Journal for Preachers* 27, no. 1 (Advent 2003): 16–21.

"Using God's Resources Wisely: A Commentary on Isaiah 65:17–25." *Earth Letter* (Nov. 2003): 6–7, 10. Excerpted from *Using God's Resources Wisely: Isaiah and Urban Possibility*. Louisville, KY: Westminster/John Knox Press, 1993.

"The 'Us' of Psalm 67." In *Palabra, Prodigio, Poesía: in Memoriam P. Luis Alonso Schökel, S.J.*, edited by Vincente Collado Bertomeu, 233–42. Rome: Editrice Pontificio Istituto Biblico, 2003.

"We Are Takers"; "Their Plowshares Are Beat into Swords"; "We Notice Your Giving." First published in *Awed to Heaven, Rooted in Earth: Prayers of Walter Brueggemann*, edited by Edwin Searcy, 33, 113, 142. Minneapolis: Fortress Press, 2003; reprinted in *Living God's Justice: Reflections and Prayers Compiled by The Roundtable Association of Diocesan Social Action Directors*, 84, 105, 136. Cincinnati: St. Anthony Messenger Press, 2006.

"Wise Beginnings, Surprising Endings." *Books and Culture* 9, no. 6 (Nov.–Dec. 2003): 32–33.

"At the Mercy of Babylon: A Subversive Rereading of the Empire." Reprinted in *Reading the Book of Jeremiah: A Search for Coherence*, edited by Martin Kessler, 117–34. Winona Lake, IN: Eisenbrauns, 2004.

"Breaking the Cycle of Enmity: A Case Study." *Living Pulpit* 13, no. 1 (Jan.–March 2004): 10–12.

"The Creatures Know!" In *The Wisdom of Creation*, edited by Edward Foley and Robert Schreiter, 1–12. Collegeville, MN: Liturgical Press, 2004.

"Environment as Creation." *Books and Culture* 10, no. 1 (Jan.–Feb. 2004): 42.

"Evangelism and Discipleship: The God Who Calls, the God Who Sends." *Word and World* 24, no. 2 (Spring 2004): 121–35.

Foreword to "A Psalm of Praise and Pleading on the Eve of War or The Last Enemy Is Death." *Journal for Preachers* 27, no. 2 (Lent 2004): 51–52.

"Foreword." *Journal for Preachers* 27, no. 3 (Easter 2004): 1–2.

"Foreword." *Journal for Preachers* 27, no. 4 (Pentecost 2004): 1–3.

"Healing and Its Opponents." In *I Am the Lord Who Heals You: Reflections on Healing, Wholeness, and Restoration*, edited by G. Scott Morris, MD, 1–6. Nashville: Abingdon Press, 2004.

"The Non-Negotiable Price of Sanity." *Journal for Preachers* 28, no. 1 (Advent 2004): 28–36.

"Noted Texts: Choosing a Study Bible." *Christian Century* 121 (2004): 36–41.

"Prayer at the Death of Gregory Peck." *Theology Today* 61 (2004): 82–83.

Preface. *Reading the Book of Jeremiah: A Search for Coherence*, edited by Martin Kessler, ix–x. Winona Lake, IN: Eisenbrauns, 2004.

"Psalms as 'Mother Tongue.'" *Benedictine Bridge* 15 (Ordinary Time 2004): 6–8.

"Scripture: Old Testament." In *The Blackwell Companion to Political Theology*, edited by Peter Scott and William T. Cavanaugh, 7–20. Oxford: Blackwell Publishing Ltd., 2004.

"Take and Read: Old Testament." *Christian Century* 121 (2004): 31.

"As the Editor Retires . . . ." *Theology Today* 61, no. 4 (Jan. 2005): 438–42.

"Authority in the Church (Part I)." In *On the Way: The Teaching Church*, edited by Frederick R. Trost, 11–17. Minneapolis: Kirk House Publishers, 2005.

"Authority in the Church (Part II)." In *On the Way: The Teaching Church*, edited by Frederick R. Trost, 18–23. Minneapolis: Kirk House Publishers, 2005.

"Authority of the Pastoral Office." In *On the Way: The Teaching Church*, edited by Frederick R. Trost, 24–27. Minneapolis: Kirk House Publishers, 2005.

"The Chance for a Sub-Version." In *Awakened to a Calling: Reflections on the Vocation of Ministry*, edited by Ann M. Svennungsen and Melissa Wiginton, 65–72. Nashville: Abingdon Press, 2005.

"Concluding Reflections." In *Shaking Heaven and Earth: Essays in Honor of Walter Brueggemann and Charles B. Cousar*, edited by Christine Roy Yoder, 157–63. Louisville, KY: Westminster John Knox Press, 2005.

"Counterscript: Living with the Elusive God." *Christian Century* 122, no. 24 (2005): 22–28.

"A Disaster of 'Biblical' Proportions" *Christian Century* 122, no. 20 (2005): 23.

"Foreword." *Journal for Preachers* 28, no. 3 (Easter 2005): 1–2.

"Foreword." *Journal for Preachers* 28, no. 4 (Pentecost 2005): 1–2.

"Holy Intrusion: The Power of Dreams in the Bible." *Christian Century* 122 (2005): 28–31.

"Isaiah: Critical Notes." In *The Renovaré Spiritual Formation Bible: New Revised Standard Version*, edited by Richard J. Foster, 981–1078. San Francisco: HarperSanFrancisco, 2005.

"A Myriad of 'Truth and Reconciliation' Commissions." *Journal for Preachers* 28, no. 2 (Lent 2005): 3–9.

"Off by Nine Miles." Reprinted in *Living by the Word: Meditations from* The Christian Century, edited by Debra Bendis and David Heim, 16–18. St. Louis: Chalice Press, 2005.

"The Psalms as Limit Expressions." In *Performing the Psalms*, edited by Dave Bland and David Fleer, 31–50. St. Louis: Chalice Press, 2005.

"Psalms in Narrative Performance." In *Performing the Psalms*, edited by Dave Bland and David Fleer, 9–29. St. Louis: Chalice Press, 2005.

"The Re-emergence of Scripture: Post-liberalism." In *The Bible in Pastoral Practice: Readings in the Place and Function of Scripture in the Church*, edited by Paul H. Ballard and Stephen R. Holmes, 153–73. London: Darton, Longman and Todd Ltd., 2005.

"Sabbath: A Bold Alternative in Today's Society." *Liguorian* (July–Aug. 2005): 8–12.

"Take and Read: Hebrew Bible/Old Testament." *Christian Century* 122 (2005): 25–27.

"The Trusting Path from Certitude to Fidelity." *Insights* 121, no. 1 (Fall 2005): 19–23.

2006–2011

"A Culture of Life and the Politics of Death." *Journal for Preachers* 29, no. 2 (Lent 2006): 16–21.

"Foreword." *Journal for Preachers* 29, no. 3 (Pentecost 2006): 1–2.

"Foreword." *Journal for Preachers* 29, no. 4 (Easter 2006): 1–2.

"From Windows Overlooking the Street." *Journal for Preachers* 29, no. 3 (Easter 2006): 55–56.

"An Indispensable Upstream Word: The Gift of Prophecy." *Reflections* 93, no. 1 (2006): 46–49.

"Message of Inclusion Not Just 'Disputed'—It's 'Urgent.'" *United Church News* (Dec.–Jan. 2006): A7.

"Old Testament Theology." In *The Oxford Handbook of Biblical Studies*, edited by J. W. Rogerson and Judith M. Lieu, 675–97. Oxford: Oxford University Press, 2006.

Panel Review of Rolf Rendtorf's *The Canonical Hebrew Bible: A Theology of the Old Testament.* In *Horizons in Biblical Theology* 28 (2006): 11–17.

"The Summons to New Life: A Reflection." In *Repentance in Christian Theology*, ed. by Mark J. Boda and Gordon T. Smith, 347–69. Collegeville, PA: Liturgical Press, 2006.

"Take and Read: Old Testament." *Christian Century* 123 (2006): 24.

"Advent: Departure and Homecoming." *Journal for Preachers* 31, no. 1 (Advent 2007): 11–19.

"Alien Witness: How God's People Challenge Empire." *Christian Century* 124 (2007): 28–32.

"Ancient Israel on Political Leadership: Between the Book Ends." *Political Theology* 8, no. 4 (Oct. 2007): 455–69.

"Can We Hope? Can Hope Be Divided?" In *Contesting Texts: Jews and Christians in Conversation about the Bible*, edited by Melody D. Knowles, Esther Menn, John Pawlikowksi, OSM, and Timothy J. Sandoval, 139–63. Minneapolis: Fortress Press, 2007.

"The Church's Practice of Memory." *Vantage: History Matters* (Summer 2007): 5.

"Dialogic Thickness in a Monologic Culture." *Theology Today* 64 (2007): 322–39.

"Foreword." *Journal for Preachers* 30, no. 3 (Easter 2007): 1–2.

"Foreword." *Journal for Preachers* 30, no. 4 (Pentecost 2007): 1–2.

Foreword to *Character Ethics and the Old Testament: Moral Dimensions of Scripture*, edited by M. Daniel Carroll R. and Jacqueline E. Lapsley, vii–xi. Louisville, KY: Westminster John Knox Press, 2007.

"Life-Giving Speech amid an Empire of Silence." *Michigan Law Review* 105, no. 6 (April 2007): 1115–32.

"Psalms as Subversive Practice of Dialogue." In *Diachronic and Synchronic: Reading the Psalms in Real Time: Proceedings of the Baylor Symposium on the Book of Psalms*, edited by Joel S. Burnett, W. H. Bellinger Jr., and W. Dennis Tucker Jr., 3–25. New York: T. & T. Clark, 2007.

"Response to *How Are the Mighty Fallen?*" *Horizons in Biblical Theology* 29 (2007): 17–28.

"A Response to Rickie Moore's 'The Prophet as Mentor.'" *Journal of Pentecostal Theology* 15, no. 2 (April 2007): 173–75.

"Sabbath as Resistance." The Thoughtful Christian, August 1, 2007, http:// www.The ThoughtfulChristian.com.

"2 Kings 5: Two Evangelists and a Saved Subject." *Missiology: An International Review* 35 (2007): 263–72.

"To Whom Does the Land Belong?" *Journal for Preachers* 30, no. 3 (Easter 2007): 28–35.

"What Would Jesus Buy?" *Sojourners* 36, no. 10 (Nov. 2007): 8–15.

"Against Cheap Labor: Prayers of Protest and Solidarity." In *Prayers for the New Social Awakening*, edited by Christian Iosso and Elizabeth Hinson-Hasty, 31–32. Louisville, KY: Westminster John Knox Press, 2008.

"Erskine: A Most Careful Listener." *Vantage* 100, no. 1 (Fall 2008): 20–22.

"Evangelism and Discipleship: The God Who Calls, the God Who Sends." Reprinted in *The Study of Evangelism: Exploring a Missional Practice of the Church*, edited by Paul W. Chilcote and Laceye C. Warner, 219–34. Grand Rapids, MI: Eerdmans, 2008.

"Faith in the Empire." In *In the Shadow of Empire: Reclaiming the Bible as a History of Faithful Resistance*, edited by Richard A. Horsley, 25–40. Louisville, KY: Westminster John Knox Press, 2008.

"Foreword." *Journal for Preachers* 31, no. 3 (Easter 2008): 1–2.

"Foreword." *Journal for Preachers* 31, no. 4 (Pentecost 2008): 1–2.

"Lament as Wake-Up Call: Class Analysis and Historical Possibility." In *Lamentations in Ancient and Contemporary Cultural Contexts*, edited by Nancy C. Lee and Carleen Mandolfo, 221–36. Symposium Series 43. Atlanta: Society of Biblical Literature, 2008.

"Prophetic Ministry in the National Security State." *Theology Today* 65 (2008): 285–311.

"The Recovering God of Hosea." *Horizons in Biblical Theology* 30 (2008): 5–20.

"Stereotype and Nuance: The Dynasty of Jehu." *Catholic Biblical Quarterly* 70 (2008): 16–28.

"A Truth-Teller for Dangerous Times." *Reflections: Between Babel and Beatitude: The Bible in the 21st Century* (Spring 2008): 49–51.

"Vulnerable Children, Divine Passion, and Human Obligation." In *The Child in the Bible*, edited by Marcia I. Bunge, Terence E. Fretheim, and Beverly Roberts Gaventa, 399–422. Grand Rapids, MI: Eerdmans, 2008.

"When We Grow Our Own." *This Point* 3, no. 2 (Fall 2008), http://www.atthispoint.net/ professional-responses/when-we-grow-our-own/190/.

"Wrath and Reason: Part 1." *Reform* (July 2008): 20-21, www.urc.org.uk.

"Antidote to Amnesia." In *Reclaiming the Imagination: The Exodus as Paradigmatic Narrative for Preaching*, edited by David Fleer and Dave Bland, 7–25. St. Louis: Chalice Press, 2009.

"The Colleague with Abiding Tenure: Tribute to Lee Carroll." *Vantage* 101, no. 1 (Fall 2009): 16–17.

"Come to the Water—Isaiah 55: God Summons Us This Lent to a Recovered Identity." *Celebration* 38, no. 3 (March 2009): 3–4.

"Continuing the Conversation Sermon: Gnats to You!" In *Reclaiming the Imagination: The Exodus as Paradigmatic Narrative for Preaching*, edited by David Fleer and Dave Bland, 33-40. St. Louis: Chalice Press, 2009.

"Die Liturgie der Fuelle—der Mythos des Mangels," in *Wir haben Genug: Neu von der Fuelle sprechen lernen*, edited by Claudia Jahnel, 5-11. Evangelisch-Lutherischen Kircke

Bayern (Rothenberg: Schneider-Druck GmbH, 2009). Appeared as "The Liturgy of Abundance, the Myth of Scarcity." *Christian Century* 116 (1999): 342–47.

"Elisha as the Original Pentecost Guy." *Journal for Preachers* 32, no. 4 (Pentecost 2009): 41–47.

"Empire Books." *Christian Century* 126 (2009): 48–50.

"Foreword." *Journal for Preachers* 32, no. 3 (Easter 2009): 1–2.

"Foreword." *Journal for Preachers* 32, no. 4 (Pentecost 2009): 1–2.

Foreword. In *Encounters at the Counter: What Congregations Can Learn about Hospitality from Business*, Alan Johnson, vii–x. Cleveland: Pilgrim Press, 2009.

Foreword. In *Fatal Embrace: Christians, Jews, and the Search for Peace in the Holy Land*, Mark Braverman, xiii–xx. Austin, TX: Synergy Books, 2009.

Foreword. In *Psalms for Preaching and Worship: A Lectionary Commentary*, edited By Roger E. Van Harn and Brent A. Strawn, xv–xvii. Grand Rapids, MI: Eerdmans, 2009.

"From Anxiety and Greed to Milk and Honey." *Sojourners* 8, no. 2 (Feb. 2009): 20–24.

"From Biblical Narrative to Economic Policy." *National Catholic Reporter* (August 21, 2009): 1, 22–24.

"Getting Ready for the Unexpected." *Sojourners* 38, no. 11 (Dec. 2009): 56–57.

"The God with the Personal Name." *Reform* (Jan. 2009): 14–16.

"Lee Roy Martin, the Unheard Voice of God: A Pentecostal Hearing of the Book of Judges." *Journal of Pentecostal Theology* 18 (2009): 15–19.

"Psychological Criticism: Exploring the Self in the Text." In *Method Matters: Essays on the Interpretation of the Hebrew Bible in Honor of David L. Petersen*, edited by Joel M. LeMon and Kent Harold Richards, 213–32. Atlanta: Society of Biblical Literature, 2009.

"Recovery from the Long Nightmare of Amnesia." In *The Bible and the American Future*, edited by Robert Jewett, 1–21. Eugene, OR: Cascade Books, 2009.

"The Answering God." *Sojourners* 39, no. 2 (Feb. 2010): 48–49.

"A Cast of Emancipated Characters." *Sojourners* 39, no. 6 (June 2010): 48–49.

"The Bible, the Recession, and Our Neighbor." *Health Progress* 91, no. 1 (Jan.–Feb. 2010): 49–52.

"Come, Rejoice with Me." *Sojourners* 39, no. 9 (Sept.–Oct. 2010): 48–49.

"Departure, but Not Yet Arrival: Performance in Exodus 15:22–26." *Journal of Scriptural Reasoning* 9, no. 1 (Dec. 2010): 1–8.

"Easter in the Very Belly of Nothingness." *Journal for Preachers* 33, no. 3 (Easter 2010): 42–43.

"Epilogue: On Fathers Filled with Sadness and Joy." In *Letters to Peter: On the Journey from Grief to Wholeness*, Donald E. Mayer, 165–73. Eugene, OR: Cascade Books, 2010.

"Foreword." *Journal for Preachers* 33, no. 3 (Easter 2010): 1.

"Foreword." *Journal for Preachers* 33, no. 4 (Pentecost 2010): 1–2.

Foreword. In *Believing Aloud: Reflections on Being Religious in the Public Square*, by Mark Douglas, vii–x. Eugene, OR: Wipf and Stock, 2010.

Foreword. In *Connecting to the Gospel: Texts, Sermons, Commentaries*, James Boyd White, ix–xii. Eugene, OR: Wipf and Stock, 2010.

Foreword. In *Equipping the Saints: Best Practices on Contextual Theological Education*, edited by David O. Jenkins and P. Alice Rogers, xi–xiv. Cleveland: Pilgrim Press, 2010.

Foreword. In *Grounded in the Living Word: The Old Testament and Pastoral Care Practices*, Denise Dombkowski Hopkins and Michael S. Koppel, ix–x. Grand Rapids, MI: Eerdmans, 2010.

"God Delivers and Protects." *Presbyterian Outlook* 192, no. 22 (Nov. 1, 2010): 31.

"God Is All-Knowing." *Presbyterian Outlook* 192, no. 23 (Nov. 15, 2010): 30.
"God Is Forever." *Presbyterian Outlook* 192, no. 22 (Nov. 1, 2010): 30.
"God Is in Charge." *Presbyterian Outlook* 192, no. 20 (Oct. 4, 2010): 27.
"God Provides Safety." *Presbyterian Outlook* 192, no. 20 (Oct. 4, 2010): 26.
"God Promises an Awesome Thing." *Presbyterian Outlook* 192, no. 18 (Sept. 6, 2010): 27.
"God's Law as a Covenantal Agreement." *Presbyterian Outlook* 192, no. 17 (Aug. 23, 2010): 27.
"God's Law Sustains." *Presbyterian Outlook* 192, no. 19 (Sept. 20, 2010): 43.
"God's Majesty and Human Dignity." *Presbyterian Outlook* 192, no. 19 (Sept. 20, 2010): 42.
"God's Presence Comforts and Assures." *Presbyterian Outlook* 192, no. 21 (Oct. 18, 2010): 42.
"God's Reign Cracks into Our World." *Sojourners* 39, no. 10 (Nov. 2010): 48–49.
"God's Revelation to Moses." *Presbyterian Outlook* 192, no. 17 (Aug. 23, 2010): 26.
"God versus 'gods.'" *Presbyterian Outlook* 192, no. 18 (Sept. 6, 2010): 26.
"Have You Heard the Good News?" *Sojourners* 39, no. 11 (Dec. 2010): 48–49.
"Heir and Land: The Royal 'Envelope' of the Books of Kings." In *The Fate of King David: The Past and Present of a Biblical Icon*, edited by Tod Linafelt, Claudia V. Camp, and Timothy Beal, 85–100. New York: T. & T. Clark, 2010.
"The Highway for Our God." *Presbyterian Outlook* 192, no. 23 (Nov. 15, 2010): 31.
"I Am Your God." *Presbyterian Outlook* 192, no. 24 (Nov. 29, 2010): 26.
"I Am Your Redeemer." *Presbyterian Outlook* 192, no. 25 (Dec. 13, 2010): 27.
"I Will Be with You." *Presbyterian Outlook* 192, no. 25 (Dec. 13, 2010): 26.
"Lent Is 'Come to Jesus' Time." *Sojourners* 39, no. 3 (March 2010): 48.
"The 'Low Holy Days' of Summer." *Sojourners* 39, no. 8 (August 2010): 48–49.
"Marked by Ashes." Reprinted from *Awed to Heaven*. *Journal of Preachers* 33, no. 2 (Lent 2010): 42.
"The Mission of the Servant." *Presbyterian Outlook* 192, no. 24 (Nov. 29, 2010): 27.
"The Power of Suffering Love." *Sojourners* 39, no. 4 (April 2010): 48–49.
"The Psalms and the Life of Faith: A Suggested Typology of Function." Reprinted in *Soundings in the Theology of the Psalms: Perspectives and Methods in Contemporary Scholarship*, edited by Rolf A. Jacobson, 1–25. Minneapolis: Fortress Press, 2011.
"Psalms, Book of." In *The Cambridge Dictionary of Christianity*, edited by Daniel Patte, 1031. New York: Cambridge University Press, 2010.
"Reassurance for God's People." *Presbyterian Outlook* 192, no. 26 (Dec. 27, 2010): 27.
"Refusing the Deathly World of Anxiety." *Sojourners* 39, no. 5 (May 2010): 48–49.
"A Season of Generosity and Gratitude." *Sojourners* 39, no. 7 (July 2010): 48–49.
"Sometimes Wave, Sometimes Particle." *Currents in Biblical Research* 8 (June 2010): 376–85.
"Turn to Me and Be Saved." *Presbyterian Outlook* 192, no. 26 (Dec. 27, 2010): 26.
"Walk Humbly with Your God." *Journal for Preachers* 33, no. 4 (Pentecost 2010): 14–19.
"Wholly Dependable." *Presbyterian Outlook* 192, no. 21 (Oct. 18, 2010): 43.
"Wondrous, Inexplicable, Demanding Newness." *Sojourners* 39, no. 1 (Jan. 2010): 48–49.
"Worship in Ancient Israel." In *The Cambridge Dictionary of Christianity*, edited by Daniel Patte, 1334–35. New York: Cambridge University Press, 2010.
"Healed by His Bruises." *Presbyterian Outlook* 193, no. 1 (January 10, 2011): 27.
"On Relinquishing and Receiving: A Christian Approach to Tikkun Olam." *Tikkun* (Winter 2011): 34.
"The Servant's Mission in the World." *Presbyterian Outlook* 193, no. 1 (Jan. 10, 2011): 26.
"Walking in the Light." *Sojourners* 40, no. 1 (Jan. 2011): 48–49.

Book Reviews

1961–1975

Servants of the Word: The Prophets of Israel by James D. Smart. *Union Seminary Quarterly Review* 16, no. 4 (1961): 408–10.

Ancient Israel: Its Life and Institutions by Roland de Vaux. *Theology and Life* 5, no. 3 (1962): 248–49.

The Old Testament: Its Formation and Development by Artur Weiser. *Theology and Life* 5, no. 2 (1962): 171–72.

Treaty of the Great King: The Covenant Structure of Deuteronomy: Studies and Commentary by Meredith G. Kline. *Theology and Life* 7, no. 3 (Fall 1964): 247–48.

History Sacred and Profane by Alan Richardson. *Theology and Life* 8, no. 1 (1965): 77–79.

Job by Marvin H. Pope. *Theology and Life* 8, no. 2 (1965): 158–59.

Psalms I, 1–50 by Mitchell Joseph Dahood. *Theology and Life* 9, no. 2 (1966): 176–77.

Israel's Sacred Songs: A Study of Dominant Themes by Harvey H. Guthrie. *Interpretation* 21, no. 2 (1967): 217–19.

Amos and Isaiah: Prophets of the Word of God by James M. Ward. *Religion in Life* 39, no. 1 (1969): 145–46.

A Guide to the Prophets by Stephen F. Winward. *Journal of Biblical Literature* 88, no. 4 (1969): 501.

Isaiah 40–66 by Claus Westermann. *Religion in Life* 39, no. 1 (1969): 141–42.

Weisheit in Israel by Gerhard von Rad. *Interpretation* 25, no. 3 (1971): 347–49.

Poets, Prophets, and Sages: Essays in Biblical Interpretation by Robert Gordis. *Journal of Biblical Literature* 91, no. 2 (1972): 258–60.

Studies in Israelite Poetry and Wisdom by Patrick William Skehan. *Journal of Biblical Literature* 91, no. 2 (1972): 258–60.

The Politics of God and the Politics of Man by Jacques Ellul. *Journal of Biblical Literature* 92, no. 3 (1973): 470–71.

The Serpent Was Wiser: A New Look at Genesis 1–11 by Richard S. Hanson. *Journal of Biblical Literature* 92, no. 3 (1973): 470–71.

Idea of Purity in Ancient Judaism: With a Critique and a Commentary by Mary Douglas by Jacob Neusner. *Review of Books and Religion* 4, no. 2 (1974): 11.

Old Testament Covenant: A Survey of Current Opinions by Dennis J. McCarthy. *Journal of the American Academy of Religion* 42, no. 3 (1974): 553–54.

Old Testament Form Criticism edited by John H. Hayes. *Religious Studies Review* 1, no. 1 (1975): 8–13.

Plainer Translation: Joseph Smith's Translation of the Bible by Robert J. Matthews. *Review of Books and Religion* 5 (Nov. 1975): 14.

1976–1985

Judges by Robert G. Boling. *Review of Books and Religion* 5 (Jan. 1976): 3.

Studies in Ancient Israelite Wisdom by James L. Crenshaw. *Journal of Biblical Literature* 95, no. 4 (1976): 690–91.

The Architecture of Jeremiah 1–20 by William Lee Holladay. *Interpretation* 31, no. 3 (1977): 327–28.

Die sogenannten Hymnenfragmente im Amosbuch by Werner Berg. *Interpretation* 31, no. 2 (1977): 195–98.

The Psalms in Christian Worship by Massey Hamilton Shepherd. *New Review of Books and Religion* 1, no. 7 (1977): 16.

Biblical and Post-Biblical Defilement and Mourning by Emanuel Feldman. *Journal of Biblical Literature* 97, no. 4 (1978): 593–94.

Jeremia und die falschen propheten by Ivo Meyer. *Catholic Biblical Quarterly* 40, no. 1 (1978): 95–97.

Tradition and Theology in the Old Testament by Douglas A. Knight et al. *Interpretation* 32, no. 1 (1978): 89–92.

Dynamic of Transcendence: The Correlation of Confessional Heritage and Contemporary Experience by Paul D. Hanson. *Journal of the American Academy of Religion* 47, no. 3 (1979): 442–43.

The Old Testament without Illusion by John L. McKenzie. *Christian Century* 96 (1979): 566.

Scripture in History and Theology: Essays in Honor of J. Coert Rylaarsdam edited by Arthur L. Merrill and Thomas W. Overholt. *Journal of Religion* 59, no. 2 (1979): 244–46.

The Elusive Presence: Toward a New Biblical Theology by Samuel L. Terrien. *Journal of Biblical Literature* 99, no. 2 (1980): 296–99.

God Has a Story Too by James A. Sanders. *Religion in Life* 49, no. 1 (1980): 120–22.

An Introduction to Old Testament Study by John H. Hayes. *Journal for the Study of the Old Testament*, no. 18 (1980): 108–11.

Persönliche Frömmigkeit und offizielle Religion by Rainer Albertz. *Catholic Biblical Quarterly* 42, no. 1 (1980): 85–87.

Temples and Temple Service in Ancient Israel by Menahem Haran. *Journal of the American Academy of Religion* 48, no. 3 (1980): 455–56.

The Tribes of Yahweh: A Sociology of the Religion of Liberated Israel by Norman K. Gottwald. *Journal of the American Academy of Religion* 48, no. 3 (1980): 441–51.

Prophecy and Society in Ancient Israel by Robert R. Wilson. *Interpretation* 35, no. 3 (1981): 290–93.

Hosea by Francis I. Andersen. *Journal of Biblical Literature* 101, no. 2 (1982): 281–82.

James Barr and the Bible: Critique of a New Liberalism by Paul R. Wells. *Journal for the Study of the Old Testament*, no. 22 (1982): 148–51.

Moses and the Deuteronomist by Robert Polzin. *Interpretation* 36, no. 3 (1982): 288–91.

Theologie der Psalmen by Hans-Joachim Kraus. *Journal of Biblical Literature* 101, no. 2 (1982): 283–84.

Wie wird Man Prophet in Israel: Aufsätze zum Alten Testament by Bernhard Lang. *Catholic Biblical Quarterly* 44, no. 1 (1982): 124–25.

The Wise King: Studies in Royal Wisdom as Divine Revelation in the Old Testament and Its Environment by Leonidas Kalugila. *Catholic Biblical Quarterly* 44, no. 4 (1982): 650–51.

Theology as Thanksgiving: From Israel's Psalms to the Church's Eucharist by Harvey H. Guthrie. *Interpretation* 37, no. 2 (1983): 191–93.

Geschichte der historisch-kritischen Erforschung des Alten Testaments by Hans-Joachim Kraus. *Catholic Biblical Quarterly* 46, no. 4 (1984): 764.

Hauptprobleme des alttestamentlichen Theologie im 20ten Jhdt by Henning Graf Reventlow. *Catholic Biblical Quarterly* 46, no. 2 (1984): 323–26.

Let the Earth Rejoice: A Biblical Theology of Holistic Mission by William A. Dyrness. *International Bulletin of Missionary Research* 8, no. 3 (1984): 137.

The Structure and Ethos of the Wisdom Admonitions in Proverbs by Philip J. Nel. *Interpretation* 38, no. 4 (1984): 430–32.

The Territorial Dimension of Judaism by W. D. Davies. *Journal of Biblical Literature* 103, no. 2 (1984): 278–79.

Das Land Israel in biblischer Zeit edited by Georg Strecker. *Catholic Biblical Quarterly* 47, no. 2 (1985): 384–86.

The Hidden God: The Hiding of the Face of God in the Old Testament by Samuel E. Balentine. *Catholic Biblical Quarterly* 47, no. 2 (1985): 310–11.

Second Samuel by P. Kyle McCarter Jr. *Journal of the American Academy of Religion* 53, no. 3 (1985): 503–4.

1986–1995

The Art of Biblical Poetry by Robert Alter. *Christian Century* 103 (1986): 247–48.

The Esther Scroll: The Story of the Story by David J. A. Clines. *Interpretation* 40, no. 2 (1986): 202.

Feminist Interpretation of the Bible edited by Letty M. Russell. *Theology Today* 43, no. 2 (1986): 282–84.

Genesis: With an Introduction to Narrative Literature by George W. Coats. *Journal of Biblical Literature* 105, no. 1 (1986): 130–31.

Old Testament Criticism in the Nineteenth Century: England and Germany by John W. Rogerson. *Horizons* 13, no. 2 (1986): 416–17.

Old Testament Theology in a Canonical Context by Brevard S. Childs. *Theology Today* 43, no. 2 (1986): 284, 286–87.

Praising and Knowing God by David F. Ford. *Theology Today* 43, no. 1 (1986): 99–100.

Tor der Gerechtigkeit: Eine literaturwissenschaftliche Untersuchung der sogenannten Einzugsliturgien im AT: Ps 15; 24:3–5; Jes 33:14–16 by Sigurdur Örn Steingrimsson. *Catholic Biblical Quarterly* 48, no. 2 (1986): 322–23.

Das Bilderverbot: Seine Entstehung und seine Entwicklung im Alten Testament by Christoph Dohmen. *Journal of Biblical Literature* 106, no. 2 (1987): 314–15.

The Book of Jeremiah: A Commentary by Robert P. Carroll. *Theological Studies* 48, no. 2 (1987): 343–47.

Form and Validity in the World and God: A Christian Perspective by Trevor Williams. *Theology Today* 43, no. 4 (1987): 584–86.

From Sacred Story to Sacred Text by James A. Sanders. *Theology Today* 44, no. 3 (1987): 398.

H. Richard Niebuhr: A Lifetime of Reflections on the Church and the World by Jon Diefenthaler. *Theology Today* 44, no. 3 (1987): 417.

Imaging God: Dominion as Stewardship by Douglas John Hall. *Theological Studies* 48, no. 2 (1987): 405.

The Just Demands of the Poor: Essays in Socio-Theology by Marie Augusta Neal. *Theology Today* 44, no. 3 (1987): 418.

Liebe deinen Nächsten wie dich selbst: Untersuchungen zum alttestamentlichen Gebot der Nächstenliebe (Lev 19, 18) by Hans-Peter Mathys. *Catholic Biblical Quarterly* 49, no. 4 (1987): 647-648.

Till the Heart Sings: A Biblical Theology of Manhood and Womanhood by Samuel L. Terrien. *Catholic Biblical Quarterly* 49, no. 1 (1987): 129–31.

The Book of Jeremiah: A Commentary by Robert P. Carroll. *Interpretation* 42, no. 3 (1988): 268–80.

A Critical and Exegetical Commentary on Jeremiah, v 1: Introduction and Commentary on Jeremiah 1–25 by William McKane. *Interpretation* 42, no. 3 (1988): 268–80.

Eschatology in the Old Testament by Donald E. Gowan. *Critical Review of Books in Religion* (1988): 165–68.

Fear Not Warrior: A Study of 'al tîr ' Pericopes in the Hebrew Scriptures by Edgar W. Conrad. *Catholic Biblical Quarterly* 50, no. 3 (1988): 493–95.

God and His People: Covenant and Theology in the Old Testament by Ernest W. Nicholson. *Critical Review of Books in Religion* (1988): 178–80.

God of My Victory: The Ancient Hymn in Habakkuk 3 by Theodore Hiebert. *Catholic Biblical Quarterly* 50, no. 3 (1988): 493–95.

A History of Ancient Israel and Judah by John H. Hayes. *Interpretation* 42, no. 1 (1988): 73–76.

Hidden Histories in the United Church of Christ edited by Barbara Brown Zikmund. *Theology Today* 45, no. 2 (1988): 236, 238–39.

Household of Freedom: Authority in Feminist Theology by Letty M. Russell. *Theology Today* 44, no. 4 (1988): 538–39.

Isaiah 34–66 by John D. W. Watts. *Review and Expositor* 85, no. 4 (1988): 715–17.

Jeremiah 1: A Commentary on the Book of the Prophet Jeremiah Chapters 1–25 by William Lee Holladay. *Interpretation* 42, no. 3 (1988): 268–80.

The Risk of Interpretation: On Being Faithful to the Christian Tradition in a Non-Christian Age by Claude Geffré. *Theology Today* 44, no. 4 (1988): 556.

United and Uniting: The Meaning of an Ecclesial Journey by Louis H. Gunnemann. *Theology Today* 45, no. 2 (1988): 236, 238–39.

The United Church of Christ: Studies in Identity and Polity edited by Dorothy C. Bass and Kenneth B. Smith. *Theology Today* 45, no. 2 (1988): 236, 238–39.

Beyond the Written Word: Oral Aspects of Scripture in the History of Religion by William A. Graham. *Missiology* 17, no. 3 (1989): 360–61.

The Book of God: A Response to the Bible by Gabriel Josipovici. *Theology Today* 46, no. 3 (1989): 323–24.

Congregation: Contemporary Writers Read the Jewish Bible edited by David Rosenberg. *Theology Today* 45, no. 4 (1989): 468–74.

The Identity of the Individual in the Psalms by Steven Croft. *Catholic Biblical Quarterly* 51, no. 2 (1989): 314–16.

Midrash and Literature edited by Geoffrey H. Hartman and Sanford Budick. *Theology Today* 45, no. 4 (1989): 468–74.

Oracles of God: Perceptions of Ancient Prophecy in Israel after the Exile by John Barton. *Theology Today* 46, no. 2 (1989): 216.

Todesbilder im Alten Testament oder: "Wie die Alten den Tod gebildet" by Matthias Krieg. *Catholic Biblical Quarterly* 51, no. 3 (1989): 522–23.

Amos: A New Translation with Introduction and Commentary by Francis I. Andersen. *Theological Studies* 51, no. 2 (1990): 325–26.

The Confessions of Jeremiah: Their Interpretation and Role in Chapters 1–25 by Kathleen M. O'Connor. *Hebrew Studies* 31 (1990): 226–28.

Cosmopolis: The Hidden Agenda of Modernity by Stephen Toulmin. *Presbyterian Outlook* 172, no. 34 (1990): 10–12.

Divine Initiative and Human Response in Ezekiel by Paul Joyce. *Critical Review* 3 (1990): 139–41.

History and Ideology in Ancient Israel by Giovanni Garbini. *Interpretation* 44, no. 3 (1990): 301–3.

Jeremiah 2: A Commentary on the Book of the Prophet Jeremiah, Chapters 26–52 by William L. Holladay. *Interpretation* 44 (1990): 410–2.

Toward a Theology of Inculturation by Aylward Shorter. *Theology Today* 47, no. 1 (1990): 80–82.

What Language Shall I Borrow? God-Talk in Worship: A Male Response to Feminist Theology by Brian A. Wren. *Theology Today* 46, no. 4 (1990): 432, 434–35.

The Book of J by Harold Bloom and David Rosenberg. *Theology Today* 48 (July 1991): 234–40.

Creation and the Persistence of Evil by Jon D. Levenson. *Journal of Near Eastern Studies* 50, no. 2 (1991): 143–44.

Exodus by Terence Fretheim. *Word and World* 11, no. 3 (Summer 1991): 332–33.

Hebrew Bible or Old Testament? Studying the Bible in Judaism and Christianity edited by Roger Brooks and John J. Collins. *Theology Today* 48, no. 1 (April 1991): 89–92.

Imagining God: Theology and the Religious Imagination by Garrett Green. *Religious Studies Review* 17, no. 1 (1991): 51.

The Political Meaning of Christianity: An Interpretation by Glenn Tinder. *Theology Today* 47, no. 4 (1991): 436–40.

The Religion of the Landless: The Social Context of the Babylonian Exile by Daniel L. Smith. *Interpretation* 45, no. 1 (1991): 76.

The Window of Vulnerability: A Political Spirituality by Dorothee Soelle. *Presbyterian Outlook* 173, no. 18 (May 13, 1991): 6.

Born of a Woman: A Bishop Rethinks the Birth of Jesus by John Shelby Spong. *Episcopal Life* 3, no. 11 (Nov. 1992): 27.

Care of Persons, Care of Worlds: A Psychosystems Approach to Pastoral Care and Counseling by Larry Kent Graham. *Pastoral Psychology* 41, no. 2 (Nov. 1992): 114–18.

Das Bundesbuch (Ex. 20, 22–23,33): Studien zu seiner Entstehung und Theologie by Ludger Schwienhorst-Schönberger. *Journal of Biblical Literature* 111, no. 1 (Spring 1992): 126-28.

Wolf in the Sheep Fold: The Bible as a Problem for Christianity by Robert P. Carroll. *Theology Today* 49, no. 1 (1992): 124–29.

The Book of Genesis: Chapters 1–17 by Victor P. Hamilton. *Catholic Biblical Quarterly* 55, no. 1 (1993): 113–15.

The Book of Job as Skeptical Literature by Katherine J. Dell. *Journal of Biblical Literature* 112 (1993): 137–39.

Born of a Woman: A Bishop Rethinks the Birth of Jesus by John Shelby Spong. Reprinted in *Cathedral life* 3, no. 3 (April–May 1993): 9.

The Song of the Sea: Ex. 15:1–21 by Martin L. Brenner. *Journal of Biblical Literature* 112 (1993): 126–28.

Theologie des Alten Testaments, Band 1: JHWHs erwählendes und verpflichtendes Handeln by Horst Dietrich Preuss and *Theologie des Alten Testaments, Band 2: Israels Weg mit JHWH* by Horst Dietrich Preuss. *Critical Review* 6 (1993): 174–77.

The Bible in Theology and Preaching by Donald K. McKim. *Presbyterian Outlook* 176, no. 11 (March 21, 1994): 8–9.

Biblical Faith and Natural Theology: The Gifford Lectures for 1991 by James Barr. *Modern Theology* 10, no. 2 (April 1994): 219–21.

The Death and Resurrection of the Beloved Son: The Transformation of Child Sacrifice in Judaism and Christianity by Jon D. Levenson. *Theology Today* 51 (July 1994): 295–97.

Engaging the Powers: Discernment and Resistance in a World of Domination by Walter Wink. *Horizons* 21, no. 1 (Spring 1994): 181–82.

The Garden of Eden and the Hope of Immortality by James Barr. *Hebrew Studies* 35 (1994): 102–4.

The Hebrew Bible, the Old Testament, and Historical Criticism: Jews and Christians in Biblical Studies by Jon D. Levenson. *Catholic Biblical Quarterly* 56 (1994): 623–24.

History and Prophecy: The Development of Late Judean Literary Tradition by Brian Peckham. *Compass: A Jesuit Journal* 12, no. 2 (May–June 1994): 40–43.

Individualism Reconsidered: Readings Bearing on the Endangered Self in Modern Society, edited by Donald Capps and Richard K. Fenn. *Pastoral Psychology* 42, no. 3 (Jan. 1994): 203–9.

Religionsgeschichte Israels in alttestamentlicher Zeit, vols. 1 and 2, by Rainer Albertz. *Journal of Biblical Literature* 113 (1994): 116–20.

The Unity of the Hebrew Bible by David Noel Freedman. *Journal of Religion* 74, no. 3 (July 1994): 380–81.

Virtuoso Theology: The Bible and Interpretation by Frances Young. *Theology Today* 50, no. 4 (Jan. 1994): 660–61.

Facing the Abusing God: A Theology of Protest by David R. Blumenthal. *Interpretation* 49, no. 1 (Jan. 1995): 102.

Suffering and Sin: Interpretations of Illness in the Individual Complaint Psalms by Fredrik Lindström. *Catholic Biblical Quarterly* 57 (1995): 562–64.

1996–2005

The Bible in Modern Culture: Theology and Historical-Critical Method from Spinoza to Käsemann by Roy A. Harrisville and Walter Sundberg. *Theology Today* 53 (1996): 414–18.

The Collapse of History: Reconstructing Old Testament Theology by Leo G. Perdue. *Journal of Religion* 76 (1996): 349–53.

Figuring the Sacred: Religion, Narrative, and Imagination by Paul Ricoeur. *Theology Today* 53 (1996): 95–98.

Imagination Shaped: Old Testament Preaching in the Anglican Tradition by Ellen F. Davis. *Theology Today* 17 (1996): 254–56.

Journeying with God: A Commentary on the Book of Numbers by Katharine Doob Sakenfeld. *Theology Today* 17 (1996): 268–69.

Priests, Prophets, Diviners, Sages: A Socio-Historical Study of Religious Specialists in Ancient Israel by Lester L. Grabbe. *Journal of Biblical Literature* 115 (1996): 728–30.

Reclaiming the Bible for the Church edited by Carl E. Braaten and Robert W. Jenson. *Theology Today* 53 (1996): 235–38.

Sage, Priest, Prophet: Religious and Intellectual Leadership in Ancient Israel by Joseph Blenkinsopp. *Journal of Biblical Literature* 115 (1996): 726–28.

The Task of Old Testament Theology: Substance, Method, and Cases by Rolf P. Knierim. *Catholic Biblical Quarterly* 58 (1996): 580–81.

Theology of the Pentateuch: Themes of the Priestly Narrative and Deuteronomy by Norbert Lohfink. *Interpretation* 50 (1996): 306.

The Bible and Liberation: Political and Social Hermeneutics, revised edition, edited by Norman K. Gottwald and Richard A. Horsley. *Missiology* 25, no. 1 (1997): 107.

A God of Vengeance? Understanding the Psalms of Divine Wrath by Erich Zenger. *Catholic Biblical Quarterly* 59 (1997): 366–76.

Preaching the Just Word by Walter J. Burghardt. *Theology Today* 54 (1997): 444–46.

Psalm 102 im Kontext des vierten Psalmenbuches by Gunild Brunert. *Biblica* 78 (1997): 112–15.

Sixty-One Psalms of David by David R. Slavitt. *Hebrew Studies* 38 (1997): 155–57.

The Curse of Cain: The Violent Legacy of Monotheism by Regina M. Schwartz. *Theology Today* 54 (1998): 534–37.

Economics, Ecology, and the Roots of Western Faith: Perspectives from the Garden by Robert R. Gottfried. *Sewanee Theological Review* 41, no. 2 (1998): 175–76.

Ethics and the Old Testament by John Barton. *Interpretation* 52, no. 3 (July 1998): 306–7.

Leap over a Wall: Earthy Spirituality for Everyday Christians by Eugene H. Peterson. *Theology Today* 55 (1998): 132–34.

Planting and Reaping Albright: Politics, Ideology, and Interpreting the Bible by Burke O. Long. *Theology Today* 54 (1998): 565–69.

The Prophetic Tradition and Radical Rhetoric in America by James Darsey. *Theology Today* 55 (1998): 474–75.

Text and Truth: Redefining Biblical Theology by Francis Watson. *Theological Studies* 59, no. 2 (June 1998): 324–26.

Vision of Transformation: The Territorial Rhetoric of Ezekiel 40–48 by Kalinda Rose Stevenson. *Catholic Biblical Quarterly* 60, no. 2 (April 1998): 348–49.

Wilderness Wanderings: Probing Twentieth-Century Theology and Philosophy by Stanley M. Hauerwas. *Theology Today* 55 (1998): 100–104.

The Bible and the Comic Vision by J. William Whedbee. *Theology Today* 56 (1999): 132–34.

Creation and Reality by Michael Welker. *Presbyterian Outlook* 181, no. 19 (June 7, 1999): 13.

The David Story: A Translation with Commentary of 1 and 2 Samuel by Robert Alter. *Christian Century* 116 (1999): 1122–24.

The Faces of David by K. L. Noll. *Catholic Biblical Quarterly* 61 (1999): 135–36.

Great Books: My Adventures with Homer, Rousseau, Wolff and Other Indestructible Writers of the Western World by David Denby. *Theology Today* 56 (1999): 280–84.

Kaddish by Leon Wieseltier. *Theology Today* 55 (1999): 614–15.

King David and the Wise Woman of Tekoa: The Resonance of Tradition in Parabolic Narrative by Larry L. Lyke. *Catholic Biblical Quarterly* 61 (1999): 132–33.

Like a Tree Planted: An Exploration of Psalms and Parables through Metaphor by Barbara Green. *Review of Biblical Literature* (1999), http://www.bookreviews.org.

The Original Torah: The Political Intent of the Bible's Writers by S. David Sperling. *Catholic Biblical Quarterly* 61 (1999): 558–59.

The Ethos of the Cosmos: The Genesis of Moral Imagination in the Bible by William P. Brown. *Interpretation* 54, no. 1 (Jan. 2000): 69–72.

A Necessary Evil: A History of American Distrust of Government by Garry Wills. *Journal for Preachers* 24, no. 1 (Advent 2000): 56–58.

The Secular Mind by Robert Coles. *Theology Today* 57, no. 1 (April 2000): 120–22.

Torture and Eucharist: Theology, Politics, and the Body of Christ by William T. Cavanaugh. *Theology Today* 57, no. 3 (Oct. 2000): 406, 408–9.

The Bible, Theology, and Faith: A Study of Abraham and Jesus by R. W. L. Moberly. *Theology Today* 58, no. 2 (2001): 257–58.

Called by Stories: Biblical Sagas and Their Challenge for Law by Milner S. Ball. *Theology Today* 58, no. 1 (April 2001): 94, 96–97.

The Prophets: A Liberation-Critical Reading by Carol J. Dempsey. *Catholic Biblical Quarterly* 63, no. 1 (Jan. 2001): 104–6.

Psalms by Craig C. Broyles. *Hebrew Studies* 42 (2001): 352–53.

Psalms by James Limburg, edited by Patrick Miller and David L. Bartlett. *Theological Studies* 62, no. 4 (Dec. 2001): 825–26.

The Social Visions of the Hebrew Bible: A Theological Introduction by David Pleins. *Princeton Seminary Bulletin* 22, no. 2 (2001): 221–23.

Between Cross and Resurrection: A Theology of Holy Saturday by Alan E. Lewis. *Journal for Preachers* 25, no. 2 (Lent 2002): 45–47.

Jeremiah by Terence E. Fretheim. *Word and World* 22, no. 4 (Fall 2002): 438–40.

Practicing Theology: Beliefs and Practices in Christian Life edited by Miroslav Volf and Dorothy C. Bass. *Theology Today* 59, no. 3 (Oct. 2002): 502–6.

The Bible in a World Context: An Experiment in Contextual Hermeneutics by Walter Dietrich. *Review of Biblical Literature* (June 2003), http://www.bookreviews.org.

History, Justice, and the Agency of God: A Hermeneutical and Exegetical Investigation on Isaiah and Psalms by Christoph O. Schroeder. *Princeton Seminary Bulletin* 24, no. 1 (2003): 152–55.

Psalms, Part 2, and Lamentations by Erhard S. Gerstenberger. *Journal of Semitic Studies* 48, no. 1 (Spring 2003): 180–82.

"A Response to Gerstenberger." In *Horizons in Biblical Theology* 25, no. 1 (June 2003): 78–87. Review of Erhard S. Gerstenberger's *Theologies in the Old Testament.*

Covenant as Context. Essays in Honour of E. W. Nicholson edited by A. D. H. Mayes and R. B. Salters. *Journal of Theological Studies* 55, no. 2 (Oct. 2004): 602–4.

The Forgotten God: Perspectives in Biblical Theology, Essays in Honor of Paul J. Achtemeier on the Occasion of His Seventy-Fifth Birthday edited by A. Andrew Das and Frank J. Matera. *Interpretation* 58, no. 2 (April 2004): 204.

The Heart of Christianity by Marcus J. Borg. *Christian Century* 121 (2004): 50–51.

In the Shadow of Your Wings: New Readings of Great Texts from the Bible by Norbert Lohfink. *Review of Biblical Literature* (Jan. 2004), http://www.bookreviews.org.

Old Testament Theology. Vol. 1, *Israel's Gospel* by John Goldingay. *Theology Today* 61, no. 3 (Oct. 2004): 380–81.

The Psalms: Strophic Structure and Theological Commentary by Samuel Terrien. *Theology Today* 61, no. 1 (April 2004): 130–32.

The Westminster Theological Wordbook of the Bible edited by Donald E. Gowan. *Theology Today* 61, no. 2 (July 2004): 284–85.

The God of Old: Inside the Lost World of the Bible by James L. Kugel. *Interpretation* 59, no. 1 (Jan. 2005): 64–66.

The Hebrew God: Portrait of an Ancient Deity by Bernhard Lang. *Biblical Interpretation* 13 (2005): 64–66.

The Kingdom Is Always but Coming: A Life of Walter Rauschenbusch by Christopher H. Evans. *Journal for Preachers* 28, no. 2 (Lent 2005): 61–62.

Major Poems of the Hebrew Bible: At the Interface of Prosody and Structural Analysis. Vol. 3. *The Remaining 65 Psalms* by J. P. Fokkelman. *Journal of Hebrew Scriptures* 5 (2005), http://www.purl.org/jhs.

2006–2011

Constituting the Community: Studies on the Polity of Ancient Israel in Honor of S. Dean McBride Jr. edited by John T. Strong and Steven S. Tuell. *Interpretation* 60, no. 3 (July 2006): 342–43.

Did God Have a Wife? Archaeology and Folk Religion in Ancient Israel by William G. Dever. *Christian Century* 123 (2006): 37.

God as an Absent Character in Biblical Hebrew Narrative: A Literary-Theoretical Study by Amelia Devin Freedman. *Review of Biblical Literature* (Jan. 2006), http://www.bookreviews.org.

Überpower: The Imperial Temptation of America by Josef Joffe. *Christian Century* 123 (2006): 47–50.

Alone in the World? Human Uniqueness in Science and Theology by J. Wentzel van Huyssteen. *Christian Century* (2007): 28–30.

AWOL: The Unexcused Absence of America's Upper Classes from Military Service—and How It Hurts Our Country by Kathy Roth-Douquet and Franky Schaeffer. *Christian Century* 124 (2007): 54–56.

God's Joust, God's Justice by John Witte Jr. *Christian Century* 124 (2007): 36.

Resurrection and the Restoration of Israel: The Ultimate Victory of the God of Life by John D. Levenson. *Christian Century* 124 (2007): 31–33.

Abraham's Curse: The Roots of Violence in Judaism, Christianity, and Islam by Bruce Chilton. *Christian Century* 125 (2008): 36–38.

The Age of American Unreason by Susan Jacoby. *Christian Century* 125 (2008): 36–38.

The Book of Psalms: A Translation with Commentary by Robert Alter. *Christian Century* 125 (2008): 50–54.

Christ and Empire: From Paul to Postcolonial Times by Joerg Rieger. *Christian Century* 125 (2008): 34–35.

Failing America's Faithful: How Today's Churches Are Mixing God with Politics and Losing Their Way by Kathleen Kennedy Townsend. *Christian Century* 125 (2008): 42–44.

Isaiah edited and translated by Robert Louis Wilken. *Christian Century* 125 (2008): 38–43.

Resurrection: The Power of God for Christians and Jews by Kevin J. Madigan and Jon D. Levenson. *Christian Century* 125 (2008): 38–40.

The Violence of God and the War on Terror by Jeremy Young. *Christian Century* 125 (2008): 36–38.

The Way of the Lord: Essays in Old Testament Theology by Patrick D. Miller. *Review of Biblical Literature* (Jan. 2008), http://www.bookreviews.org.

Approaching Yehud: New Approaches to the Study of the Persian Period edited by Jon L. Berquist. *Christian Century* 126 (2009): 41–43.

The Clash within: Democracy, Religious Violence, and India's Future by Martha C. Nussbaum. *Christian Century* 126 (2009): 37–40.

The Deed and the Doer in the Bible: David Daube's Gifford Lectures. Vol. 1, *Christian Century* 126 (2009): 39–41.

The Eucharist: Bodies, Bread, and Resurrection by Andrea Bieler and Louise Schottroff. *Christian Century* 126 (2009): 55–59.

Genesis by James McKeown. *Theology Today* 66 (April 2009): 91–94.

Predestination: The American Career of a Contentious Doctrine by Peter J. Thuesen. *Christian Century* 126 (2009): 44–45.

Reading the Hebrew Bible after the Shoah: Engaging Holocaust Theology by Marvin A. Sweeney. *Christian Century* 126 (2009): 32–33.

Sacramental Poetics at the Dawn of Secularism: When God Left the World by Regina Mara Schwartz. *Christian Century* 126 (2009): 55-59.

Sacred Attunement: A Jewish Theology by Michael Fishbane. *Horizons in Biblical Theology* 31 (2009): 210–14.

The Unheard Voice of God: A Pentecostal Hearing of the Book of Judges by Lee Roy Martin. *Journal of Pentecost Theology* 18, no. 1 (2009): 15–19.

America's Prophet: Moses and the American Story by Bruce Feiler. *Christian Century* 127, no. 7 (2010): 49–50.

The Imperial Cruise: A Secret History of Empire and War by James Bradley. *Christian Century* 127 (2010): 41–42.

The Judaizing Calvin: Sixteenth-Century Debates over the Messianic Psalms by G. Sujin Pak. *Christian Century* 127, no. 18 (2010): 54–55.

Old Testament Theology. Vol. 2, *Israel's Faith* by John Goldingay. *Scottish Journal of Theology* 63 (2010): 117–19.

The Reader-Oriented Unity of the Book of Isaiah by Archibald L. H. M. Wieringen. *Biblica* 91, no. 1 (2010): 116–19.

Reason, Faith, and Revolution: Reflections on the God Debate by Terry Eagleton. *Christian Century* 127, no. 6 (2010): 39–42.

Saving Creation: Nature and Faith in the Life of Holmes Rolston III by Christopher J. Preston. *Christian Century* 127 (2010): 37–39.

Sin: A History by Gary A. Anderson. *Christian Century* 127, no. 5 (2010): 39–40.

The Ten Commandments by Patrick D. Miller. *Christian Century* 127 (2010): 48–50.

CPSIA information can be obtained at www.ICGtesting.com
Printed in the USA
BVOW022303131112

305462BV00005B/18/P